Education and Informatics Worldwide

The State of the Art and Beyond

Education and Informatics Worldwide
The State of the Art and Beyond

*Jacques Hebenstreit, Bernard Levrat, Alfred Bork, David Walker,
André Poly, Fatima Seye-Sylla, Samir Qasim Fakhro, Mike Lally,
Neil Hall, Dentcho Batanov, Peter Gorny, Robert Lewis,
Marco Murray-Lasso and Rhys Gwyn*

Jessica Kingsley Publishers / UNESCO

Jessica Kingsley Publishers ISBN 1 85302 089 3
UNESCO ISBN 92 3 102798 0

First published in 1992 by Jessica Kingsley Publishers,
116 Pentonville Road, London N1 9B
and
The United Nations Educational,
Scientific and Cultural Organization
7 Place de Fonteroy
75700 Paris, France

British Library Cataloguing in Publication Data
    available on request

    ISBN 1-85302-089-3

Printed and bound in the United Kingdom by
Bookcraft Ltd, Midsomer Norton, Avon

Preface

Between the early 1960s, when computers first began to be used in education as a research activity, and the early 1990s we have seen education and informatics evolve from wishful thinking to a day to day reality. The important role of informatics in education as both a teaching and learning tool had emerged clearly by the early 1980s, attracting the attention of educators throughout the world. At the same time education has ceased to be regarded as uniquely the transfer of information but is seen rather as a more dynamic transactional process wherein both the teacher and the learner are changed. In this new context, informatics comes into its own in education, providing learners with both access to knowledge and opportunities to apply the knowledge in other situations. As informatics became more and more important to education, education and informatics quickly assumed a greater place in UNESCO's programme and numerous activities were undertaken.

Informatics is constantly changing, constantly evolving. The present sourcebook therefore makes an attempt to look beyond the immediate future and envisages a closer interaction between education and informatics at both international and regional levels.

Education and Informatics has its origins in the deliberations of the international congress on 'Education and Informatics; Stengthening International Co-operation', organized in 1989 by UNESCO with the support of the Intergovernmental Informatics Programme (IIP) to draw up recommendations to the Director-General of UNESCO and the international community on the use of computers in improving educational processes and systems, and on international co-operation to secure these objectives.

The congress brought together more than 400 participants from 93 countries and 29 international organizations. Its programme was organized around five themes – Present Situation and Objectives, Strategies, Co-operation with Industry, Applications and Prospects – which were discussed at roundtables.

After the congress, UNESCO decided that the discussion merited greater reflection and dissemination than would result from simply issuing the *Proceedings* and *Final Report* (both of which are available on request from UNESCO). Thus it was decided to commission articles from several experts in the field of informatics and education.

This book is expected to serve as a source not only for educators using informatics in formal and non-formal education but also for those working in related industries whose co-operation is essential in order to strengthen the impact of teaching-learning through computer and other means of information and communication.

UNESCO would like to express its appreciation to the authors of the five chapters making up this publication: Dentcho Batanov, Alfred Bork, Samir Qasim Fakhro, Rhys Gwyn, Peter Gorny, Neil Hall, Jacques Hebenstreit, Mike Lally, Bernard Levrat, Marco Murray-Lasso, Fatima Seye-Sylla and David Walker. UNESCO would also like to thank André Poly of the Ecole Normale Supérieure (Fontenoy St Cloud, France) who reviewed Chapter 3 and Professor Robert Lewis of the University of Lancaster (United Kingdom) who reviewed the section of Chapter 4 dealing with Europe and North America. Finally, UNESCO would like to acknowledge the contribution of Frank Lovis who edited Chapters 1 and 2. The ideas presented are those of the authors and do not necessarily reflect UNESCO's views.

Contents

CHAPTER ONE

Where are we and how did we get there?

J. Hebenstreit

A short history of the use of computers in education

How it started

The use of computers in education started as a research activity on a very limited scale in the early 1960s. At that time computers were large and very expensive machines, and the communication procedure with these machines was difficult and lengthy; one had first to prepare a set of punched cards which then had to be brought to the computing centre; after a day or two, a print-out was delivered by the computing centre, provided there was no punching error in the set of cards.

The price of the equipment and the procedures made the use of computers in the classroom sound completely unrealistic. Despite the complete absence of interactivity (in the modern sense) with the computer, a few experiments were made using mainly the multiple-choice-question technique where children answered questions by using a pencil to punch pre-perforated cards. This was supposed to make marking various exercises automatic, without any loss of time for the teacher.

In the late 1960s however, the situation improved with the advent of the minicomputer and the invention of the time-sharing mode whereby many users at individual terminals could share the same computer at the same time.

In the early 1970s, the decreasing price of equipment and the increasing availability of time-sharing systems led to small-scale experiments in schools in France, in the United Kingdom and in the United States which were funded by the government or by governmental agencies. These three countries share a number of characteristics with other developed countries. Their computer industries date from the early 1950s; they have a great number of computers installed in industry, commerce and administration, a great number of professionals in computer science at all levels and well-established curricula in computer science at universities, schools of engineering, polytechnics, etc.

The present situation regarding the use of informatics in education in these countries is, however, different from other developed countries in three respects: research into the use of computers in education started before 1970, experiments in schools started as early as the late 1960s or the early 1970s, and the present ratio of number of computers to the total school population is higher than one to fifty. Because these countries started quite early and have accumulated over thirty years of experience we shall call them the 'advanced countries'.

The advent of the microcomputer in the late 1970s, its low price and its rapidly increasing use in industry, commerce and administration in developed countries has led an increasing number of these countries to plan the introduction of computers in schools. In this chapter, 'developed countries' excludes France, the United Kingdom and the United States. There is no strong distinction between advanced and developed countries, the difference being introduced for the sake of simplicity as these two groups of countries do not face exactly the same problems.

Pedagogical objectives

In the early 1960s, when computers were hidden in air-conditioned computing centres, the idea of using computers in education was, at the very best, a form of science fiction or wishful thinking. The advent of the time-sharing mode where each learner could sit at a terminal (first a typewriter and later on a cathodic screen and a keyboard) and get immediate feedback from the computer was the real starter of a theoretical and practical activity in the area of research on computers in education. Various proposals were made at that time for the 'best' use of computers to 'improve' education but the general trend was to replace the teacher by a computer.

The arguments for using computers that way were: (a) computers, contrary to teachers, are available all the time and at any time the learner wishes to learn; (b) computers are never 'tired' and never 'lose their temper'; they are 'infinitely patient'; (c) the learner can learn at his or her own speed and is not constrained by the speed of learning of the other children in the class; and (d) some learners are less scared by machines then by teachers.

This was generally summed up by saying that learning with computers allowed a 'personalized' process as opposed to the standardized process of the classroom and, last but not least, it was shown that computer learning was less expensive than institutional education. Various ways of using computers in the educational process, each based on a different pedagogical theory, were proposed and implemented.

TUTORIAL MODE

The subject to be taught is divided in elementary pieces of knowledge (called 'items') which are organized logically and presented in turn at the request of the learner. Immediately after the presentation of each item, a question is asked to check whether the learner has memorized correctly the item followed by an immediate feedback – negative ('You are wrong, try again') or positive ('You are correct, go on'). Apart from the difficulty of decompos-ing all facts, concepts, methods or techniques to be taught in a linear sequence of items, there is the problem of analysing by software the learner's answers.

The well-known technique of multiple-choice question can and has been used on computers, but it is not completely satisfactory. On one hand, it does not always make sense to ask learners to only choose from among four or five proposed answers and, on the other hand, if learners choose a wrong answer, they do not improve their learning if the computer's reply is 'You are wrong, try again' until the right answer is finally given.

The situation is worse when students are allowed to type their personal answers freely on a keyboard: analysing a free answer is, in fact, an exercise in understanding natural language and this problem is far from solved on computers.

To try to increase the 'personalization' of the teaching-learning process, it was proposed to use 'branching'. This means that for each wrong answer the learner is automatically directed towards a 'help-sequence' where the item which has not been correctly understood is itself split up into a sequence of sub-items; if this sequence is successfully completed, the learner is brought back to the point where the main sequence was left.

Because no two students follow the same path through the learning material, it was said that the branched-tutorial mode was a highly individ-ualized mode of learning and therefore much superior to what is going on in a classroom where all students have to adapt to the teacher's lecture. Many arguments have been given against the tutorial mode. First, the method leads to an 'atomization' of the acquired knowledge: to decompose a piece of knowledge into items and to teach them one by one does not guarantee that the learner will be able to understand correctly the initial piece of knowledge. Second, learning is not a purely intellectual activity; it has social, emotional, sentimental, etc. components. Finally, learning in the tutorial mode is a very repetitive (hence boring) activity and will not be continued by any student beyond a short time except in the case of very strong motivation.

The tutorial mode was the first effort at using computers in education. The computer is used to simulate the most visible part of a teacher's activity – to transmit knowledge and check whether the knowledge has been correctly transmitted.

Despite its many shortcomings (such as no initiative to the learner and no questions from the learner) and despite the rigidity of most tutorial software (no possibility to skip parts of a lesson, to change the level of difficulty, to go back to a previous part of the lesson, to change a previous answer, etc.), the tutorial mode has proven effective in a number of cases. It has been and still is used successfully to teach subjects which have a check-list structure (repair and maintenance of all sorts of complex devices as mechanical and electrical engines, electronic equipment, etc.), mainly for on-the-job training in various companies. It is not much used in schools and universities.

DRILL AND PRACTICE

Another frequent activity in schools is to test the level of understanding and the ability to use the tools and methods which have been taught through the use of aptitude tests concerned with students' ability to solve exercises and problems.

Exercises and problems can, of course, be proposed by the computer in a sequence of increasing difficulty. In case of a wrong answer, either the reply from the computer is 'You are wrong, try again' (in this case, the computer offers no advantage over a book of exercises where the answers are given) or the computer offers some help. The latter is generally not done because it is extremely difficult and, in most cases, impossible to infer from an error made in an exercise the kind of mistake which has led to that error. There are however subjects, mainly in elementary and secondary education, which lend themselves to that kind of software (arithmetic, grammar, history, etc.). In scientific disciplines drill and practice is, in most cases, more or less mixed with the simulation mode.

SIMULATION

Simulation has long been used in research and industry whenever the study of a device or a system proved either too expensive to be built for experimental purposes or too complex to be studied or designed through the usual mathematical approach.

This led many people in education to the conclusion that the only interest of simulation is its possibility to replace real experiments whenever these are impossible in the classroom. Most of the time, these same educators add that simulation is a 'worst case' situation which should be avoided as far as possible because it is or may be dangerously misleading for the students.

If the objective in education were just be to replace real experiments by simulation because it is easier or faster or less expensive, the above arguments would be perfectly valid. But this is not the point. Recent research results have shown that modelling and simulation have some deep cognitive aspects and the fundamental problem educators should be interested in is how these cognitive aspects could be used to improve education.

In *The Nature of Explanation*, Kenneth Craik wrote:

> If the organism carries a small-scale model of external reality and of its own possible actions within its head, it is able to try out various alternatives, conclude which is the best of them, react to future situations before they arise, utilize the knowledge of past events in dealing with the present and future, and in every way to react in a much fuller, safer, and more competent manner to the emergencies which face it (Craik, 1943).

More recently, Johnson-Laird (1983) said:

> If you know what causes a phenomenon, what results from it, how to influence, control, initiate, or prevent it, how it is related to other states of affairs or how it resembles them, how to predict its onset and course, what its internal or underlying 'structure' is, then to some extent you understand it. The psychological core of understanding, I shall assume, consists in your having a 'working model' of the phenomenon in your mind.

According to this school of thought, modelling and simulation are very basic built-in intellectual mechanisms in all human beings and even if they are, most of the time, subconscious, they are nonetheless the very basis of 'understanding'.

If it is agreed that education can less and less be a process of accumulation of knowledge – because our knowledge increases exponentially which makes such a process hopeless – then the only alternative is to transform education from a process of accumulation of knowledge into a process which relies on the built-in mechanism of modelling and simulation with the purpose of extending it, broadening it, etc., so as to increase each student's ability in every way to react to emergencies in a much fuller, safer and more competent manner.

Not all students will be able to reach the same level of sophistication in their aptitude to model and simulate. However, modelling and simulation on digital computers are most probably the best possible choice for improving this aptitude.

Our teaching, most of the time, goes too quickly to formulae and procedures, and does not help children to acquire the kinds of analytical and representational skills they need. Teaching qualitative analysis in science is of course difficult and time consuming. It does not make much sense if children are not involved in the task of making sense of procedures and formulae through extensive experimentation. But how is extensive experimentation possible in the classroom?

However, because carefully prepared, simulated experiments are conducted at the child's initiative, because they can be proposed at various levels of abstraction (from the purely qualitative to the completely quantitative), because they can include a wide spectrum of special cases, because they allow to explore many different examples in a short time and because they can be conceived to force students to pit their 'naive theories' against the ones they are being asked to learn, they are certainly a major tool to overcome the difficulties mentioned above (Resnick, 1983).

This does not mean a retreat from real experiments made in the laboratory or from the teaching of computational procedures or scientific formulae or from the basic factual information in any discipline. There is definitely an important role for the traditional aptitude to conduct real experiments and for the traditional skills in mathematics and the facts that underlie them.

What simulation brings, when carefully planned, is an answer to the recent findings in the psychology of learning. It does not replace anything; it is a new tool allowing types of activities which were not possible before and which can increase tremendously the efficiency of the teaching/learning process.

The 'dangers' of simulation. It is often said that the use of simulation in education has a number of potential 'dangers'.

It is not the 'real thing' and gives, therefore, a wrong appreciation of the difficulties involved in real experimentation. This would be a danger if simulation were intended to replace real experiments, which is not the case. Simulation should be used for its own sake and with objectives different from those of experimentation. Moreover, even so-called 'real experiments' in the classroom are organized in a pedagogical way so as to hide a number of difficulties and to show with great evidence what the teacher wants to demonstrate.

Simulation does not develop various aptitudes and crafts which are necessary for real experiments like reading meters, adjusting knobs, measuring elapsed time, judging change of colour, etc. Again, simulation is not intended to and should not replace real experiments just because it is easier or cheaper. Simulation is a new tool and should be used as an add-on to develop different attitudes and aptitudes.

No model on a computer can include all the complexity of the real world and simulation gives, therefore, an over-simplified image of the real world. This is a two-sided argument; in fact, any model in science is a simplified representation of the real world (most 'laws' in physics are described by linear relations which are, actually, first-order approximations because no phenomenon in nature is linear) and, moreover, the explanatory power of a model stems directly from its simplified representation.

> What must be emphasized, however, is that one does not necessarily increase the usefulness of a model by adding information to it beyond a certain level.

> Your model of a television set may contain only the idea of a box that displays moving pictures with accompanying sound, alternatively, it may embody the notion of a cathode-ray tube firing electrons at a screen, with the beam scanning across the screen in a raster controlled by a varying electro-magnetic field... A person who repairs television sets is likely to have a more comprehensive model of them than someone who can only operate one. A circuit designer is likely to have a still richer model. Yet, even the designer may not need fully understand the full ramifications of quantum-electrodynamics which is just as well because nobody completely understands them (Johnson-Laird, 1983).

The abstract/concrete aspects of simulation. Because of the very nature of simulation, its use induces in the learner an intermediate level of abstract thinking which is not accessible without simulation. The model which is implemented in the software is, most of the time, a set of mathematical relations or equations which describe the behaviour under various circumstances of the phenomenon or system being modelled. Hence, the most abstract aspect is contained within the computer but completely hidden from the user.

The user can act on the model by specifying the values of various parameters at the keyboard or through the use of a 'mouse', which is a physical action, but not the one able to influence the physical phenomenon or system; it is rather a description of an action to be executed by the computer on the model, and this again implies a level of abstraction which can not be accessed without a computer.

Moreover, once the action is specified, the behaviour of the model on the screen – as a moving picture of the real phenomenon or system as taken by a film-camera, or in a symbolic simplified representation or, even more interesting, as a set of curves in various systems of co-ordinates (which could, of course, be done by hand) – appears as the answer of the model to the stimulus the user has applied.

From a cognitive point of view, the model becomes for the user an entity at least as real as any other phenomenon or system because it reacts as if it had an autonomous existence, any action by the user leading to a reaction of the model in the form of an information displayed on the screen.

While the model has a certain level of reality, it is unlikely that the user will confuse a program embodying a piece of physics with the actual physical process that is being simulated. A program that represents a wave breaking on the shore is manifestly different from a real wave and it would be absurd to criticize the program on the ground that it was not wet. Moreover, no sane person is likely to assume that the real wave is controlled by a computer programs: it is governed by physical forces that are simulated by a program.

The interest of simulation lies in the pedagogical value of that intermediate level of abstraction between the real phenomenon and the abstract model in the form of a set of relations describing the behaviour of that phenomenon, and that level is not accessible without the use of computers. The pedagogical value of that intermediate level of abstraction, has, however received little attention up to now.

We have seen that simulation and modelling in the general sense are fundamental activities in the thinking process as they are in science, but without simulation on computers, the concept of model remains an abstract definition. Through computer simulation, a model acquires a certain level of reality because users can act upon it and observe its reactions.

Moreover, through simulation, the user can investigate the behaviour of the model in a number of ways which are not directly possible in the real phenomenon: no moving body can materialize its trajectory, whereas it is easy to do so on a screen; no moving body will display, on request, a graph showing its speed or acceleration as a function of time or position; no real phenomenon will contract or expand time to allow detailed investigation; and no real system will ever answer instantly to the question 'what happens if?' but will request lengthy procedures to change the conditions of an experiment, thereby discouraging the user to go on in his investigations.

Because simulation allows the display of a lot of useful information in various forms in a very fast dialogue, users are encouraged to make educated guesses to see 'what happens if?' and, moreover, the teacher or the tutor is able to check the list of successive actions taken by the student to verify if these actions are coherent and convergent or if they are of the trial and error type, in which case a remedial lesson on experimental methodology would be necessary.

The advent of the microcomputer

Up to the late 1970s only the three advanced countries had made significant efforts to introduce computers into general education. In the universities of almost all developed countries at that time various degrees were available in computer science and in many countries, after some bitter fights, computer science was finally considered as a subject or a discipline. Computers were still expensive and their massive use to improve education seemed still unrealistic. New arguments were, however, given by some specialists who tried to prove that computer science was at least as universal as mathematics and represented a kind of intellectual quantum-leap which should be taught to all children.

The advent of the microcomputer in the late 1970s changed drastically the problem of the use of computers in education, not only because of its price but also because of its volume, weight and absence of air-conditioning which made it transportable in any place including the classroom (Lewis, 1982).

THE 'COMPUTER LITERACY' WAVE

Microcomputers were first introduced as expensive user-friendly toys and electronic games were a major use at the beginning.

The use by IBM of the name PC (Personal Computer) as a trade mark for its microcomputers had a tremendous impact on the use of these small machines in society at large. It led to the idea that computers were 'personal' tools and in many companies and administration this led in turn to the concept of 'a microcomputer on each desk'. This 'personal' argument became overwhelming with the advent of a variety of new software such as spreadsheets, word processing, small databases, etc., and within a few years a majority of offices became 'electronic offices', including those receiving customers such as banks, post-offices, travel agencies, etc.

The fast increasing number of clerks and employees using microcomputers in public places had a number of social consequences mainly because it led, at least in developed countries, to a kind of growing public awareness of the key-role of informatics for the society of tomorrow. The mass media and many official speeches contributed considerably to this phenomenon. This in turn led governments in almost all developed countries to proposals or decisions to introduce computers throughout the education system, from kindergarten to university.

Despite some dissimilarities in scope and methods, proposals or projects to introduce computers in education can all be classified as follows:

Computer awareness/computer literacy. In the first scenario, all children should be taught about computers, how they work, how they are used, their social impact, the way they change jobs and, last but not least, children should be taught programming (even micro-electronics were included in the British Micro-electronics in Education Project), and all this at ages 12 to 15.

This scenario looks like a kind of emergency decision to face the massive arrival of microcomputers. It is oversimplified because it does not make much sense to teach the state of the art of informatics to children who will be adults ten years from now, given that nobody is able to predict what informatics will look like in a decade's time (who was able ten years ago to predict $500 computers, computer networks, integrated service networks, electronic mail, extensive data-banks, multiple windows, pull-down menus, etc.).

This scenario may even become harmful because the time spent on these topics could be better used to teach much more fundamental subjects like mathematics, sciences or oral and written expression, which are more than ever necessary to turn out the highly adaptive people needed by our modern and fast changing society. In some places, it is suggested to go even further and to teach programming and/or algorithms.

The teaching of programming. Some people argue that it is necessary to be able to program a computer on the grounds that (a) if you don't know a programming language you will be like an invalid in a computerized society and (b) if you know a programming language you will be able to find a well-paid job. These two arguments were valid years ago but are no longer so. First, citizens of the computerized society will not write programs; they will use computers with pre-written cheap software because it will be sold by the hundred thousand copies (one should remember that the LOTUS 1-2-3 software has sold over 5 million copies). Second, if companies can afford to buy microcomputers, they cannot afford the cost of having their employees write programs instead of doing their work. Moreover, those people who will be hired to write programs will be required to be specialists in programming, which has little to do with the simple knowledge of a programming language.

Others argue that programming has intellectual virtues and they compare it to mathematics or even Latin. Training in programming is supposed to teach children to 'think logically' (whatever this means), to formulate solutions in a clear, exhaustive and unambiguous way, to be meticulous and handle all details, etc. The truth is that we would like future programmers to have the above qualities but experience has shown that the teaching of programming, even intensively, has been unable to develop these qualities in those who did not have them beforehand.

Finally, some people argue that the above was true up to now because previously we were not able to teach 'good' programming but the 'new' programming methods or such and such new 'miracle-language' or 'miracle-system' is going to change the situation.

> However, advocates of teaching programming to students argue that it is an important skill that can improve problem solving abilities and has wide applicability to many areas of the curriculum, but research on the cognitive consequences of programming has produced mixed results (OTA, 1988).

Moreover, which language should be taught – the respectable one (FORTRAN), the easy one (BASIC), the pedagogical one (PASCAL), the useful one (COBOL), the versatile one (C) or the modern ones (LISP, PROLOG, SMALLTALK, etc.) – and which will be the standard one ten years from now?

Some specialists agree with the above arguments that a programming language is not really important, but they insist on teaching algorithms.

The teaching of algorithms. The teaching of algorithms should teach children to formulate correctly a problem, to analyse the problem and decompose it in relevant sub-problems, and to solve the problem by writing the correct algorithms, all this being also sometimes called 'problem solving'.

Now, problem-solving is an interesting concept because since its formalization in the seventeenth century by René Descartes in his *Discours de la méthode* where he suggested decomposing a problem in to sufficiently small sub-problems which can be solved at a glance, the only thing we have done is to add new keywords such as 'step-wise refinement' or 'divide to conquer'.

This is no surprise because the general concept of problem-solving is so broad as to be almost semantically empty, apart from academic problems and, even in that case, the solving method of any problem depends heavily on the relevant discipline in which the problem is formulated and is strongly isomorphic with the handful of paradigms characteristic of that discipline. There is very little in common between solving a problem in astronomy and solving a problem in biology, except the fact that in each case there is a 'problem-solving' problem. At that level of generality we can consider the concept of problem-solving semantically empty except if it is applied to a given discipline and in that case problem-solving is much more a bag of tricks than it is a method.

In fact, what is common between the proposals of teaching programming and teaching problem-solving is the idea that there are 'informatics methods' for solving problems and that the ultimate in problem-solving is writing a computer program that solves the problem.

Unfortunately, the general activity of problem-solving is not reducible to the specific work of automation of symbol-handling procedures (what programming fundamentally is) and therefore the teaching of programming and/or algorithms is of little use except for professionals in informatics.

From the early 1980s, especially in the United States, the teaching of computer awareness/computer literacy has been very popular and in many places it was the only use of the microcomputers available in schools. During the last few years the situation has progressively changed and the recent trend is towards the use of the so-called universal tools (word processing, spreadsheets, databases, etc.) and an increasing interest for educational software of various types (tutorial, drill, simulation, etc.).

THE COMPUTER AS AN INTELLIGENCE AMPLIFIER

Most psychologists believe that children learn about the world through their interaction with the world and Piaget goes even further by saying that children develop their 'logico-mathematical tools' through abstraction from their daily experiments with the world.

If we accept the idea that children learn about the world by doing and that therefore their vision of the world depends on the variety of their experiments, then the use of computers raises a number of questions because with computers children can make types of experiments which are completely impossible without computers. What are these new experiments and how do they (if at all) change the way children perceive the world? (Hebenstreit, 1986)

There are simple drawing-software with which it is possible to make drawings on a screen with a light pen. In its simplest form such a software draws, for instance, a straight line through any two successive positions of the light pen. How do children use that possibility? How do they explain the automatic drawing of a straight line as soon as the second point is given?

A bit more sophisticated are icon-driven drawing software where two points can define a rectangle, a square or a circle depending on the icon chosen. Moreover, a drawing or a part of it can be moved all over the screen, can be made larger or smaller, etc. All these possibilities do not exist on paper. How do children use these possibilities? How much do they like it? How do they explain what they see?

If different basic drawings are available through icons in a menu (houses, trees, flowers, ships, windmills, boys, girls, animals, etc.), do children use the icons separately or together to draw a landscape? After having used this drawing software, do they still draw on paper and, if so, what is the influence of the software on their future drawings?

What is the impact of a text processing package on the speed of learning of writing and spelling? What is kept and what is lost when children switch to hand writing? Is there a transfer between both activities?

The description of an action to be executed by a device later on upon request can be done either by pressing functional keys, as in the case of the toy called 'Big Track', or by typing instructions on a keyboard. Which way is the easiest for children? Why?

What difference do children see between a mobile executing a list of instructions by moving on the floor and a mobile in the form of a triangle simulating a real mobile and moving on a screen (generally vertical)? What kind of relationship do they see between the mobile and its simulation?

To make a drawing on a screen, storing it in memory and calling it again at a later time is one level of abstraction higher than drawing on a piece of paper and storing it in a physical location where it can be found again. How does this different approach change the way a child conceives the concept of storing for later access? What difference does a child make between storing in a computer and storing in a physical location? How does a child understand the necessity of naming an object before storing it in memory?

There are many more questions along these lines and they are all open questions, mainly because little research has been done on these and other fundamental problems. There is a historical reason for that lack of fundamental research. Years ago some computer scientists developed various pieces of software and/or hardware aimed at the child-computer interaction and promoted these (mostly for commercial reasons) as the only tools for interaction. Psychologists and teachers were not sufficiently competent in computer science to define their own hardware/software tools for investigating the child-computer interaction in terms of psychology and pedagogy; the only research they did therefore was to investigate the properties and possibilities of the products designed by the computer scientists, tending to draw universal conclusions as if these products were the only possible ones.

Recently, as more and more psychologists and teachers have become familiar with computers, an increasing number of them are defining by themselves their subjects of research in the area of child-computer interaction and are developing by themselves the hardware/software tools they need for their specific investigations.

This will hopefully bring to a stop stories about 'Children love computers', 'They cannot stop typing on the keyboard', 'They take the computer to bed' which may be true for some but hide the fact that counter examples of children completely reluctant to handle computers can be mentioned as well and in equal number. Statistically children do not love or hate computers; when they can access one, they play a while with it and then they change for other games.

It will also hopefully bring to a stop stories about the wonderful properties of miracle programming languages such as LOGO (which are supposed to make children become creative, and explore and find out lots of things by themselves) as opposed to the use of software packages which are accused of 'programming the child'. To believe or advocate that the use of any specific programming language can make people become creative is either a naive view or an over optimistic view of mankind in general and of children in particular, reminiscent of Jean-Jacques Rousseau's 'gentle savage' corrupted by civilization.

That so many optimistic assertions about the psychological impact of using LOGO, made without any element of proof as to their general validity, have been accepted by psychologists and teachers and that nobody ever mentioned a single drawback or dared raise an objection, can only be explained by the dominant social status of computer scientists and the general lack of competence in computer science of psychologists and teachers.

COMPUTER-ASSISTED ACTIVITIES

In this scenario, the role of the computer is the role of an assistant; a set of resources and services. In other terms, future users of a computer will not be more concerned by computers per se than are citizens of our 'electronified' society by electronics.

What they will be interested in is the quality and variety of services available at their terminals which will be an outlet of a complex network system for communication, information and processing, and the use of such a terminal will be socially accepted if, and only if, its use is sufficiently simple, which means compatible with the usual behaviour of people in our society.

The history of informatics over the last twenty years shows – with evidence – that a considerable effort has been made by professionals to simplify the use of computers so as to put the machine at the service of man, instead of obliging people to learn a complex set of relevant details of the machine which in fact was putting man at the service of the machine. We have still to go further in that direction to accomplish the statement of Arno Penzias (Nobel Prize in 1978): 'We must teach computers to understand people'. The computer as a source of services and resources is going to play a major role in education and in many countries there are now projects in progress in that direction.

Computer-aided teaching. Very little has been done in this direction up to now and therefore very few software packages (which I shall call 'teachware') are available to help teachers to improve their teaching in the classroom.

One interesting application is the 'electronic blackboard' where the teacher uses the screen to show texts and pictures. Many different uses are possible: increasing the number of examples, simulation of experiments, presentation of cases where an unknown rule is applied and asking the class to find the rules, etc.

Some experimental teachware has been developed in France and has given extremely interesting results.

What is important here is the emergence of a new type of teaching where the computer, in the hands of the teacher, plays an active role. Also important is the change introduced in the relationship between the teacher and the pupils whereby teachers cease to be those who dispense the truth and give bad marks for wrong answers. On the contrary, they encourage the intuition, the imagination and the creative thinking of pupils, leaving it to the computer to show whether a pupil's proposal is right or wrong, with the subsequent demonstration which helps pupils to understand why some ideas are right and others not.

Another possible use of the computer to assist the teacher in the classroom is 'guided discovery' which is the teacher's version of a game called *Microworld*. For that purpose, the teacher uses a software package simulating an experimental phenomenon (physics, chemistry, biology, demography, geography, etc.). Pupils work in groups on a terminal where they can change the parameters of the phenomenon and carry out experiments; they are asked to discover the laws governing the phenomenon. The teacher goes from one group to another.

There are four objectives. The first is to put children in a research situation, which leads to the construction of an explanatory model of what has been observed. This requires inductive reasoning and creative thinking at a rather high level of abstraction (children are working on a symbolic representation of a real event). The second is to verify that children apply correctly the experimental method: experiment, hypothesis, verification of the hypothesis through experimentation, new hypothesis, etc., with examples and counter examples. The third is to verify that children apply a strategy in order to ensure that their experiments converge towards a conclusion rather than arrive there through trial and error. The fourth is to help children to become autonomous in a situation which requires constructive thinking in the search for a solution.

Another interesting possibility for the teacher is small data-banks which can be used in many disciplines, the main purpose being to show that there are methods for asking the right questions and for refining these progressively, and that there are also methods for making a distinction between relevant and non-relevant facts in the answers given by the computer.

Computer-aided learning. Here, we are interested in the assistance a computer can give to the pupil. I shall only mention video-games or the so-called educational games; aside from what has been said previously about the psychological impact of the specific properties of the computer, they have on the whole little pedagogical value.

Besides these, the tutorial mode or the drill and practice mode can help the less gifted children at home to improve their results provided their parents pay attention (few children volunteer for working after class hours even on a computer when it becomes daily routine).

More interesting is a text-processing system with dictionary, which can be used to improve spelling or can encourage children to write, either because it comes out neatly printed or it can be sent directly through electronic mail. Dictionaries or encyclopædias on computers including video-disks are much more likely to be used by children because they are much more appealing than big heavy books with entries in alphabetical order; instead, they give immediate answers to any question with moving pictures on the screen.

Finally, the most interesting is probably still to come, as shown by a recent experiment in France. The example is in elementary chemistry but it can be used in any discipline. The software is an expert-system in chemistry but it is not used to answer questions. Instead of asking a question, the user submits a chemistry problem to the computer and asks the computer to explain step by step how it solves the problem. This is a good example of learning how to solve a problem by watching a computer solving that problem while giving step by step the rules which are followed to find the solution. This new direction seems very promising, at least for simple problems, and should be further investigated.

Where are we now?

Information technology and educational change

Over the last years it has become a general consensus in many countries that as education systems are no longer well adapted to our present world and even less to the foreseeable future, it is becoming more and more urgent to find ways and methods to improve them.

One of the main suggestions is to introduce computers into schools as a first step towards a generalized use of 'information technology' (video-cassette recorders, compact and video disks, electronic networking, etc.) whereas recent results in cognitive psychology give some hints as to how to use that technology (CEC, 1987; UNESCO, 1986).

For a long time instruction has been considered as a process of information transfer. The teaching-learning process is seen as one of transferring knowledge from the teacher to the learner. This view naturally puts the main emphasis on memorization of facts and on the aptitude of answering factual questions. The measure of efficiency of the process is defined by the quantity of information which has been transferred in a given time to a given number of learners, including an evaluation of the retention time (length of time after which the answers are still correct). As already noted, the initial use of computers in education supported that view through the tutorial mode.

Whereas a part of education is undoubtedly based on transfer of information (which explains why many activities in the classroom reflect that view), there is a recent tendency to consider education as an interactive process in which the teacher and the learner are both actors of the learning process. This is tightly linked to the recognition of the existence of 'naive theories' in students minds and to the necessity to start from these 'naive theories' to define a pedagogical strategy which will allow the building in the student's mind of a correct model of the outside world. This implies providing more opportunities for discussion, small group interaction, personal expression and collaborative instructional activities in the classroom.

A somewhat more dynamic view is emerging in which learning is defined as a transactional process in which the teacher and the learner are defined as two interacting systems, both of which are changed by the interaction (the teacher improves his model of the learner and the learner improves his understanding of the subject). In that perspective, the learning environment should provide the learners with access to knowledge and to opportunities to apply that knowledge to other situations. Open-ended educational software such as simulations of various situations and systems which allow students to define their own models for simulation purposes are relevant here.

Teacher training

Whether information technology is introduced into education for its own virtues (computer awareness, computer literacy, computer studies, etc.) or with the purpose of improving the teaching of various disciplines, experience has shown that nothing happens without teacher training (Lovis and Tagg, 1984).

Simply providing hardware to a school, even if it comes with very good software, will not suffice to change the teacher's daily practice for a number of reasons: even 'user friendly' computers are not easy to use for a newcomer, software documentation (technical and pedagogical) is usually poor, most software still has many 'bugs' which are strong deterrents for a beginner and preparing a lecture where computers are used is much more work for the teacher (at least in the early days). Teacher training is the only way to overcome these difficulties and is therefore an absolute prerequisite to the introduction of information technology in schools. However, it raises a number of problems.

There are different levels of teacher training depending on the purpose of the training. A first level is generally a short course on computer hardware and how it works, including bits, bytes, ROM, RAM, input/output, loading a disk and running a pre-written program. This kind of course is mostly technical and takes somewhere between two days and a full week. A second level is often about algorithms and elements of a programming language, with some information about the role of the operating system. The time required to complete that course depends on the objective. A one-week course is considered as a short introduction but if the participants are supposed to become able to write programs by themselves, it may take up to three or six months full-time. A third level is a course in educational software design. This normally includes: definition of pedagogical objectives, choice of a pedagogical strategy, defining a teaching/learning method, programming, debugging and testing methods, description of various available authoring systems, pedagogical evaluation methodologies, etc. In the very early stages of the use of computers in education it was generally thought that a majority of teachers should be able to write educational software, but as time went on the difficulty of designing and writing software became more evident and today this kind of course is normally given only to a minority of teachers. It takes a few months full-time (including lab work) to complete such a course. A fourth level is a course for training teacher-trainers as such people did not normally exist in the area of computer use in education. The curriculum of such a course is normally composed of elements of the three previous courses with varying levels of in-depth coverage.

Teacher training has been and still is the most important part of any policy for introducing computers into education because nothing will happen in schools without the teacher's approval. It is also, at least during the first few years, the most expensive and, unfortunately, the least visible part of such a policy (as compared to the visibility of bringing computers in classrooms). Local, regional and national authorities who funded the introduction of computers in education have therefore had a tendency to invest heavily in the visible part of such a policy (buying hardware) and to leave little funding for teacher training and for software (we shall come back to software later). This lack of training is the main reason why quite a number of schools have dust-covered computers in cupboards.

By way of example, the expenses for teacher training in France have been approximately as follows (in millions of United States dollars): 1982 – 5.5, 1983 – 9.5, 1984 – 20, 1985 – NA, 1986 – 9.5 and 1987 – 10.5, whereas during these same years some US$80 million has been spent on hardware (not including the expenses for the special project Informatics for All in 1985 which is mentioned later on).

Generally speaking the most difficult has been the very beginning, because there was nobody able to train teacher's teachers. In almost all advanced countries the very first courses for teachers were given by scientists from computer science; this is one of the reasons why, at the beginning, there was a very strong bias towards computer science in general and towards programming in particular.

Teachers had a tendency to consider that the difficult part in educational software was programming. It was only when they started to test their software with students that they became progressively aware that the most difficult problem was not programming but the teaching content. In fact it took time to admit that a trivial teaching method, even if it is difficult to program, remains a trivial method.

The way in which teacher training has been organized depends on the country, and primarily on the extent of government control over the education system.

Hardware problems

As already noted, the first experiments in schools were made in the late 1960s on terminals linked to time-shared mainframes or minicomputers, but these experiments remained few and isolated because most schools could not afford computers. The advent of the microcomputer changed the situation and the policy of buying hardware became strongly dependent on the level of control the central government had on schools.

In countries such as France, where everything in education is decided centrally and where private schools are few, the hardware-buying policy is decided by the government and it is legally impossible for schools to buy computers on their own. The drawback of such a policy is that it cannot take into account the specific needs of local situations – the model and the number of computers to be put in each school are imposed. On the other hand, such a policy has advantages because it makes all schools 'equal' (the number of computers given free is the same for each school and does not depend on the local economic situation) and, moreover, imposing a single computer hardware to all schools minimizes considerably the software portability problem from one school to another.

In countries such as the United Kingdom, where central control exists but is less tight, and where funding is mainly local, schools could choose their computer from among a few models, but the central government paid half the cost if the school chose the model 'recommended' by the government. Almost all schools bought the recommended model.

In countries such as the United States, where there is little federal control over education, where most of the funding is local and where there are many private schools, private initiatives under the pressure of local vendors or of heavy discounts from manufacturers or various lobbies have brought to school almost every existing model of microcomputer in the low price range with all the problems which this implies in terms of software portability, available educational software, hardware repair and maintenance, etc.

In countries that were fighting for a national computer industry, efforts were made for obliging (France) or 'convincing' (United Kingdom) schools to buy computers manufactured nationally. The 'national policy' of some countries was based on the assumption that schools represented a potential large market for microcomputers. Experience has shown that the argument is partly wrong in the sense that it is a market but not a large one, and in any case not sufficient to be used as a base for building a national microcomputer industry. In the advanced countries the computer/pupil ratio is between 1:30 and 1:50, which amounts to a few hundred thousand computers in the schools of each country. Most of these computers has been bought over the last ten years, and experts generally agree that about half are obsolete and will have to be replaced shortly. Most of them are by today's standards 'toy computers' (small RAMs, low speed, poor definition screen, no networking possible, exotic operating systems, etc.) for which no one wants to write educational software; some of them have been or are being discontinued.

Furthermore, pressure from parents for more computers in schools is decreasing partly because their children tell them that they already use a computer at school and partly because their children are not very enthusiastic about what they have been shown on computers for school purposes.

As a consequence there are today few nationwide plans to add another hundred thousand computers to those which already exist. Thus, it can be seen that the school market for microcomputers is not large compared to those of commerce, industry and administration and it is not going to grow significantly within the next few years. This does not mean that the educational market for information technology is not going to grow – it probably will, but not as an extension of the present institutional school market.

We shall come back later on to the revolution coming with the 'pocket-computer' which will be bought by parents and not by schools (as is already the case with programmable pocket-calculators).

Regarding hardware in general, past experience has shown that there is no need for a computer specifically dedicated to education; any commercially available microcomputer will do provided it has the following characteristics: large RAM (at least 1 Mb), fast CPU with floating point coprocessor, large capacity diskette reader and large (40 Mb) internal disk, hardware for networking, videodisc capacity, high definition graphics and standard operating systems with a rule which is little followed because it seems to go against common sense: 'the smaller the child the bigger the computer' or, put differently, the less smart the user, the more help that user requests from the computer which implies larger and more sophisticated software which in turn implies, if the computer reaction time is to be kept short (small children have no patience), a more powerful computer to be able to execute larger programs in less time.

The software problems

SPECIFICITY OF EDUCATIONAL SOFTWARE

Educational software shares some important problems with general software, i.e. portability, maintainability, importance of man-machine interface, etc., but these technical aspects are minor; pedagogy is the main issue.

Writing and testing general software is a rather easy task because, with a few exceptions, the problem to be solved is almost always well-defined and even if it is not so, the program can be easily tested by checking if it solves the problem in specific cases where the answer is known.

With educational software the aim may be well-defined in some cases (teach rules of grammar, etc.) but the method to achieve the aim is a total guess because nobody knows how students learn! General software acts on data and prints results whereas educational software is supposed to act primarily on the user himself (change his knowledge, his know-how, his behaviour, etc.).

We are, in fact, unable to check the efficiency of educational software as compared to traditional education because it depends heavily on individuals and, moreover, it is extremely difficult to define what traditional education is. The nearest we come to evaluation is by comparing statistically the results of two groups of students, one working with computers and one without. This is fine, but what do we measure? The quality of a piece of software as compared to the quality of the teacher working with the other group? The 'Hawthorne effect'? The excitement of the students being part of an experiment? The absence of any definite criteria as to the pedagogical value of a piece of educational software explains why trends in aim, design and evaluation have changed over the years – and are still changing – as a function of how fashionable a given pedagogical strategy is at any given time.

Table 1. Distribution of software by type in the United States (7325 software)

Type	Percentage [1]
Drill	15
Skills practice	51
Tutorial	33
Concept demonstration	3
Concept development	4
Hypothesis testing	1
Educational games	19
Simulations	9
Tool programs	11

[1] The sum is >100% because some programs are assigned more than one type.

Source: Office of Technological Assessment (OTA), July 1987, Washington, D. C.

Moreover the existing educational software looks like a big patchwork made of completely unrelated bits and pieces (a bit of Mendel's laws, a piece of French grammar, a bit of nuclear physics, a bit of biological simulation, etc.) made by different people with different aims in mind and using different approaches or strategies.

Designing educational software

The lack of available educational software is one of the main complaints of teachers working with computers; furthermore, many teachers also complain about the poor quality of what exists. Globally speaking it is true that in all countries educational software is a scarce resource. By the end of the 1980s there were some 10,000 software packages in the United States, about 2,000 in the United Kingdom and 1,000 in France. Moreover, between 70 and 80 per cent of these are either rote drill or elementary skills practice or

**Table 2. Distribution of educational software by subject in the
United States (same 7325 software)**

Subject	Percentage [1]
Comprehensive	6
Computers	5
English language	12
Foreign languages	5
Mathematics	27
Reading	12
Science	16
Social sciences	8
Others	18

[1] The total is >100% because of multiple assignments.

Source: Office of Technological Assessment (OTA), July 1987, Washington, D. C.

tutorials with multiple choice questions or educational games; most are therefore considered by teachers to be completely trivial from a pedagogical point of view.

Educational software design is a very difficult task. It is a recently established area of activity, little is known as to what contributes to quality and there are no established know-how, rules or experience. Most authors know very little about the methodology of programming in general and too many authors do not invest the necessary efforts to make their program attractive to use and easy to run through appropriate input-output procedures ('friendly' man-machine communication requires impressive amounts of lines of code). Many authors think that they are finished when their program runs bug-free. This is however often a rather small part of the total job as the program has first to be tested with students to check acceptance, interest, results, etc. The results of the tests lead generally to modifications of various parts of the program followed by a new set of tests. Finally, to facilitate use of the program, it should come with pedagogical documentation (objectives, methodology, expected results, etc.), practical documentation (user's guide, user's manual) and technical documentation (structure of the software, structure of files and access methods, list of parameters which are accessible to the use, etc.). The total time required by all these activities explains why the design of educational software is a lengthy process (which means an expensive one) leading to high prices per copy. This tendency is further exacerbated because the market for educational software is small.

This situation is well described in a report by the Office of Technological Assessment:

> OTA finds that software manufacturers tend to play it safe. They produce what teachers will buy and teachers usually buy products that are familiar. The potential result is a relatively homogenous set of products that fall short of the possibilities provided by the new learning tool. The problem of a fragmented market is aggravated by information barriers, difficulties in enforcing intellectual property rights and the incompatibility of hardware and operating systems... Unauthorized duplication of software programs, as well as theft of broad software design principles, continue to plague the industry and the presence of different computers in the schools, with different operating systems raises development costs for publishers in pursuit of market share. The commercial market may be viable but there is substantial concern for the long-term quality and diversity of its products (OTA, 1988).

SOFTWARE EVALUATION

Different groups of people are interested in software evaluation, but the interest in the various aspects of evaluation varies from group to group (Winship, 1988). Classroom teachers want information allowing them to make a choice between existing software either for use in their classroom or for making recommendations for purchasing software. School directors and inspectors will probably select software for various grades and subject areas, and therefore rely more upon available evaluations than do teachers. Software authors and publishers need evaluations for improving their products. A publisher will probably discontinue products getting bad evaluations or encourage authors to design products more or less similar to those getting good evaluations (the 'remake' or 'play-safe' policy).

The necessity of evaluating the quality of educational software showed up very early among teachers. In the beginning it took the form of more or less informal bulletins or, as the majority of software was developed by teachers, sessions in professional meetings. As software became available commercially, more formal evaluation structures appeared – committees inside the Ministry of Education (in the case of centralized countries like France) or clearinghouses making their evaluation available to other educators either in printed form or through a terminal connected to a computer network (examples of the latter include Educational Products Information Exchange, MicroSIFT and the York University Faculty of Education On-Line Service).

> 'There has been no other kind of teaching and learning resource in the history of education that has prompted such widespread efforts at evaluation', but it is fair to add that 'the efforts [to design and disseminate software in schools] are without precedence in size and scope in the development of educational material' (Owston, 1987).

All surveys of quality have shown that the overall level is rather low. A study done at Columbia University Teacher's College concluded that most available software is poorly designed and does not take advantage of the possibilities of the microcomputers. It has frequently been said (EPIE, York University, Alberta Education) that no more than 5 to 10 per cent of the existing software can be considered as acceptable.

Another reason for evaluating software is the difficulty of obtaining copies from software producers for previewing. Producers are reluctant to send out copies for previewing because they fear that the software may be illegally copied. On the other hand, teachers are not used to buying teaching resources without having seen them. As regards choosing software, reading evaluations is the only source of information.

In fact different companies have different policies, and because of the competition, more and more companies try to improve their service to teachers by making copies of their software available for inspection generally in the form of a down-graded version with limited possibilities.

The impossibility of previewing is not the only reason for software evaluation; the sheer volume of available software makes previewing an impossible task for any single teacher. Software evaluation therefore plays an important role by providing a means of sifting through a large number of software to choose a small number for closer inspection.

Whereas there is still no agreement on a universal evaluation grid for educational software most institutions which evaluate regularly have developed their own questionnaire (EPIE, MicroSIFT, ministerial document in various countries such as Canada or France, various specialized magazines, etc.). This does not solve the evaluation problem at the most general level but it has the advantage that all software are evaluated, for a given institution, against the same grid or scale.

However, regardless of the method used, all current approaches tend to present a number of weaknesses. First, current approaches tend to be comparative in the sense that evaluators are asked to grade software by their level of agreement with various statements like 'strongly agree', 'agree', 'disagree', 'strongly disagree' that the presentation of software is simple, clear, fit to the learner's level, etc. As there are no objective standards in this area, evaluators have a tendency to answer by comparing with the software they know or have used. Second, current approaches tend to be subjective in the sense that, even if the questions asked of the evaluators seem or look or try to be objective, the answers are neccessarily a function of the evaluator's beliefs, habits, qualification in his discipline, his pedagogical talent, etc. The subjective aspects of evaluation can be minimized by comparing evaluations made by different evaluators but the difficulty remains. Finally, current approaches tend to give an 'atomic' evaluation in the sense that the set of answers to the forty or fifty questionnaire items do not allow an overall judgement about a software. They give hints about various aspects which are, of course, important but they cannot capture the complex interactions of the many parameters which, in combination, are often an important characteristic of quality software.

Case studies in 'advanced countries'

History and state of the art in the United States

The American system of education is very decentralized (the federal government has little influence on it) and responsibility is mainly exercised by state governments and local authorities. It is therefore difficult to give a precise account of what happened in schools throughout the country owing to the considerable contrasts between different states.

Generally speaking, however, the introduction of computers into schools has been the result of local or regional efforts, and we shall therefore limit this report to the description of some well-known large scale projects and to statistical results when it comes to the whole country.

TWO MAJOR PROJECTS

The PLATO project. This project was started at University of Illinois at Urbana in the early 1960s on the Illiac I computer with a single terminal to investigate the possible roles of the computer in the pedagogical process and the possibility of building a computer system with a powerful processing unit and many terminals, capable of competing, in terms of cost per hour and per user, with the traditional education system. Through successive extensions, the PLATO system, which has been commercialized for many years by Control Data Corporation (CDC), uses a very powerful central processing unit with hundreds of terminals spread throughout the country and linked to the central site through telephone lines. It is also available in other countries such as the United Kingdom, Belgium and France.

A recent version, Micro-PLATO, tries to lower the cost of the use of telephone lines; instead of renting a simple terminal which must remain connected to the central site during a whole lesson, CDC is renting out a PLATO microcomputer into which the software for any lesson requested by the user can be down-loaded at high speed through a telephone line from the central processing unit. The processing for the whole lesson is thereafter done locally without any further use of the telephone line.

One of the characteristics of PLATO is the use of a single programming language, TUTOR, (also known as an 'author language') for writing all the courseware packages. This was supposed to simplify the task of writing courseware packages by avoiding the necessity of learning a standard programming language such as BASIC, FORTRAN or PASCAL. In fact successive extensions have made TUTOR at least as difficult to master as any other programming language. There are over 4000 lessons available in over seventy different subjects.

PLATO has been reasonably successful in the United States as well as in other countries. For instance the University of Delaware adopted PLATO in 1975 and during the academic year 1982–1983, for instance, about 29,000 students have used the system with a mean use of three hours per student. The University has about twenty on-campus and ninety off-campus terminals.

The TICCIT Project. This project, funded by the National Science Foundation, was started in the early 1970s by the MITRE Corporation and the Institute for Computer Uses in Education at Brigham Young University at Provo (Utah).

The TICCIT (Time Shared Interactive Computer Controlled Information Television) project did not succeed and was abandoned after a few years of research. It is, however, interesting because its aims and scope were completely different from the PLATO project and, in many ways, complementary. The hardware consisted of two NOVA 800 minicomputers, disk-drives, 128 terminals composed of high resolution colour-television receivers with added graphic possibilities and a keyboard incorporating a set of 'learner control' keys as well as a standard typewriter keyboard. These terminals had to be on-site which means within 300 meters of the central processing unit (CPU).

PLATO and TICCIT are not only opposites in their scales (minis versus maxi, on-site versus remote access); they are also opposites in the sense that TICCIT is an integrated project in which the courseware is supposed to come as a standard part of the system.

Specific to TICCIT is the complete separation between course content and computer programming. More than that, course content and teaching strategy are also separated. This allows the strategy to be incorporated into a computer program at the operating system level, written by programming experts which in turn permits a team of specialists including instructional psychologists, subject matter experts, design technicians, packaging specialists and programmers to co-operate in writing an integrated system.

Because of the variety of system outputs and the small memory available on the computer, the task of the software group was much more complex than initially planned and the system took two more years to complete than expected.

TICCIT was tested in the mid-1970s in a few places such as the Phoenix Community College and the Northwestern Virginia Community College, but the high cost of producing courseware in the TICCIT environment and various delays in the debugging of the system finally led to the project's being abandoned.

THE PRESENT SITUATION

Since the advent of the microcomputer in the late 1970s the situation has changed as more and more microcomputers have come into schools. Moreover, the computer industry is helping through high discount rates and sometimes even free computers for schools. The production of courseware is left almost completely to private companies and there is no general policy for teacher training.

Over the last five years the general trend has been towards using computers to teach 'computer literacy' which in most places included computer structure, programming in BASIC or in LOGO, the impact of computers in commerce, industry and administration and on society at large with more or less emphasis on the different subjects, depending on places.

Recently, there has been a change in emphasis and there is now a trend towards 'computer literacy in disciplines' with emphasis on how to teach a discipline using a computer, how use of computers changes the content of what is taught in a discipline, etc.

Primary education (6 to 11 years old). Over 90 per cent of all primary schools own at least one computer and of these 70 per cent own at least five microcomputers or more. Because of the decentralization of the American education system, schools and local authorities can choose freely their equipment. However, some school districts have set up technical centres to help administrators and heads of schools to choose the right equipment and courseware. For instance, the state of Minnesota has created the Minnesota Educational Computing Consortium (MECC) which has recently become a private company which evaluates and distributes courseware packages as well as thousands of microcomputers for all levels of teaching. The same kind of service is available in other places, for instance the 'Houston Independent School District', the 'New York State Center for Learning Technologies', the 'Educational Collaboration Center of Greater Boston', etc.

In primary education the general trend is to give access to the greatest possible number of children to the existing equipment, which in turn implies that each child has a rather short access time to the computer.

Statistically, in primary schools, a microcomputer is used about eleven hours a week (a little over two hours a day). In fact, the practical use varies widely from school to school. In a typical primary school, 80 per cent of the children have access to a computer during less than thirty minutes each week while one child out of fifty has more than one hour of access each week. Typically about 40 per cent of the time the computers are in use is spent for exercises in mathematics, spelling and memorizing. Another third is spent by teachers for copying and evaluating courseware and the rest is used for pedagogical games.

Secondary education (12 to 18 years old). Between 90 and 95 per cent (depending on sources) of all secondary schools own at least one microcomputer. Of these, 90 per cent own at least five microcomputers or more.

Secondary schools have, for computer access, quite a different policy from primary schools. They choose to restrict the access to computers but to give to some of their pupils a longer access time.

Statistically, in secondary schools, microcomputers are used about thirteen hours a week. Here again the real use of computers varies widely from school to school. Some 20 per cent of the schools say that they use each computer over five hours each day while another 20 per cent use each computer only one hour each day. Typically, the majority of children in a secondary school have access to a computer for forty-five minutes each week; two children out of five have more than one hour access per week. About 70 per cent of the computer time used by the children is for 'computer literacy', 18 per cent for drill and practice, and the rest for pedagogical games, text processing and laboratory work.

In many secondary schools informatics is taught as a subject during three hours each week for twenty weeks to children over 14 (mainly programming) while the use of computers for teaching mathematics, sciences and foreign languages increases as the corresponding courseware packages increase in quality.

The courseware problem. Since the beginning, states and local school authorities have paid for most of the hardware but have not participated significantly to the funding for courseware development.

Some packages have been written by university professors with funds from the federal government but most of the existing courseware packages have been produced by private companies and the mean quality of these products is generally considered as rather low. This is probably due to the fact that the companies are small and cannot afford the right manpower to produce high quality products.

About 750 companies are producing software packages to be sold to schools and many thousand packages are available. Most are produced by book publishers such as Addison Wesley, Giner and Co., Random House, Mac Graw Hill, Scott Foresman, etc., but show-business companies are also entering the market, for instance Walt Disney and Children Television Network.

Several institutions have been created to try to help schools in their choice of hardware or software. These include the Minnesota Educational Computing Consortium, the National Co-ordinating Center for Curriculum Development (part of the State University New-York at Stony Brook), the Northwestern Regional Laboratory (its information centre, 'MICROSIFT', gathers and evaluates available software packages to inform teachers in schools about the content and the value of the packages) and the Conduit Consortium (Iowa) a non-profit making organization formed by a group of about a dozen different universities for selling software packages at a low price ($10 to $50). The originality of the Conduit Consortium is that it does not produce courseware but has a number of experts for reviewing proposed packages; it sells only those which have been accepted by those experts.

The availability of courseware for the classroom is one of the main difficulties as most of the existing courseware, except those for the teaching of reading, generally do not fit existing curricula in schools.

Trends and perspectives. Since the early 1980s public opinion in the United States has been very favourable to the introduction of computers into schools and this is why the number of computers has steadily increased. Some experts do not hesitate to say that computers in schools is the only possible answer to some of the difficulties of the United States education system as described in *A Nation at Risk* (National Commission on Excellence in Education, 1983); the main argument is that massive use of computers by children could help to overcome the insufficient level of training of teachers at a lower cost than retraining all teachers.

However, quite recently a number of articles have appeared which question the role of computers in education as a universal panacea and insist on the fact that there is no use putting computers in a school, even if they are given free, as long as the teachers do not know for what educational purpose they are going to use them.

> Clearly the teachers are central to full development of technology in education. Teachers are not the problem and without them there can be no solution. Most teachers want to use technology but few have found ways to exploit its full potential. The technology will not be used and certainly not used well, unless teachers are trained in the use of technology, provided goals for new applications, supported in doing so, and rewarded for successes in meeting these goals (OTA, 1988).

Moreover some university professors warn that computers in education may well follow the fad-and-reject cycle which has already been the case for previous technological tools, for instance the film and television, a new technology being rejected and put aside as soon as the excessive predictions of improvement of education do not show up in practice.

The United Kingdom experience

THE SCHOOL SYSTEM

The school system in the United Kingdom can be divided into a system covering England, Wales and Northern Ireland, and a system for Scotland. Both systems are very decentralized in the sense that there does exist a Department of Education and Science (DES) at the government level but the school system depends much more on local educational authorities (LEAs) than on the central government.

There is however a strong link between DES and the school system through the Schools Council (created in 1964), an independent body funded equally by DES and the LEAs. The Schools Council develops the curricula, undertakes educational research, approves new A-level syllabuses (final examination of secondary education) and advises the Secretary of State on the examination system.

THE NDPCAL PROJECT (1973-1978)

Aims and scope. The National Development Program in Computer Assisted Learning (NDPCAL) has been a remarkable innovation in the area of financing educational change. In 1973 DES decided to earmark £2 million for testing and developing the use of the computer as an aid to teaching.

A small Directorate for NDPCAL was established by Richard Hooper that year; its number fluctuated but never exceeded seven people, including secretarial support. Overall direction and control of policy remained with a Program Committee of twenty-two members, including representatives of seven government departments and of bodies such as the Council for Educational Technology, Schools Council, University Grant Committee and Social Science Research Council and an important group of co-opted advisers from academic, technical and industrial organizations. This committee received proposals for projects after they had been developed jointly by the Directorate and the projects staff; these proposals had to be approved by the Program Committee.

From the beginning it was decided to have two external evaluation reports on the project, one educational evaluation (carried out by a team led by Barry Mc Donald of the Centre for Applied Research in Education at the University of East Anglia) and one financial evaluation (carried out by John Fielden and Philip Pearson, members of a Management Consultant Office).

Moreover, the aim for NDPCAL being 'to develop and secure the assimilation of computer assisted and computer managed learning on a regular institutional basis at reasonable cost' (Richard Hooper) all institutions which submitted a project were invited to fund their project with an amount equal to that provided by NDPCAL. It was hoped that this policy would encourage the use of computers in education even after the end of the project. Finally, NDPCAL had two objectives: Computer Aided Learning (CAL) and Computer Managed Instruction (CMI).

The CAL projects. Altogether there have been seventeen CAL projects funded by NDPCAL: nine in higher and further education, three in secondary schools, two in industrial training and three in military training (one Royal Navy, one Army, one Royal Air Force). The programs written to implement the projects are in the form of packages (450 altogether) but the size of the packages are widely spread from 100 lines of code to over 10,000, the mean being around 700 lines of code per package. The programming languages used were FORTRAN, BASIC and special 'author-languages'.

It is important to note that the time devoted by academic staff to writing the packages was generally no more than 10 to 20 per cent of the total time; the bulk of the job was done by programmers hired on NDPCAL funds. When one also notes that it was estimated that no more than 20 to 30 per cent of the staff funded by NDPCAL would be funded by the institutions after the end of NDPCAL, a serious problem emerges for institutionalization of CAL in the absence of outside funding, unless CAL is ranked high in institutional priorities.

In agreement with findings in most places, the time needed to develop a one-hour interaction package has been found to be in the order of 100 to 300 hours. Moreover, no real learning curve in package development was found, which means that as programmers and academic staff gained experience of CAL there was no decrease in the time needed to develop new packages. The reason is that, as time goes on, packages become more and more complex, and programmers as well as academic staff seek new challenges once they have mastered the easy work.

The average use per terminal in hours has been well under the level of the forecasts made at the beginning. Whereas a feasibility study made by the National Committee for Educational Technology predicted in 1969 an average use of 2000 terminal hours each year, experience has shown that the real use has been somewhere between 150 and 500 hours per year depending on the institutions.

The three CAL projects in schools are not significant. Two are in history and one in geography, and in all three cases computers were used through inquiries sent through the postal service to be processed in batch mode and then sent back to the schools. They are also not significant in terms of funding, the funding from NDPCAL being less than 6 per cent of the total resources for CAL.

The two projects in the area of industrial training are also of little interest as they offer no base for generalization and used together no more than 6 per cent of the total budget of NDPCAL for CAL.

Despite the fact that it was believed towards the end of the NDPCAL project that CAL would probably not be used, over 35,000 student-terminal-hours were recorded, which amounted to over 10 per cent of the time of each student in 1976/1977. A significant part of the projects started with the help of NDPCAL have continued in a number of institutions.

The CMI projects. Computer Managed Instruction (CMI) also called Computer Managed Learning (CML) deals with the use of computers as an aid to educational management where computers are used, at frequent intervals, for recording, marking, assessing, directing or recommending and reporting.

The computer plays the role of a tutor, delivering tests and, depending on the marking of the tests, indicating a set of learning modules to be taken by the student. A complete system of this kind is generally a large project taking a long time to implement and involving complex system software but partial systems implementing only a subset of all functions mentioned are also possible.

Moreover, a CMI system can be either specialized or 'content-specific' for one particular application or it can be 'content-free' in the sense that it has no in-built course content or type of reporting but is easily adaptable to any particular need.

The most important CMI development within NDPCAL is a software package called *CAMOL* (Computer Management Of Learning), a large content-free system initially developed by International Computers Limited (ICL) in the United Kingdom. Part of the system and most of the educational material for applications have been developed with NDPCAL funds. There are two main applications. The first, at the New University of Ulster (course on curriculum design and development partly based on material produced by the Open University and partly on locally prepared material), concerns about 200 students each year and represents one-third of the students workload for half of an academic year. The second is at Brighton Polytechnic where CAMOL is mainly used for test-marking, question analysis and record keeping for about 600 students each year (150 and 500 hours per year depending on the institutions).

Dissemination. NDPCAL has funded two small organizations for exchanging and disseminating CAL products. They were intended to collect packages, test and eventually modify them, and distribute them upon request to their members.

The Physical Sciences Program (PSPE) disseminates small packages, mainly in Physics and Chemistry, to its members who are professionals able to modify or even translate the packages in another programming language. Membership is about 50 and the requests for programs are in the range of 30 a month. Given the small staff of PSPE, the cost of a package is around £10.

The Geographical Association Package Exchange (GAPE) has a membership with no or little knowledge of computers. It has a small central staff for soliciting, testing and amending packages, with distribution based on a number of regional centres in colleges, polytechnics and universities and from them to local schools. At the end of the NDPCAL project they had already distributed 270 copies of packages to 70 schools, colleges, polytechnics and universities.

Costs. The total cost of the NDPCAL project from 1973 to 1978 was £2.5 million, broken down as follows: computers, terminals – £400,000; staff working on projects – £160,000; travel – £100,000; and other – £400,000. The matched funding from the institutions amounted to about £2 million, half of which was spent on hardware.

Careful analysis by an evaluation group has led to the following conclusions. First, cost-benefit techniques are not relevant to CAL and CMI – outcomes cannot generally be quantified. Second, projects vary greatly in unit cost terms; some CAL applications cost less than £5 a student-hour and others over £20. Finally, CAL and CMI do not replace anything; they represent and add-on cost.

THE MICRO-ELECTRONICS EDUCATION PROGRAMME (MEP)

As early as 1979 the British Government announced at £12.5 million programme of support for micro-electronics education in schools. This programme did not materialize but in March 1980 DES started the 'Micro-electronics Education Programme' with a total funding of £9 million for four years (Thorn, 1987).

About a year later Richard Fothergill, director of MEP, supported by a small team of seven people was operating from offices based in Newcastle upon Tyne.

The programme is responsible to the Departments of Education of England, Northern Ireland and Wales and it operates through contracts administered by the Council for Educational Technology. MEP is aimed at primary and secondary schools in England, Northern Ireland and Wales, and there is a different programme for Scotland (Scottish Micro-electronics Programme).

Aims and objectives. MEP has two main objectives: first, it investigates the most appropriate way of using the computer as an aid to teaching and learning, as a guide to the individual child, as a learning aid for small groups of children or as a system which involves the whole class. Software can be developed for computer-based learning across the curriculum but MEP will give priority to applications in mathematics, the sciences, craft/design technology, geography and courses related to business or clerical occupations. Second, it introduces new topics in the curriculum, either as separate disciplines or as new elements of existing subjects. The new topics (at varying levels of specialization) include (1) micro-electronics in control technology, (2) electronics and its applications in particular systems, (3) computer studies, (4) computer-linked studies, including computer aided design, data-logging and data processing, (5) word processing and other electronic office techniques, and (6) use of the computer as a means of information retrieval from data-bases.

In order to implement MEP, three main needs were identified which had to be met for the programme to succeed: to inform teachers about activities and developments in the field, to train teachers in the methodology of using computers effectively in the classroom, and to develop materials to be used by the teachers and examine the whole issue of computers in the curriculum.

Despite the small number of microcomputers in schools, it had been agreed that MEP resources would not be used for the purchase of large quantities of equipment. In fact a special project 'Micros in Schools' was started by the Department of Industry to help secondary schools buy computers. Through this project (£1 million) secondary schools which chose to buy one of the two British-made micros paid half price, the other half of the price being paid by the project. By the end of 1982, about 5,000 secondary schools had bought a microcomputer under this scheme. Moreover in July at that year a second 'Micros in Schools' project was launched for the 27,000 primary schools under the same conditions. Today almost every primary school has at least one computer.

One important feature of these schemes has been their insistence on having at least two teachers receive basic training on the equipment as a condition of purchase.

Management. Because of the small amount of money available, it was impossible to work directly with the 109 LEAs. The LEAs were therefore grouped into fourteen regions. It was decided that two-thirds of the funding would go to regional and one-third to national initiatives.

Each regional centre has an information centre containing a software library and other relevant teaching material for use in the classroom including videotapes, slides, audio-cassettes, books and electronic devices. Many of these are produced by MEP but commercially developed materials are also available.

In each region there are four training centres, normally based in LEAs where courses are given on four main themes: technology, including electronics, control technology and industrial applications; computers, including computer studies and the computer as a device; computer-based learning, including the use of equipment as an aid to teaching across the whole curriculum; and communication and information, including business studies and the changing role of information.

Each region has a regional co-ordinator in each of the four fields; there is also a national co-ordinator for each field.

A variety of courses is normally available: one-to-three day courses for beginners, one-week courses for those having already taken the beginner's course, three-month courses for those who want to specialize or to write courseware, and courses for teacher trainers.

For each region £60,000 are reserved each year for organizing courses; the daily cost is evaluated at £25, which means about 2,400 teacher-days per year and per region. In addition, distance courses are given by the Open University, the British Broadcasting Corporation and the National Extension College.

Courseware. Because of the delays and cost in producing courseware, this is the least available resource. Evaluations of the necessary resources made in the United Kingdom indicate that in order to provide each school with one course per week using the computer, about 1,000 different packages are needed; if the computer is to be used during one course every day, then about 5,000 packages are needed. Today there are about 2,000 packages available commercially.

The dissemination of software packages is one of the roles of the mentioned regional information centres which are invited to work along the lines of two organizations set up during NDPCAL: Project CEDAR (Computers in Education As a Resource) at the Imperial College and the different SATROS (Science and Technology Regional Education) which are organizations for disseminating to all their members the packages written by some of the members. Other organizations which help to disseminate available packages include MUSE which publishes a journal called *Computers in School* and which centralizes and sells about fifty packages at prices between £1 and £2 (exceptionally £10) and MAPE (Micros and Primary Education) which publishes the journal *Micro-Scope*.

Finally, to encourage the use of computers in education, for each microcomputer bought by a primary school, MEP provides thirty free packages.

The last period. By the end of March 1988 the government decided that time had come for local authorities to take over the activities and MEP was closed down. To help the transition an intermediate institution called Microelectronics Education Support Unit – MESU – was set up with half the annual budget of MEP.

MESU has a staff of about fifty and gives help to LEAs in various aspects of information technology in schools, including examples of good practice, publications, reviews, hardware and software development, training for pre- and in-service, standard protocols for software and software portability. The staff works in small teams to keep contact with the 110 LEAs and the about 90 teacher-training institutions.

Currently DES funded 660 information technology 'advisory teachers' (ATs) for two years. These ATs are recruited by the LEAs for their proven subject expertise rather than for their knowledge of information technology and MESU is funded to train them both in information technology and in their role as change agents. In their advisory role, these ATs will help disseminate MESU's many publications (books, training packs, curriculum materials, programs, etc.).

Recently the government decided to merge MESU with the National Council of Education Technology to become the National Council for Educational Technology.

CONCLUSION

After project NDPCAL from 1973 to 1978 where over 50áper cent of the funds available was spent for staffing and which left a number of on-going CAL activities after the end of the project, MEP again has emphasized the importance of teacher-training. The buying of equipment was encouraged with the objective of one computer per school. This aim was almost met.

Despite efforts made by NDPCAL and MEP, courseware packages remain a scarce resource and will probably continue so for some years, thereby constituting an obstacle to rapid spreading of the computers in schools. Much remains to be done because, in the words of the Director of MESU:

> There is still a long way to go before we can say that most teachers are comfortable with a computer in the classroom and that we are using the computer in all subject areas, at all levels of attainment with all age groups, wherever it is appropriate to do so (Foster, 1989).

The French experience

SETTING THE SCENE

The way computers have been introduced in education in France is strongly related to the structure of the French system of education; a few words of introduction are therefore necessary for those readers not familiar with this system.

The entire French education system is strongly centralized with a hierarchy ranging from the teacher up to the Minister. All teachers, from kindergarten up to university level, are government employees; all curricula are completely defined down to the least detail by the Ministère de l'Éducation Nationale and are compulsory for all schools. The curriculum for each school-year is therefore the same in all schools throughout France. Moreover, for teachers, the number of teaching hours per week are also determined centrally. Finally, all examinations are national which means, for instance, that for the *Baccalauréat* (the examination all students take at the end of secondary school, at about age 18), all 200,000 students have to go, the same day and at the same hour, to examination centers where they have to work on exactly the same subject.

The Ministère de l'Éducation Nationale with its 600,000 teachers and professors, 500,000 civil servants working in offices and about 13 million pupils and students has been called the biggest company in France; its budget is approximately 18 per cent of the total budget of the country.

For the last few years a real effort has been made to de-concentrate and decentralize this enormous monolith. The country has been divided in twenty-seven academic regions (*rectorat*) under the authority of a *recteur* nominated by the Ministre. Each region is, again, subdivided in smaller districts (100 altogether) under the authority of an *inspecteur* who is, again, nominated by the Ministre.

Although it has some drawbacks, such a centralized education system has advantages when it comes to decision-making and implementation of changes, as shown during the introduction of computers within the French education system.

THE COLD START (1970-1976)

In 1970 a commission preparing the 6th Five Year Governmental Plan discussed the introduction of computers in education and the official report of that Commission *La formation en informatique pendant le 6ème Plan – 1971*) made a distinction between (a) training computer specialists, (b) introduction to computer science and (c) more general information to make informatics familiar to a large number of students. For obvious reasons, this last objective had to be achieved in secondary schools through general education.

Without waiting for the conclusions of the Commission, the Ministre de l'Éducation appointed Professor W. Mercouroff as Chargé de mission à l'Informatique; his role was to implement the different conclusions of the Commission's report.

The pedagogical objectives of the first phase. Professor Mercouroff agreed that computer science was definitely not a subject to be taught in general secondary education because computer structure and programming were technical skills and, therefore, not relevant to general secondary education.

Moreover, programmed learning was discouraged and teachers were asked to develop courseware based on simulation and modelling in all disciplines.

Operation. Naturally, the different operations carried on overlapped, but they were launched successively.

Teacher training. Some 530 secondary-school teachers of various disciplines were trained in universities, for a full academic year, on a volunteer basis, between 1970 and 1976. In addition, during the same period, over 5000 teachers took a correspondence course in computer science specially established and oriented toward applications in secondary education.

After training, the teachers resumed their teaching duties in their schools. Each was asked to implement a pedagogical use of the computer in his discipline and to try it out with pupils. All these projects were co-ordinated by the Institut National de la Recherche Pédagogique (INRP), the French national pedagogical institute.

Choice of programming language. In order to disseminate the courseware written by teachers and to avoid spending time and money in rewriting programs from one language to another, a specific programming language was created by the Computer Department at the Ecole Supérieure d'Electricité.

This is the *langage symbolique d'enseignement (LSE)*. It is a French-speaking, highly interactive, ALGOL-like language, simple enough for beginners yet sufficiently sophisticated to be effective for experienced programmers.

Computers installed. A standard hardware configuration was defined and several minicomputers – the MITRA 15 from the Compagnie Internationale pour l'Informatique and the T 1600 from La Télémécanique – were ordered in 1972. In 1976, fifty-eight such minicomputers were installed in secondary schools (and gave the name to the experiment). These computers were time-shared, and accommodated eight terminals and a printer; later, a floppy disk drive was added.

Results. The experiment of the fifty-eight secondary schools was rather unique. Its development was stopped in 1976, but it lasted until 1980 with the same equipment. At the same time, a team from INRP started an evaluation of the experiment. The main results of this evaluation are: (1) during the experiment, 45,000 students (one out of two) and more than 1,000 teachers (one out of six) used a computer each year in the equipped schools; (2) the computers were used an average of 32 hours per week, 25 weeks per year (800 hours in a year); (3) a set of more than 400 courses written by teachers was centralized, evaluated, documented and distributed by INRP; (4) general information on informatics was effectively given; moreover, some volunteer students received an initiation into computer science; and (5) lastly, the introduction of informatics has been achieved through all disciplines, not only in mathematics and science.

There are, however, additional remarks. Despite official instructions, there is an important number of packages using programmed learning (mainly in French grammar or foreign languages). The majority of course-ware packages in experimental sciences are using simulation and modelling. During the one-year full-time training, too much emphasis was put on computer structure and programming per se, and not enough on the peda-gogical use of computers; this produced some harmful results. For instance, a non-negligible number of teachers have been fascinated by the machine and have become unconditional computerniks, lending credence to the idea that it is important to teach computer science as a separate discipline (the probable reason behind this attitude is that it is more fun to play around with computers than to teach algebra or history). Another harmful result comes from the fact that many teachers had great difficulties in mastering the use of a programming language and had, therefore, a tendency to consider that the challenging part in a courseware package was the writing of the program and not the definition of the pedagogical objectives. The net results are some packages of little real value because their objectives are trivial or could be achieved with pencil and paper or in book form. Finally, despite the fact that almost all teachers realized that producing a package was a difficult and time-consuming activity, many of them had a very critical attitude towards packages written by others (the not-made-here syndrome).

Since few similar projects have existed on the same scale, it is difficult to compare France's experimental use of computers in education with experiences elsewhere. Perhaps the only comparable experience is the NDPCAL Project, which lasted from 1973 to 1979, and had a budget of the same order of magnitude. NDPCAL, however, was mainly aimed at the university level. Out of seventeen projects, only three were in secondary education, and all three were in history and geography.

Even so, similar remarks can be made regarding both projects. About 60 per cent of NDPCAL's budget was spent for staffing, whereas in France about 70 per cent of the budget was spent for the same purpose: teacher-training and package-writing. The evaluation of terminal use during NDPCAL showed a mean use of 500 hours/year; during France's experiment, the terminals were used about 800 hours/year. During both projects, the amount of time needed to write a one-hour interactive program was somewhere between 100 and 300 hours. In both cases, the best packages generally were produced by teachers working in teams. For both projects, the emphasis in teaching mode was on modeling and simulation, and the attitudes of students were very positive – in these modes, the student has the initiative in dialogue. Again from both projects, experts concluded that CAI will not replace anything but will add on to what already exists.

THE 10,000 MICROCOMPUTERS PLAN

By 1979, the first generation of microcomputers had arrived, mainly based on 8-bit microprocessors using floppy disks as auxiliary memories. They were far from professional standards in terms of versatility, reliability and sophistication of operating system. Nevertheless, it was evident that second-generation microcomputers – including all necessary features – were close at hand.

For this reason, the ministries of education and industry jointly launched a five-year plan in 1979 to install 10000 microcomputers within secondary schools for use with students aged 11 to 18.

The decision to implement that plan had to take into consideration the situation as it stood at the beginning of 1979. At that time, experience was accumulating in the instructional use of time-shared systems; however, no experience existed in such use of personal computers. Under the earlier project, 600 teachers had been fully trained to the level of being able to write courseware packages and about 5,000 teachers had completed a correspondence course on the basics of computer science and the use of computers in education. Furthermore, a bank of more than 500 fully portable courseware packages already existed. It was also obvious that first-generation microcomputers were not the best choice for use in education. Finally, a national data transmission net – including home terminals – was under way.

These considerations led to four major decisions. The first was to install 1200 microcomputers during the coming two years – 400 in 1980 and 800 in 1981 – each time choosing the best machines available.

Second, it was decided that after two years of experience with personal computers, it would be possible to make a thorough comparison of personal computers and local time-shared systems from a pedagogical point of view and, as a result, define the best kind of equipment to use.

The third decision was to make *LSE* a standard language. To this end, a request for a standard was introduced before the Association Française de Normalisaton (AFNOR). Apart from avoiding the obvious problem and expense of translating programs from one language into another, there are two other reasons supporting this decision. First, it allowed maximum use to be made of the existing bank of about 500 programs which were already fully documented and tested, 70 per cent of which had been ranked by users as being 'fairly good' to 'excellent'. The second reason was pragmatic – it is easier to convince a teacher of the value of using a computer in the teaching/learning process by providing him with an easy-to-use courseware package designed for his discipline than it is by requiring a lengthy and complex process of education in the basics of computer science and the subtleties of programming. Moreover, it is fairly evident that in the future the majority of teachers will be users of packages and only a minority will be involved in the design and writing of packages.

Finally, for the academic year 1979–1980, forty teachers – selected from those who earlier received a year of training – were given a year of release time on full pay to visit and direct short seminars with other teachers at those schools which will receive the microcomputers (eight per school) mentioned earlier. A three-week seminar, held in October 1979 for these forty teachers, provided them with the necessary training for directing these seminars.

In 1981, after the election of President Mitterand, the 10,000 microcomputer project was frozen for a few months and Professors C. Pair and Y. Le Corre were commissioned to write a new report. This report concluded that the project should go on with the same aims and objectives as before and recommended the setting up of a small experiment (twelve secondary schools) to evaluate the teaching of informatics as an optional subject for students aged 16 to 18.

Simultaneously, the report recommended that the short seminars to be given in the schools receiving the equipment should not be less than 100 hours spread over two weeks and defined the content of a full-time course (thirty weeks) for teacher-trainers to start in October 1981.

This same year, eleven *centres de formation à l'informatique et à ses applications pédagogiques* (centres for education in informatics and its pedagogical applications) were set up, mainly in universities for teacher-trainers, with a curriculum of 750 hours (300 hours for general informatics, programming methods, etc., 300 hours for CAI and 150 hours for planning future activities in teacher training).

In 1982, about 230 teachers were trained in the eleven centers. In 1983 the number of centers went up to fifteen with 300 teachers trained for thirty weeks (the 230 teachers of 1982 were used full-time for teacher training in the schools receiving equipment).

In 1984, there were twenty centres and about 500 teachers altogether had been trained during a full academic year.

The objective was one centre in each *Académie* (twenty-seven altogether). During that same time, the number of teachers trained in short seminars (100 hours) has increased. From 1981 to 1983, about 20,000 teachers were trained and another 20,000 teachers during the academic year 1983–1984.

While the rhythm of teachers training increased since 1981 so did the amount of hardware put in schools. While at the end of 1981 in all there were about 1,200 computers installed (eight microcomputers costing about US$2,500 plus a line printer in each school); this number went up to 6,000 at the end of 1983.

In that same year, the Ministre de l'Éducation Nationale announced that the 10,000 microcomputers project was cancelled and replaced by a new and more ambitious 100,000 microcomputers project including the training of 100,000 teachers, to be achieved in 1988. As part of that new plan, some 12,000 computers were installed in 1984 not only in *lycées* (2,500 of these in France) but also in *collèges* (12 to 15 age group), of which there are about 5,000 and finally in elementary schools, of which there are about 36,000.

INFORMATICS FOR ALL, 1982–1985

	1982	1983	1984
Equipment cost (in US$million)	7.8	8.8	24.7
Cost of training of teachers (in US$million)	5.5	9.5	20.0
Number of teacher trained	4200	11000	20000
Number of microcomputers installed (cumulated)	3000	15000	40000

During the last few years, the programme of the French Government may be summarized as follows:

During a press conference held in Paris on 25 January 1985, the Prime Minister at the time, Laurent Fabius, officially announced a plan aimed at introducing another 120,000 microcomputers in schools and training 100,000 teachers before the end of 1985.

This has brought the total number of computers to about 160,000 for a total school population of about 11 million and the number of trained teachers to about 150,000 (about 25 per cent of the total teaching body).

The total cost of about US$200 million for the fiscal year 1985 was split approximately as follows:

Equipment	US$150 million
Teacher training	US$25 million
Courseware	US$25 million

The aims. The scope of the new plan was much wider than just adding another 120,000 computers to those already in use in schools. *Informatics for all* aimed to familiarize the whole population with the use of computers; for that purpose, it was decided that the schools would be open after class hours to allow citizens free access to the computers under the supervision of the school teachers who have already been trained.

Teacher-training. The training of teachers was organized during school holidays to avoid interferring with normal schooling and was on a voluntary basis. Three periods were available: the Easter holiday, the summer holiday and a one week holiday in early November.

The training was organized for groups of about twenty to thirty teachers and lasted five full days. During that period, teachers were taught to manipulate the equipment and how to use the different kinds of software which came to schools together with the equipment (details below on this topic under Software).

During the two weeks of the Easter holiday in 1985, it was initially planned to train 500 groups of teachers, but the great number of volunteers led the Ministry of Education to organize about 620 groups all over France, a total of about 19,000 teachers; about 5,000 sessions in 1000 centres were planned during the summer holiday (14 July to the end of August) and the last sessions were to be organized at the beginning of November where there is a one week holiday for schools.

To encourage teachers to attend training sessions during their holidays and to help them cover travel (generally short distances because of the decentralized organization of the sessions) and related expenses, each participating teacher received from the Ministry an amount of about US$130.

Software. From the beginning, it was decided that each school receiving equipment would receive at the same time a software box including some fifty software packages. All French and foreign companies in France were invited to propose their products to the Ministry. A small software committee of experts, chaired by the author, was set up by the Ministry to choose among the proposals received.

This software committee laid down eight guidelines. First, over 60 per cent of the software box should be educational software in the strict sense: mathematics, physics, biology, history, geography, French, foreign languages, arts, etc., excluding games. Second, between 10 and 20 per cent of the software box should be general tools or home application oriented: text-processing, spreadsheets, database applications, computer-aided drawing, etc. Third, every selected package should be tested technically (bugs, deadlocks, ergonomy, etc.) and pedagogically for soundness. Fourth, any submitted package using a foreign language selected by the Committee should be translated into French. Fifth, only half of the total budget for software should be spent on software boxes. The other half should be used by the schools as an open credit to make their own choice in a coming official software catalogue to be put together by the software committee before the end of the year, with the same criteria as above. Sixth, all equipment should run either under CP/M or MS DOS or, at least, should be compatible with these two; also three languages should be in each box: BASIC, LSE and LOGO. Seventh, one or two author-languages should be available. Finally, only a very few educational games should be in the software box, mainly for the purpose of attracting the visitors coming in during after class hours.

A total of 696 software packages were submitted, including about 200 packages from the Centre National de Documentation Pédagogique, an institution of the Ministry itself and whose products are, therefore, free for the Ministry.

The commercial terms for buying software packages varied from company to company (buying the packages and the documentation directly from the manufacturer at a discount price, including the right to copy the software inside a school, buying a license for the product from the manufacturer with the right to make a certain number of copies, etc.).

Hardware. Different types of equipment, about 98 per cent French-pro-
duced, were given to schools; the remaining 2 per cent was left open for
foreign computers.

Some 33,000 schools with fewer than 400 pupils received one Thomson
T07-70 (64kb memory, 8-bit microprocessor, standard colour television set,
using a magnetic tape cassette recorder for secondary storage and/or ROM
cartridge and a printer).

Some 11,770 schools (6 to 11 years old) and *collèges* (12 to 15 years old)
and 500 *lycées* (16 to 18 years old) received what is called a *Nano-réseau*,
which is a local network made of a professional (IBM-PC compatible)
microcomputer used as a server linked to six microcomputers of the home-
computer type (these six can be up-graded up to thirty-one). Moreover, each
lycée received three microcomputers of the professional kind.

The end of the 1980s saw 20,000 additional microcomputers in elementary and secondary schools, a significant increase in the number of educational software packages developed by private companies, the development
of a policy of signing commercial deals between the Ministry of Education
and private software companies to get discount prices for packages bought
in great numbers, a decreasing interest on the part of parents, mass media,
politicians, unions, etc. for computer-in-school problems which, apparently,
came to be seen as no more important than all the other problems in
education (lack of classrooms, shortage of teachers, etc.).

Conclusion

The ways in which computers have been introduced into schools are very
different in the three 'advanced countries' because their education systems
are different. In the United States teacher training was completely left to
local initiatives while in the United Kingdom two teachers per school, at
least, had to be trained to entitle a school to get a 50 per cent discount on the
equipment; in France, teacher training has been considered very important.

In all three countries the policy of using computers is almost the same:
to improve education and to familiarize children with the use of computers.
In all three countries also, because of the increasing awareness of the impact
of computers on education among teachers and because of the increasing
number of computers available, research has been going on for some time
into how the widespread use of computers will change the content of the
subjects taught and how it may change the curricula. Again in all three
countries, the availability of courseware remains a bottleneck in quantity as
well as in quality, and there are no short-term solutions in sight.

In all three countries the present ratio of one computer for about thirty children is considered as a first step and some experts are already trying to extrapolate to what education will become when each child will have his own portable computer as he has today his pocket-calculator.

THE DEVELOPED COUNTRIES

In this group of countries, some are rather near to the group of 'advanced countries' whereas others are just starting to define a policy for the use of computers in education (MINEDEUROPE IV, 1988).

In countries such as the Netherlands, Australia, New Zealand and Denmark, from 50 to 90 per cent of all secondary schools own at least one microcomputer but they are mainly used to teach informatics as a discipline or for data processing applications in professional training. This is why in these same countries there are very few computers in primary (6 to 11 years old) or lower secondary (12 to 15 years old) schools.

In other developed countries such as Portugal, Spain and Greece governments have plans for the introduction of computers in education; they all have to solve the same problems.

THE HARDWARE PROBLEMS

Despite the low price of microcomputers (as compared to mainframe computers), their introduction into the education system rises a financial problem because of their number. In most countries the school population is about 25 per cent of the total population and to have a significant impact on education this implies installing microcomputers by the million. Because it looked like a tremendous potential market for the manufacturers the hardware problem has become in most countries a political problem.

Except the United States, most countries have policies to encourage buying nationally-manufactured computers (United Kingdom, France, Japan, Germany, etc.) when these computers are bought with governmental funding. In some countries which do not have a national computer industry, efforts are made to start such an industry based on the school market (for instance New Zealand and Australia).

In the United States the existence of this school market has started a competition between companies which either propose heavy discounts if the computers are bought in great number by a school or propose to give computers free to schools provided the government agrees on tax exemptions for the company.

Official funding policies for buying hardware for schools varies widely from country to country depending partly on the administrative structure of the country and of the structure of the educational system.

Two extreme examples are the United Kingdom where the Micros in School project (Ministry of Industry) pays half the price of a microcomputer bought by any school provided the computer is chosen between two British-made models (with the aim of having one micro in each of the about 30,000 elementary and secondary schools) and France where the computers are completely paid through official funding at the rate of eight micros in each school with the aim of reaching 200,000 micros in elementary and secondary education.

In federal countries and in those where private schools are an important part of institutional education, funding is national or regional and/or local depending on circumstances.

THE SOFTWARE PROBLEMS
In the early 1980s there was no educational software problem because most of the uses of computers in education were experimental and in that time researchers were writing their own software for their own use.

As the number of computers in education began to increase, it became evident that it did not make sense to ask each teacher using a computer to write his or her own software. However private companies were reluctant to enter the market of educational software for a number of reasons (the small number of computers in schools made the market too small to be able to sell products as a price level compatible with what schools could afford, impossibility to predict or to guess the number of copies sold in a given time, necessity of having as many versions of each program as there are computer models and/or programming languages, no provision for software in any school budget, etc.).

In many countries, therefore, the process has started through local initiatives, mostly in computer science departments of universities where the manpower was paid through research contracts with more or less official funding (National Science Foundation in the United States, NDPCAL project in the United Kingdom, off-duty time given to trained teachers in France, etc.).

It is only quite recently that private companies (mainly book-publishers) have started to invest in this area, asking interested teachers to propose detailed pedagogical scripts and hiring computer specialists to write the software.

In France there is a competition between private companies and the government-funded Centre National de Documentation Pédagogique which centralizes all the educational software written by teachers and gives away free a copy of it to any school asking for it. For the time being most companies believe that the real market for educational software is the home-computer market and try to enter that market by developing 'educational games'.

THE TEACHER-TRAINING PROBLEMS

In some places there is a feeling that there is a teacher-training problem only when teachers are asked to teach informatics or computer literacy (Lovis and Tagg, 1984).

This is true of course, but it is not the full picture. Even if there is no teaching of informatics or computer literacy per se but only the use of educational software, there is still a teacher-training problem, and it is perhaps more difficult in the last situation; it is rather easy, in terms of content of the training, to teach about computers and their use (there are already well-established curricula for that purpose, at least for professionals) whereas it is extremely difficult to teach about the proper pedagogical use of computers in the classroom for the very simple reason that there is no previous experience on which to rely.

It has been said that computers can improve education if they are used at the right place, at the right time, with the right amount and in the right way, but to meet all these conditions teachers have to be trained to use the computer that way. The mere presence of computers in schools does not guarantee that education will be improved – the unskilled use of computers in education can be worse than not using them at all.

While heavily emphasized in the *Carnegie Report* on 'the fourth revolution' as early as 1972, the need for teacher training *before* starting activities in CAI is only being slowly recognized, probably because the idea of teacher training to meet the needs of technological progress is something new in institutional education in most countries and also perhaps because of the scale and the difficulties of the problem. Whatever the reason for that slow recognition of the problem, teacher training today is almost everywhere an important part of any plan to introduce computers in education. In the United Kingdom, in the fourteen regions into which England was divided for the MEP project, there are a variety of courses available in each regional centre: a three-day course, a one-week course, a three-month course and a teacher-trainer course; some of these courses are compulsory for at least two teachers from each school which buys a computer at half the price with the help of governmental funding.

In France, in each school which receives a package of eight microcomputers paid by the government there is a twelve-day course in the school itself to which all teachers are invited. Moreover, twelve centres have been created in universities where about 600 teachers are trained each year during a full academic year to become either teacher-trainers or authors of educational software. About 6,000 teachers have already been trained through this scheme. The costs of teacher training are impressive.

EVALUATION PROBLEMS

As already said, CAI activities as well as teaching of computer literacy has been heavily funded through governmental aids in most countries. These financial efforts have been made by governments with the aim of improving education through the use of computers and as a consequence in most countries, committees were set up to investigate and evaluate how the funds were spent and what kind of improvements have resulted. These evaluation reports should normally compare the results of teaching with and without computers, and attempt to draw conclusions on the impact of the use of computers in education.

In fact most of these reports discuss the financial and quantitative results of the experiments (how the money was spent for hardware, software, training, staffing, etc., and how many computers were bought, how many software packages were written, how many teachers and how many students were involved, how many hours students spent weekly on a terminal, etc.) as is the case for instance in *The Program at Two* where NDPCAL is evaluated by the Centre of Applied Research of the University of East Anglia in 1975.

In those parts of the reports dealing with the pedagogical changes induced by the use of computers, emphasis is often on what is changing in the classroom (changes in the attitude of the teacher, changes in the behaviour of students, changes in the content of what is taught, etc.) much more than on the strict comparison between the same course taught with and without a computer.

The very content of the reports shows that this kind of comparison today is an exercise of academic interest only and that the problem is elsewhere.

It is considered today that the use of computers in education: allows pedagogical strategies which could not be used otherwise, allows subjects to be taught which could not be taught otherwise, allows students through proper use of CAI to be familiarized with the main applications of computers (graphics, simulation, text processing, data banks, etc.), allows students, at a given age, to handle more complex subjects and problems, and allows for improvements in the autonomy and creativity of the students.

These changes are almost impossible to evaluate because of the absence of proper terms of reference; the changes are so drastic in terms of content and teaching methodology that the state of the art of present-day teaching is not felt to be the right term of reference. This is probably the reason why, in most reports, the use of computers in education is justified by the necessity to adapt the education system to the computerized society of tomorrow rather than by evaluating the improvements brought to present day education.

Things to come

The computer-room syndrome

Thirty years ago whoever wanted to process data had to go to the computing centre, leave a deck of punched cards and come back the next day to pick up a listing with printed results.

The main trend in the evolution of the use of computers over the last thirty years has been a permanent tendency to bring the processing power as near as possible to the user, first through time-sharing of large computers and finally through the availability of a microcomputer on each user's desk.

This increase in the interactive use where computers are constantly available to users for assisting them for any length of time in their job is the general rule in commerce, industry and administration. Unfortunately, this almost never happens in schools. With some rare exceptions, the computers are locked up in a computer-room (for safety reasons) and access to that room is planned well in advance to make the best possible use of the available equipment.

This has two kinds of drawbacks. First of all, students have to go to the computer room and this gives the computer a status as a part of institutional education and not the status of a personal tool. This is further accentuated by the fact that when going to the computer room the students have to use software prepared by the teacher, which leads again to the computer being seen as a part of the institutional education environment and not as a personal tool. Moreover, because students have to go to the computer room and because walking both ways requires 15 to 20 minutes, the net result is that a student will not go there even if there is free access as long as solving a problem by hand requires less than 20 minutes (even if the computer could do it in 20 seconds). As the vast majority of questions asked in school problems do not require generally more than 15 to 20 minutes to be solved by hand, the mere existence of a computer-room where one has to go makes the computers standing there useless for the daily work of students, which is exactly computers greatest usefulness to them. The second drawback is an indirect outcome from what has just been said. Authors writing educational software are aware of the use of computers in computer rooms and to have a chance of selling their software they have to take that situation into account. This means that they will design their software to fit the constraints imposed by that use. They will avoid writing short programs designed to reduce 15 minutes handwork to 20 seconds computer time which is the widespread use of personal computers and would convince students of the usefulness of computers, and they work rather on lessons supposed to teach something during a one-hour session.

The advent of the so-called universal tools such as spread-sheets, text processing, data-bases and electronic mail on micro-computers has definitely called the attention on the importance of personal computing – the permanent availability of a personal computer for each user to solve problems large or small at any moment in real time as opposed to the computer-room type of use.

Present trends in educational software

Under the combined pressure of industry and parents, the number of microcomputers in schools has steadily increased over the last ten years. In developed countries, the ratio of the number of computers to the number of students is somewhere between 1 to 50 and 1 to 20 in primary and secondary education, which implies that the usual way of organizing computer use is still the computer-room type with all the drawbacks already mentioned.

Because authors have for commercial reasons adapted their products to that type of use we have had a quasi stagnation of the state of the art in educational software over the last few years and this is going to last as long as the computer room.

The hot items today are experts and authors asking for a methods to assess the pedagogical quality of software before and/or after writing it whereas teachers complain that they don't know what exists and ask therefore for large national and international catalogues. None of these two requests can be reasonably fulfilled today. On the one hand it is practically impossible to assess the pedagogical value or quality by examining a piece of software which does not generally cover more than a few pages of a normal school-book: the sample is too small to allow any realistic assessment. On the other hand the variety of computers (even those claimed to be compatible), of dialects of a same language, of formats and densities of diskettes, of graphic interfaces, etc., makes the portability problem of any software a real mess as long as it does not come from a colleague who has used it intensively or from a shop across the street where there are plenty of knowledgeable vendors.

Trends for the future in educational software

It is well known that people have a natural tendency to formulate solutions to their problems in terms of their daily practice. Therefore, as long as the ratio of computers to students in school lies between 1 to 50 and 1 to 10 there will be little change in the way computers are used in schools, which means that we will continue to stay with the computer-room mode with all its drawbacks.

If, however, we look ahead we may guess that in five years from now the volume, the weight and the price of what is called an 'IBM-PC clone' will have decreased to a level where each child will have its own computer. This will introduce a kind of quantum leap in the way computers are used in education because many things will change. There will be a market for personal educational software with millions of potential customers (all children will be concerned). No school book will be accepted for publication if it does not come with its diskettes showing examples and proposing interactive exercises for drill and practice to illustrate some difficult points as well as a library of standard sub-routines relevant to the usual problems of the discipline. The working methods of the students will change through the use of the computer for solving problems, writing texts, searching data bases and communicating with other people, in other words becoming able to achieve more in less time and to do things which were just impossible before or so time consuming that they were never done whatever their interest (Wenger, 1987). All this will inevitably lead to changes in the curriculum on the one hand because the use of computers will change the relative emphasis put on various subjects and on the other hand because the use of computers decreases considerably the difficulties of some topics which are at present considered as difficult (calculus is a good example, provided derivation and integration are made by using difference equations and avoiding going to the limit, i. e. leaving out the differentials).

Conclusion

In education, computers are used mainly in the stand-alone mode and gathered in computer rooms. This kind of use explains why educational software is how it is and what it is and why it is not going to change fundamentally in the near future.

Some experiments where each student has a computer are going on in higher education, mainly in the United States (MIT, Drexel, Brown, etc.) and have shown that in this case the main problem is not so much the software or the hardware than the difficulty of training and motivating teachers to consider the use of a computer as part and parcel of their pedagogical strategy.

The 'one computer per student' paradigm will come rapidly to primary and secondary education because parents will buy pocket computers and we shall face the same problems as those met in higher education. Here too, the main problems will not be to assess the quality of this or that piece of software or to choose the best program in a catalogue. The main problems will be much more difficult. What kind of software would best help specific teachers to improve their personal teaching by using a computer during their lectures? How is the pedagogical strategy used by a teacher to be changed given that the computer allows to engage children in activities which were not possible without a computer? What kind of software will improve the guided discovery mode when the teacher, the student and the computer work together? What kind of software will improve the 'learning activities' of the students as a complement to lectures and book reading? What kind of activities for the students will become feasible which are impossible today despite their great pedagogical value? What kind of library of sub-routines will help students to achieve more in less time? These are but a few of the problems which will have to be met and solved.

The advent of the personal pocket-computer announces the beginning of a new era. Computers have had a very small impact on education up to now but this is going to change in the next few years.

The most important is still to come and if we want to avoid what has been called the 'pocket-calculator disaster' (some teachers work very hard to design problems where a pocket-calculator can not be used), we better get prepared right now for the radical change lying ahead of us.

References

Commission of the European Communities (CEC) (1987) *Development in the Introduction of New Information Technologies in Education*. Luxembourg: CEC.

Craik, K. J. W. (1943) *The Nature of Explanation*. Cambridge: Cambridge University Press.

Foster, J. F. (1989) Educational Computing in England, Wales and Northern Ireland. *SIGCUE*, Vol. 20, No. 2.

Fourth Conference of Ministers of Education of Member States of the Europe Region, Paris, 1988 (MINEDEUROPE IV) (1988). *Informatics in Education: Trends and Achievements by International Organizations and Prospects for further Co-operation.* Paris: UNESCO. (ED-88/MINEDEUROPE/REF. 5.)

Hebenstreit, J. (1986) Children and Computers: Myths and Limits. In: B. Sendov and I. Stanchev (eds.), *Children in an Information Age*. Oxford: Pergamon Press.

Johnson-Laird, P. M. (1983) *Mental Models*. Boston: Cambridge University Press.

Lewis, R. (ed.) (1982) *Involving Micros in Education: Proceedings of the IFIP TC 3 and University of Lancaster Joint Working Conference, Lancaster, England, March 24–26*. Amsterdam: Elsevier.

Lovis, F. B. and Tagg, E. D. (eds.) (1984) *Informatics and Teacher Training*. Amsterdam: Elsevier. (Proceedings of the IFIP WG 3. 1 Working Conference on Informatics and Teacher Training, Birmingham, July 1984.)

National Commission on Excellence in Education. (1983) *A Nation at Risk: the Imperative for Educational Reform*. Washington, D. C.: Government Printing Office.

Office of Technological Assessment (OTA) (1988) *Power on*. Washington, D. C.: OTA.

Owston, R. D. (1987) *Software Evaluation*. Prentice-Hall Canada.

Resnick, L. B. (1983) Mathematics and Science Learning: a New Conception. *Science Education*, April.

Thorn, M. (ed.) (1987) Microelectronics Education Program. *British Journal of Educational Technology*, Vol. 18, No. 3, pp. 165 et seq.

UNESCO. (1986) *Informatics and Education: a First Survey of the State of the Art in 43 Countries*. Paris: UNESCO. (ED. 86/WS/9.)

Wenger, E. (1987) *Artificial Intelligence and Tutoring Systems*. Los Altos, Calif.: Morgan Kaufmann.

Winship, J. A. (1988) *The Search for Quality in Educational Software*. Paris: OECD-CERI.

CHAPTER TWO

Basic strategies for introducing and using informatics in education

Bernard Levrat

Introduction

Advanced countries have applied a variety of strategies, closely linked to the structure of their education system and to past history, to the problem of introducing informatics in education. More recently, a number of developing countries have conducted pilot projects, often co-financed by western countries. In spite of the rate of innovation – which makes irrelevant today what was done only yesterday – some constants emerge from all the reports: the necessity of properly preparing teachers and decision makers, the importance of planning and fully implementing pilot projects, and the need to keep up to date with the technology.

This chapter will look first to the relationship between education and the new information technologies. Before proceeding to identify the actors involved and the actions to be taken, it will look at the mechanisms of innovation in informatics in general as they worry all the managers of projects involving new technologies in business, industry and universities, showing that the problems are not restricted to the education system.

It will then be observed that the real decision makers are not the top managers but the final users. For this to happen in education, computers must reach teachers and students, and that involves large investments not only in terms of computers but also in the accompanying training and support structures. International co-operation is vital, and the new communication facilities between computers make it possible electronically.

Any strategy must be based on an analysis of the needs of a given country or region, followed by a design phase. The result of local developments must then be produced, distributed and maintained. Whether one deals with local production or one wants to buy learning material produced elsewhere, there is a need for evaluation, a particularly challenging task. When getting learning materials from outside, the issues of transfer, adaptation and standardization may spell disaster. Problems concerning language and culture are also possible.

After dealing with hardware and software procurement, attention will focus on human resources: specialists with the necessary skills must be present and the teacher population must be prepared to work with computers; several strategies will be reviewed. Teachers are also important in the development of educational software. The usefulness of computers in planning and managing school activities is also mentioned with the necessary training of administrators.

Finally, overall economic and financial constraints are taken into consideration, with a few recommendations based on experiences in dealing with the rapid obsolescence of personal computers. The evolution of investment and operational costs are calculated for a unit lab with a few personal computers linked to a server through a network, a very common solution in advanced countries. It is not possible, in general, to assess the costs of research and development.

The conclusion on cost-effectiveness and efficiency of the various projects and organizations insists on the need for pilot projects and on the extreme importance of teams of competent and dedicated people, working in co-operation with the rest of the world of education.

Education and the global challenge of the new information technologies

Teaching is a strange process, not yet well understood, in which basic skills and knowledge are transmitted along with social, cultural and ethical attitudes. When information technologies are brought in, an entirely new set of problems stems from having a new partner in the student/teacher relationship. Nothing is simple in this *ménage à trois* imposed from outside; there are tensions, expectations, frustrations and fears of rejection on the part of both human partners. Information technologies are costly and full of surprises, psychologically as well as technically. Then why bother at all?

There are two compelling reasons: first, information technologies play an increasing role in modern society and cannot be ignored by education; second, information technologies hold so many promises to overcome a large range of problems in education that policy makers at all levels try to harness them.

Teachers prefer to exercise their profession in an environment which they master completely and, in spite of the fact that their usually keen minds are constantly in search of new intellectual ventures, their teaching habits show a strong tendency to reproduce the learning environment in which they studied and an equally strong resistance to innovations affecting their day-to-day life, unless these changes result from their own endeavours.

Learners do not show the same caution once their attention has been caught. Grappling with a computer terminal will not elicit at once fear and rejection. If a reasonable degree of user friendliness can be achieved, the interactivity introduced in the learning process can be a strong incentive to explore new concepts. Since McLuhan, the importance of the form of the message is recognized; it is a part of the external environment which cannot be separated from the substance being taught.

Recent progress in computer hardware makes it possible to further enhance the quality of the message with better and better images. Animation is just around the corner with the optical disks coming of age. One can also expect voice applications, freeing the user from having to conduct the whole process of interaction through the keyboard. These developments hold many promises but will not be out of the labs and in the average school classrooms for quite a while. But even when restricted to currently available proven technology, good software can present quite attractive materials for playing or for learning.

In order for this gadgetry to be something more than a source of distraction, it must be integrated into a strategy for learning. There is an often-heard claim that, with the help of a computer and suitable programs, students could determine and control their learning strategies. While this possibility exists by design in a few of the best computer aided learning (CAL) programs, it requires that students possess the necessary cognitive level – the interpretive skills and model building skills – to interpret and assimilate the situations they experience with the computer.

It is unlikely that, given the current state of educational software, beginners can achieve much without a lot of friendly human help coming either from parents who happen to be familiar enough with computers or from specially trained teachers. But beyond turning on a machine, loading a diskette and entering a few simple commands until the stored programs take over, who knows enough cognitive psychology to monitor the progress being made and the coherence of the global models being built by the student? Proponents of intensive computerization argue that it cannot be worse than in the present day classrooms. This may be true, but it is a subject that certainly requires serious study and constant observation.

Given the chance, teachers are also learners; they must be made familiar with hardware and software before computers invade their classroom, otherwise they will not feel sure of their ground. They must accept the idea that some of their pupils will develop greater manipulative skills, even a better 'understanding' of the machines than their own, without that fact discouraging them from using computers. The teachers must subscribe to clearly established objectives for which the hardware and software were purchased, get a basic understanding of how it works and adapt their teaching methods accordingly. Although they need and deserve teacher-training programmes to do that, they are in the same position as the rest of the work force who must adapt to survive.

Indeed, everyone should be prepared to keep up with rapidly changing job requirements and with the evolution of society. Informatics is not going to be present in schools only but, if properly mastered, will be the instrument of lifelong education. A fundamental question was raised by André Danzin in his opening address to the 1989 UNESCO International Congress on Education and Informatics:

> Can it enable us to rethink the structure of education inherited from the nineteenth century Western world, so that more is learned outside school and less time is spent in the classroom with, however, more ambitious objectives for individual development, not only in terms of direct economic utility but also in those of the individual's enriched culture and personal fulfilment (International Congress..., 1989a, p. 34).

With information technology, the challenge is within as well as without. Relentlessly, progress brings new technologies in hardware and software which make the old ones obsolete and often unavailable. Decision makers do not have to make a big step once and for all, as was perhaps the case with educational television or the 'new math', but they have to hold a steady course while technology is constantly changing the rules of the game.

Observing the painful struggle which characterized the attempts of the last twenty years to introduce computers into schools in developed countries as pilot projects, one is tempted to advise those who have not started yet to leapfrog some of the stages and to fall in step with modern technology. But while spectacular progress has been made in hardware and entirely new domains of research in informatics have found their way in applications, many of the fundamental problems relating to the use of informatics in education have not yet found satisfying solutions. This chapter advocates a comprehensive approach to all the difficulties which must be faced simultanously and recurrently.

Understanding the mechanisms of innovation in informatics

Generations of hardware

In its infancy, the computer industry went through a series of generations corresponding roughly to the technology supporting the arithmetic and logic circuitry at the heart of the computer. The first generation involved vacuum tubes and was largely confined to research labs. The second generation used transistors and introduced machines doing a lot of useful work thanks to the emergence of operating systems and high level languages such as FORTRAN and COBOL. In spite of good intentions on the part of the user community, there was little portability between systems of different manufacturers. As soon as the manufacturer had been chosen, the customer was entirely in its hands, but once installed, a machine would run for a number of years without major changes.

The third generation, which introduced integrated circuits and more sophisticated, time-sharing operating systems, brought its lot of troubles. Many projects were too ambitious and resulted in major delays and cost overruns, giving software a bad reputation. The discipline of software engineering emerged from the crisis, giving users a better understanding of the life cycle of all kinds of software products, ranging from operating systems to large application programs.

IBM's domination of the computing market received unexpected challenges with the appearance of 'plug compatible' peripherals (printers, cardreaders, and disk and tape drives), sold cheaper by other companies which opened the way for all sort of clones, culminating with mainframes that would run the same operating system. The added complexity meant many headaches for the direction of the computing centre which had to balance a gain in price versus maintenance availability and reliability. The last straw came with the unbundling of software, priced separately from the hardware. Today, there are more software than hardware companies and the revenues generated by the former is taking a larger and larger share of the profits.

The fifth generation, despite an impressive research and development effort which may have advanced the state of the art, has not delivered much of significance for the average computer user.

Micro-processors, micro-computers and peripherals

Meanwhile, nobody really knows if there was a fourth generation of computers because of the appearance of the micro-processor around 1970. Product of the very large scale integration technology, the micro-processor is mass produced cheaply by extremely expensive factories. Only a few United States and Japanese companies are competing in a field where financial skills are almost as important as design and manufacturing genius. The models they make – Motorola 68000, etc., Intel 8086, 80286, etc. – are the heart of micro-computers – such as the Apple II, the Macintosh, the IBM PC and a number of workstations – such as SUNs and Apollos. When a micro-processor stops being made, the corresponding micro-computers are bound to disappear.

Around the micro-processors and their standardized interfaces, one finds a great variety of peripherals for storage ($3\frac{1}{2}$ and $5\frac{1}{4}$ inch diskettes, hard disks, optical disks and cassette tapes), for visual displays with different resolutions and graphics capabilities, and for communications. The communication ports can accommodate all kinds of printers from the cheapest pin-point head to laser-based high resolution engines. Using the same communication interfaces, the micro-computers can access remote resources through modems and telephone lines or can even be linked to a network, although special hardware may have to be bought to achieve greater communication speeds. Every issue of the magazines aimed at the vast audience of personal computer and workstation users advertises a number of new products for storage, visualization or networking.

The problem with this flood of hardware products is that they are, more often than not, mutually exclusive. Take the example of the $3\frac{1}{2}$ inch diskette, certainly more practical and robust than the older $5\frac{1}{4}$ inch floppy disks: for an organization partially equipped, installing the better solution on the personal computers being bought now makes them incompatible with the old ones. Retro-fitting the whole store with the new hardware is much too expensive. It would seem better to stick with the old $5\frac{1}{4}$ inch solution if it were not for a strong feeling that their days are numbered and that, at some point in time, they will stop being manufactured. By then, the older personal computers will be obsolete, but not the new ones. To solve the incompatibility problem, one can buy a few systems with the two kinds of disk systems or share software through a local network, the choice of which will present many more difficulties than the relatively simple diskette problem.

To summarize, one can observe that over the last twenty years the amount of computing power which can be bought for a constant sum follows an exponential curve, practically doubling every year. Except for the handling of very large amounts of data, almost any kind of application can be tackled today on a desktop computer. Innovative hardware and software developers offer an endless stream of new products which are very tempting but make present installations obsolete and, while still in good operating condition, very frustrating to use. For reasons relating to forces of the market place and to the psychology of the user, it is unreasonable to make long-term plans based on the availability of the same hardware over a long period of time.

Operating systems

The best hardware is not usable if it is not supported by software. But software itself does not exist in isolation. A program participates in an environment called an operating system, which takes over most of the tedious tasks of managing the hardware, the file system and the scheduling of different processes. If a program is successful, it will increase the sales of the platforms (hardware plus operating system) that support it. But operating systems are not static; they must cater to new hardware and new user requirements. Successful programs bring in revenues allowing the company which conceived them to keep up with new features being introduced while nobody cares to update less popular pieces, hurting the users who chose them.

Going back to the history of computing and its disruption by the advent of the micro-processor, one can observe the evolution of the proprietary operating system's which still run on large mainframes manufactured by companies such as IBM, Digital, CDC, Honeywell, ICL, Bull or Siemens. These systems present a friendlier interface than in the 1970s. They have adapted to telematics and are able to handle many simultaneous users coming in through directly coupled terminals or through personal computers attached to dedicated communication lines or to an access network, emulating the behaviour of a given terminal by program. In spite of the rise of personal computers and workstations, the large mainframes often play an important new role as software distribution centres and archiving facilities in addition to their traditional functions of number crunching and administrative data processing. Because they provide so many facilities in a unique fashion, it is almost impossible for business users to move their applications to another environment; scientific users find moving time consuming and costly. This means that mainframe computers and their proprietary operating systems are going to stay for a number of years to come. New software is being developed for them by dedicated user communities and research in some fields is almost impossible without the environment prevalent in the corresponding user community.

Software developed around micro-processors should be easier to exchange since the basic instruction sets of the different machines are the same. It is so only if one stays within one family of operating systems. At present, the market is split among several major systems, creating as many separate worlds with only tiny links between them. They all compete for the attention of software developers, knowing full well that success is linked to a rich software environment.

MS DOS, the disk operating system designed by Microsoft for the IBM PC and compatibles, runs on the Intel family of micro-processors. It is very successful and a very large number of application programs run under it. From its inception in 1980, it has overcome some of its early limitations as more user friendly software came to its rescue. It supports several windowing systems, hundreds of text processors and spreadsheets, dozens of desktop publishing programs and enough high level languages to make programmers' lives acceptable if not bright. Many educational applications have been written under MS DOS and new ones appear every week.

The future of MS DOS, as it stood, was questionable. It had a built-in limitation which restricted the programs that ran under it to being smaller than 640,000 bytes. As memory became cheaper, many programs expanded beyond this limit, offering a better interface and more functions, somehow circumventing the limitations by using different tricks. But MS DOS has now outgrown the earlier memory limitation, and can handle the larger memory needed by many commercial programs. In doing so, it has regained its attractivity.

Macintosh is the name of a family of computers offered by Apple with a very friendly user interface. Mac operating systems invite all application designers to use its powerful window and graphics system in a consistent way and this means the user feels very comfortable going from one program to another. It is often possible to cut and paste stuff from one application to another without trouble. Macintosh has integrated, from the beginning, different pieces of software useful for the office worker and its ease of use has metamorphosed mere beginners into dedicated converts. Mac was first in affordable desktop publishing, a new metaphor coined by Aldus corporation when it introduced *PageMaker* in 1985. It is a class of software for producing nice looking publications on a Laser printer while working directly on the image of the printed page on the screen. This and a number of smart and pleasing applications like *Hypercard*, a powerful information organizer, appeal to teachers as a tremendous help in preparing their classes. It is not surprising that one finds a great deal of educational material created for the Mac.

UNIX has been a popular operating system in the research community since the late 1970s. Written in the C language, it requires a minimum of adaptation to run on a wide variety of hardware platforms ranging from supercomputers to micro-processors. Its greatest use, currently, is with the powerful workstations made by DEC, IBM, HP or SUN. Because of its academic tradition, the UNIX environment carries with it a lot of freeware for the advanced programmer. Designed to handle several processes simultaneously, UNIX integrates naturally in networked applications. The tools to make UNIX more palatable, if not really user-friendly, are in the making, and more and more excellent application packages hide UNIX from the user.

Unfortunately, there is more than one flavour of UNIX, trademark of AT&T, which offers 'system V'. Berkeley has produced the very popular variants BSD 4.2 and 4.3, distributed with an impressive amount of free, very useful software. Two independent efforts tend to standardize. One involves SUN and AT&T while all the others, including IBM, subscribe to the Open Software Foundation (OSF). But even on different UNIX systems the same basic tools can be made to work, like the very powerful X-window system (X.11) developed at MIT and the Network File System (NFS) licensed by SUN.

In order to remain competitive with respect to the very aggressive Macintosh and UNIX-based workstation, vendors who are after the DOS corporate users, IBM and Microsoft have launched a new operating system for micros called OS/2. It is a multitasking system, like UNIX, with an advanced user interface called the Presentation Manager, reminiscent of the good features of the Macintosh. Given its price and the resources it requires, OS/2 is mostly used by developers for the time being, but it will offer a smooth path of evolution to current DOS users (at present they number over 25 million).

International Data Corporation (Southerton, 1989) has estimated the projected sales of Operating Systems worldwide in 1993 as follows: DOS and OS/2 – 29 per cent; UNIX – 19 per cent; Macintosh – 5 per cent; and others (including mainframes) – 47 per cent.

New software products

The term 'product' is used here instead of 'program', indicating that a piece of software should not be presented by its author(s) or given any consideration by reviewers until it reaches the stage of being usable by others, which means having an installation guide and a user's manual.

The early success stories of the application of computers are to be found in a number of scientific fields where the processing power and the graphics capabilities of the machines combine with well-designed man-machine interfaces to give users fantastic problem-solving capabilities. The most striking examples are to be found in astronomy, crystallography, chemistry, earth sciences, physics and medicine as well as in many disciplines of engineering, including the more commercial computer aided design systems.

There are lessons to be learned from the way these applications developed. The pioneers understood very well their discipline as well as the possibilities of applying computers to their problems. After initial demonstrations, the projects received appropriate funding with a strong back-up of their scientific community. It took several development cycles to reach the degree of sophistication observed today, but a conscious effort was made to ensure some degree of portability.

When the products reached the market place, often through companies with strong links to university laboratories, the psychological problems related to the man-machine interface had been solved, the usefulness of the product had been demonstrated and the whole scientific community of that discipline was aware of its existence.

The above remarks are not confined to hard sciences and engineering. There are beautiful examples in geography, sociology, history and the humanities, such as the *Thesaurus Linguae Graecae*, a compilation of all that is known about ancient Greek texts, widely distributed among scholars. It is an ongoing work which, among other things, produces and updates a CD ROM version, containing 42 million words.

With the advent of micro-computers, innovative products have made their authors rich and, sometimes, famous, turning an original idea into a multi-million industry. When Dan Bricklin and Bob Frankston (Bricklin and Frankston, 1986) introduced *VisiCalc*, they found it difficult to convince computer professionals that the idea of electronic spreadsheets would interest anybody. The response of the business community was overwhelming, helping both *VisiCalc* and the Apple II computer to become big commercial successes. New products such as *Lotus 1-2-3*, *Multiplan*, *Framework* or *Excel* have taken the place of *VisiCalc* on the shelves of computer vendors. Although it initiated a tremendous momentum towards a whole new range of software products, *VisiCalc* itself has disappeared from the currently used software products.

Another interesting story involves *Turbo-Pascal*, developed and distributed by Borland. Borland's founder idea was that the micro-computer market would respond favourably to a good but affordable programming environment for Pascal programmers. With an unprecedented advertising campaign for a product still in its infancy, *Turbo-Pascal* was launched. It met with instant success which a whole range of excellent Turbo products helped consolidate. Today, a growing number of students are initiated to good programming practice through a Turbo environment and this can be expected to continue since the Borland company invests part of its revenues in steady improvements of its products.

The few examples presented above are meant to give an idea of what the world of software development is like. Good software is both difficult and expensive to produce. Educational software is subject to the same rules as apply to other software products. It requires some sound and attractive ideas to get started, but it will not succeed without the support of a community of users willing to invest in a product they find useful or without being distributed to a very large customer base at a reasonable price in order to cover the development and maintenance expenses needed to keep a software product up-to-date.

One difficulty is that good educational material is slow to mature and does not seem likely to enjoy the same universality as popular packages for electronic spreadsheets or text processing. Although many projects and products pertaining to education have been developed in different countries, very few have enjoyed a worldwide audience. It may be that problems are perceived quite differently from country to country, with the consequence that a design corresponding to given pedagogical goals cannot be adapted to different strategies for reasons which are not purely technical ones.

The LOGO language and the associated pedagogical efforts going with it should be mentioned among the exceptions. *Mindstorms*, Seymore Papert's stimulating articles and books in the 1970s, captured the imagination of many teachers and language interpreters were developed by a few software companies.

Books about languages such as LOGO or PASCAL, beginner's or user's manuals for popular operating systems, spreadsheets or word processors abound. They sell briskly and make publishers happy: the intended audience is well known and the material can be easily evaluated by their own specialized reviewers. Why then aren't publishers investing in the production of educational material for which they would sell books or even distribute the software themselves? Portability problems make the publishers wary of investing in teams vastly more costly than those needed to produce a book, where the essential part is done by the authors. Even when simply matching a diskette with a book, software production is a domain where publishers feel inexperienced and want to move very cautiously, all the more anxious because the ease and low cost of copying software undermines the copyright protection.

Software companies make money in the educational business. They sell language compilers, authoring languages, programming environments and packages ranging from word processor to expert systems. They yet have to launch significant programs of courseware development. The parallel often made between the production of books and the production of educational software does not stand up to a thorough examination. For textbooks used in schools, most of the basic research and development work is done at the school system's expense, drawing on the talent and experience of teachers to produce the raw material out of which the publisher team of expert designers and printers will make the attractive volumes expected on the specialized shelves of bookstores. The steps between the stage at which a prototype has been demonstrated to work with a few students and the time where a completely packaged product is ready for distribution are much more time consuming and expensive than putting a book together from a manuscript. Moreover, publishing houses do not have the educational software specialists who could compare to their graphical arts, type-setting and printing specialists.

Development of new platforms

There is no hope of insulating the education system from the fast pace of innovation. The very existence of computer systems depends on their success in the marketplace, determined mostly by business users. The quest for a really cheap machine dedicated to education has not produced convincing results so far, in spite of efforts in, among others, the United Kingdom, France and Norway.

When manufacturers propose somewhat downgraded systems to be sold cheaper to schools without undermining their commercial sales, they generate frustrations, among the teaching staff because some of the most attractive software products won't run on them and among developers who have to contend with poorer capabilities than currently available ones, especially in graphics.

Distribution

To have a chance to compete, a product must be known to its potential users. It is also true for learning materials having reached the stage of commercial products. If their development has been sponsored by a computer manufacturer or a software distributor, these may be assumed to provide the required distribution channels. However, they have trouble reaching through the computer professionals and school administrators to address practising teachers.

Products which target primarily learners as opposed to teachers will be marketed outside the school system. They will have to compete with other items for shelve space either in bookstores, in computer stores or among the educational games in general stores. In this context, there are very few success stories.

Some developers, mostly involved with higher education establishments, are willing to distribute their software for free or for a nominal fee. Although this could be a source of interesting components for other developers or a base for experimentation for teachers with computer experience, the lists of freeware products are not widely circulated and they are difficult to evaluate for someone unfamiliar with the jargon of particular subcultures.

Because software is different from books and educational software marketing is different from the marketing of other software products which are constantly reviewed in specialized publication widely read by the interested public, different mechanisms are needed to ensure that quality learning material is brought to the attention of its potential users. Some steps have been taken in that direction as regional centres or national organizations have been set up to play the role of clearinghouses, but much effort is still needed at all levels if the educational community and those who finance it are to stop reinventing the wheel while excellent materials wither away and die because they remain forever unknown by their potential users.

One may wonder why the abundant literature on computers in education and the many conferences on the subject do not cover this need. With rare exceptions, articles which are accepted describe projects rather that products, experiments rather than evaluations. Perhaps the specialized magazines will appear if home computers become a reality through their usefulness for individual learning. They may fail to address the great diversity of needs at different educational settings. Although the lack of good computer-based educational material has often been denounced, there is an equal lack of coherent effort in evaluating, adapting and distributing what is already available. New projects not yet fully prototyped, planned for advanced hardware only a few could afford, receive much more publicity than less glamorous but already operational products.

It has to be recognized that evaluating the educational value of a given product is much more difficult than testing the functions of a text processor. Yet such evaluations should be conducted, with some degree of objectivity, by distribution centres fully supported by the school authorities and made available to the international community. If the problem of disseminating not only learning material but opinion-forming guidelines on what is best to choose in a given set of circumstances does not find a solution, the use of computers as learning aids will fall short of its promises.

IDENTIFICATION OF DECISION-MAKERS

More and more, the success or failure of computer systems designed for the home, for the workplace and, to a certain extent, for schools is determined by acceptability to end users. The qualification as regards schools comes from the fact that the real end-users should be the students but acceptability rests primarily with the teachers. If it can be said for people who leave a place they don't like that they are 'voting with their feet', end users of computer systems can 'vote with their fingers', refusing to use unfriendly systems while becoming enthusiastic salespersons for the things they like, with a powerful commercial clout coming from their sheer number. The final decision makers are the teachers and the students.

For this to happen, some expertise will have to reach the lower levels of the education system either through pilot projects initiated by the government or through local initiatives by self-taught individual teachers or by university graduates who have been exposed to the new methods during their years of studying. If there is no national plan, the local decision-makers in education will then be faced with difficult choices in providing an adequate environment for the introduction of informatics in their schools given their limited resources. They should be prepared to invest not only in buying computers, but in determining what they will be used for and in providing for adequate teacher training. They will discover that although there are many opinions on what should be done, very little research exists that can guide them in establishing their priorities.

Even in a well organized national effort, the rapid progress occurring in hardware and software is at best a mixed blessing to those who are trying to make plans for a reasoned introduction of computers in a given education system over a few years period. They are dealing with large numbers of purchasing decisions spread over time and the rate of change is such that between the beginning of their project and the current situation, the original hardware they chose is not manufactured any more, the 'standards' (graphics, networking and operating systems) have evolved and even the vocabulary of the original proposal is fast becoming obsolete. In-depth studies and large-scale comparative experiments are out of date before they are completed. Observations on specific approaches lose their relevance before they are published.

Education must benefit from the vast promises of the introduction of computers in schools. The inter-relations between the scientific, engineering and commercial aspects of informatics and the needs of education must be understood, and appropriate measures should be taken to make better use of the intellectual and material resources already available today. Is educational software, which has seldom been a source of profit for a company, the victim of a fiercely competitive world where there are so many possibilities that only the most rewarding ones are pursued? Is the rate of technological change, imposed by a majority of users, more demanding than educators, such that the education system is not equipped to follow it?

The partners of the vast research and development work which must be done have been identified. They are the hardware manufacturers and the software publishers and distributors on the one hand, and the producer of educational software on the other hand. But there are many obstacles. Researchers are mainly interested in using the latest technologies and scant attention is paid to the down-scaling of applications towards lesser systems. There are very few rewards for authors of good educational software and an enormous amount of effort aimed at prototyping individual ideas goes to waste for lack of proper selection and promotion. When a national or regional effort turns out to be successful, its adaptation to a different context is nearly impossible for lack of portability and adaptability. The market forces alone will not solve these problems. In education, equality of chances will be guaranteed only by strong actions by the governments of the different countries; the equally serious problems of closing the technical gap between developing and developed nations is being addressed by UNESCO and other international organizations.

TRAINING AND SUPPORT STRUCTURES

Looking back to the introduction of informatics into the education system of the United States or of Western European countries, one can observe that pilot projects were started within a number of university departments ranging from physics to the sciences of education. The roots of the use of computers as a means of instruction are firmly planted in the United States as a result of the co-operation, begun as early as 1958, involving the private sector, federal agencies and private foundations with major universities such as Dartmouth, the University of Illinois and Stanford (see for example, Carnoy and Loop, 1986).

Through these collaborations, computer use in education developed into its major programme areas. With teams of colleagues, at Dartmouth John Kemeny developed BASIC, at Stanford Patrick Suppes presented the earliest CAI modules, while at Illinois Bitzer was attempting to show that a large coverage of the curriculum was possible. The major areas of the use of computers in education were essentially determined at that time: programming instruction, remedial programs of the tutorial type and drill and practice.

The main virtue of these early experiments is to have convinced decision-makers that computers should find their way into schools where they would be globally beneficial. No proof of the pedagogical value of the introduction of the new technologies was given and none was required. Today, several projects are pushing the limits of technology to show brilliant applications of new hardware and software, but it is not necessary for every school system to experiment with them. A visit to a trade show or the perusal of the literature provides enough material to dream about what the future may look like. Present day mass produced micro-computers offer a sufficient range of possibilities to implement different policy approaches.

Pierre Duguet, while restricting his scope to developed countries belonging to the Organisation for Economic Co-operation and Development (OECD), divides these approaches in two broad categories according to observations made on different countries in the mid-1980s:

> The first group consisted of countries which developed policies which could be called 'restricted'. The first objective of these policies was to introduce the teaching of computer science into vocational and upper

secondary education, in order to develop computer-related skills for participation in the labour market. A second objective was to teach computer literacy to all students at all other levels of education in order to provide them with a basic understanding of the way computers work and the impact of computers on society and on the individual...

The second group consisted of countries who developed 'comprehensive' policies intended, not only to promote the teaching of computer science or technological literacy but also and mainly to using information and communications technologies to improve teaching and learning processes. This last objective includes a number of different and complementary aims such as: to improve the quality of the teaching process; to enhance learning and to better understand the related cognitive processes; to review education, especially curricula; to compensate for the decline in the number and quality of teachers; to improve access to education; and to develop communications between schools intra- and internationally. The best examples of countries (or states) with 'comprehensive' policies were probably Ontario (Canada), France and the United Kingdom (Duget, 1989, p. 284).

These ambitious schemes require massive and continuous support from government agencies. It is too early to assess their effectiveness or whether the 'comprehensive' approach is bringing substantial changes in the educational systems. The fact is that they bring computers and software in to the local schools where the experiments are done finally.

When confronted with the realities of what can be accomplished with currently available products, decision makers need to set up pilot projects of a different kind, far from the glory of the computer science research lab. After setting their objectives, they must see if they can be inserted in a given context, adapted to a given culture with the personnel at hand. The people in charge of the task should not act in isolation but must be in close contact with the mainstream of the education system in which the pilot project will eventually be generalized.

Admittedly, there will be more than a single project considered at any given time, the pilot organization would gain in pulling together a variety of experts from different fields, computer and telecommunication specialists, practising teachers and psychologists in addition to specialists in computers in education. With the supporting organization which hosts it (possibly a university or a teacher-training school), the aggregate becomes a centre of competence.

Once the pilot phase is moved to an extended experiment, involving more than one school and one location, the pilot centre will become a resource centre which must provide training for teachers involved in the programme, documentation when required (from participants or from interested parties outside the programme) and on-line help when requested.

This last request implies that telematics be part of the system and indeed, networking seems to offer some hope of overcoming the chronic lack of staff that any distributed system experiences. Once a given hardware and software solution has been chosen, once the educational software has been selected and the teachers have been trained to make the best use of the whole package in a classroom situation, there are maintenance problems that appear which are not only linked to hardware failures. The success of the experiment will depend on how quickly users in difficulty can be helped.

Having a 'hot' telephone line is an expensive solution since it must be on call permanently. Moreover, the staff may be required to move around to do maintenance work or to install new users. If part of the training offered to users includes an initiation to electronic mail, many benefits can occur. Cries for help will be answered, not immediately but within a short period of time. If the failure is not hardware, quick fixes can often be suggested for the software. Psychological difficulties related to real classroom situations are reduced if they are described to specialists.

While electronic-mail is very useful in providing a direct contact with specialists and an easy way to discuss common problems with colleagues, there are other electronic means to disseminate information, keep people up-to-date and help them fight the feeling of being isolated in front of problems which seems at times quite unmanageable. The various electronic bulletin boards, computer conferences or electronic news bring together groups of people who share common interests and are potentially able to benefit from sharing their expertise.

With present technology, that might rapidly become obsolete in France when the Ministère des Postes et Télécommunications introduces the Integrated Services Data Network (ISDN), the path to electronic communications would be first of all to link all the computers located in adjacent buildings to a local area network. This can be accomplished in a number of ways, the cheapest using ordinary telephone lines or twisted pairs and the RS 232 communication ports on the personal computers, the fastest involving buying a specialized hardware and cabling system such Ethernet or a Token Ring. One of the machines will play the role of server and be equipped with a 'gateway' through a modem and a leased line linking it to the nearest link of a major educational network.

That may well be the supporting centre which itself must be linked to the rest of the world in order to be able to keep track of current developments in hardware, software and educational material adapted to the needs of its users. In the case of national centres, they will be expected to advise users throughout the country about the prospects of informatics for education and the educational challenges that come with it.

THE NEED FOR INTERNATIONAL CO-OPERATION

Developed countries already have such national or regional centres. The EEC, within the framework of the ESPRIT programme, is fostering co-operation among its national centres through a project named Start-Up. Co-operative experiments have also taken place in the Eastern European countries, in Canada and in the United States. Pooling their resources, they could create a central database and the necessary networking services to make it available all over the world.

The heart of international co-operation should be based on the exchange of information concerning products, techniques and policies in the field of education. The way to achieve such an exchange and the necessary adaptation to different contexts implies the linking of regional centres, which should be created where they do not exist. Regional centres for developing countries could play an important role in helping to start information technologies-based educational programmes.

In spite of the constant evolution of hardware, software and even standards, it would be desirable to give people with experience in the field the opportunity to advise others on how to tackle some of the problems they know best and how to avoid glaring mistakes. This could be possible by offering consulting services through the network.

Lessons from the past are of limited value only, while an awareness of the directions of current technical developments could be vital. In all cases, a structure which ensures that a constantly adapted list of preferred solutions is maintained and available would be preferable to a set of documents which would be obsolete before printing. Special educational rebates granted worldwide by a manufacturer would also be announced. Maintenance considerations and experience with the product under different conditions could enter the database at a later stage.

If such a structure can be established, one of its tasks should be to test and recommend migration paths from preferred solutions at a given time to later ones. In some developed countries, there are national and regional centres which do work in this direction: France, the Netherlands and Norway have national centres while regional centres are to be found in the United Kingdom.

The structure need not be a bureaucracy. To give an example of what is possible, one could mention the permanent informal consulting going on through the Network NEWS bulletin boards. The information is collected by a specialized piece of free software to be installed by the systems engineers. There are thousands of readers worldwide on many different machines connected to the academic networks; they can formulate queries which are posted under the appropriate headings. In most cases, there will be someone with the appropriate knowledge who will answer and the answer will be spread to all users of that interest group. Specialized columns in some trade magazines also give advice, but without the immediate feedback of their readership which exists in the NEWS. Communications with the rest of the world depend on the services of the telephone companies and on the availability of coupling devices between one's equipment and the communication facilities. A gateway to X.25 services would be the standard recommendation but some more innovative solutions could be envisioned. Full two-way communication is desirable but one could live with the fact that one receives much more information than one generates. Receiving this information through a dish antenna while sending requests via normal telephone lines would be a possible alternative.

When one looks at the flow of exchange in an electronic relationship, one finds it very much lopsided, the server sending out quite sizable amounts of information in the form of software being distributed, electronic newspapers or reports being circulated while end users may send requests consisting of a few words only, occasionally contributing an article a few pages long. This suggests that telephone lines would be perfectly adequate in one direction while the high volume of satellite transmission may be needed in the other (see Fig. 2.1). The infrastructure is already in place; all that is needed is the political determination to set up the required channels. In Europe schemes such as the Programme of Advanced Continuing Education (PACE) and the Community Action Programme for Education and Training Technology (COMETT) have encouraged the development of satellite user groups to pool resources and co-ordinate efforts for setting up various satellite program projects. Another extremely potent development has been the free broadcast time being offered by the European Space Agency (ESA) on OLYMPUS-1.

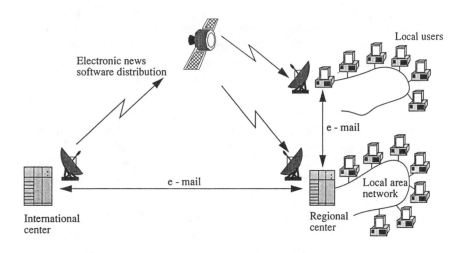

Figure 2.1: Electronic links between an international centre, a regional centre and a user LAN

It would be desirable to have an international resource base to act as a clearinghouse, offering facilities for updating knowledge of educators and educational decision-makers. Such a clearinghouse could also specify and disseminate methodologies for conducting research, feasibility and evaluation studies. It could help prepare and disseminate studies related to the effective application of information technologies in large-scale educational programmes.

It is often said that education is now a lifelong activity. Sending people to training courses is costly. The choice of courses is limited and the time they are given is imposed. Instead, telematics offer an alternative to the persons or organization who possesses the basic equipment and a certain amount of training. It is a way that ought to be actively pursued both inside a country or a region of the same culture and internationally.

The analysis of the needs

The picture showing the networked solution supposes that a first stage of computerization has been accomplished, which is the case in a large number of countries. In fact, to a certain extent, every country is trying to meet a number of objectives which the Stanford/UNESCO symposium itemized in the following way:

> a) to meet a cultural objective generally part of a broader project of modernizing the productive base; i.e. to prepare children for an 'informatics future' by developing an awareness of computers and how they work (computer literacy); b) to prepare young people, particularly at the secondary and university levels, in programming and related skills for work in the informatics industry; c) as an educational aid to improve pupils' skills in academic subjects at the university, secondary and primary levels; d) curriculum development – introducing and developing changes in the content and methods of education through informatics; and e) as an aid to teach management and other skills in private industry and the public sector (Carnoy and Loop, 1986, p. 3, para. 2.10).

In view of the limited resources available, a clear statement of the educational objectives is needed. The advent of the micro-computers has substantially lowered the entry cost of a pilot project, but it made even clearer than in the past that the initial hardware costs are only a small part of the total expenditure necessary to develop and maintain a well-functioning system of computer applications in education.

The Paris Congress recommended that:

> Primary focus in introducing new educational technology in schools should be as a learning aid to students in important courses. Student study of these technologies, informatics, can be considered at later stages (International Congress..., 1989a, p. 61).

It must be pointed out, however, that it would be a drama if a country tried to introduce computers in schools without ensuring first that enough local competence exists to provide the necessary support to computer-based school activities.

Programming languages and operating systems have been conceived and documented in the English language. Providing courseware material of top quality for the whole curriculum in another language is a major effort. Keeping it up-to-date requires careful planning and continued government support.

The choice of any course of action depends so much on the political, cultural, technical and financial background of each country that basic choices must be made and validated independently in each situation. Many people in the United States think that there is already a lack of qualified teachers for science and mathematics courses and that the situation will get worse in the years to come. They see a possible solution with the development of full computer-based parts of the curriculum (Bork, 1988). The Western European countries tend to view the contribution of CAI modules as a complement to current teaching. Several countries are gathering existing software for the different disciplines and training teachers to use it efficiently. They feel the necessity to adapt and develop new modules corresponding to their specific needs. Developing countries feel both the lack of qualified teachers in sufficient numbers and the difficulty of using material imported from other cultures.

Unfortunately, there is not much guidance to be gained from studying the great diversity of strategies already existing. This is abundantly illustrated by a recent book entitled *Computers in Third World Schools: Examples, Experiences and Issues* (Hawkridge et al., 1990). The information now available on computer-based educational material in different countries is seldom analytical or critical. Little is known about the impact of the introduction of computers in schools and how it affects the education system. Expert opinions differ on the most efficient ways of developing courseware and very little experience has been gathered in the adaptation of successful products to a different cultural environment. It is recognized that much experimenting needs to be done, in directions determined by national or regional priorities. Before these broader issues can be dealt with, it is desirable to examine the conditions necessary to the successful completion of experiments, even ones of a limited scope.

To take but a few examples, one could mention the design of a simple text processing system for its introduction in elementary schools, a generalized help facility for individual access to databanks by students, the development of a complete set of modules to assist the teaching of mathematics in high school or the adaptation of computer based learning programs for physics from the American language and metaphors to another culture by people of this culture.

The design phase

Whatever project is finally approved, it must be conducted like any large project involving sizable amount of software. A project team must be formed that will formulate objectives and needs in terms of target population, manpower, financial investments and available technology. This project team is to be composed of high-level decision makers, practitioners and experts on educational problems, and informatics specialists. Outside expertise may be required to validate some of the options, but most of the work pertains to the situation at hand and, as usual, success depends on a good perception of end-user needs.

When the project has been approved and the necessary funding granted, the full-time staff required by the project is hired. It is expected that some of the specialists of the project team will stay on the job on longer-term appointments than the study group warranted. Detailed specifications can then be worked out with the well-known methods of software engineering but with the extra constraint of satisfying the pedagogical goals as well as the external specifications.

Software developers have a number of tools at their disposal, but first they must settle the problem of communicating with the teachers doing the pedagogical design in ways that the teachers find congenial and highly motivating. The computer should play a role in the process as communication tool, as a permanent memory and as a source of information. These tools exist already in a variety of forms and the choice is best guided by the explicit effort to keep to an environment close to the expected delivery system.

The strategies implemented by the plan will find their rationale with the experience of the teachers and their knowledge of the difficulties commonly encountered in mastering each of the concepts presented in the material. Although a large amount of control rests in the hands of learners who can move at their own pace and, within limits, decide on their own learning strategy, the program will attempt to guide them on an optimal course, especially when remedial help is required. Computer-based learning material has the great advantage of being an active learning environment where all students should be able to find the learning mode which suits them best. As new techniques to include more (artificial) intelligence in the programs are discovered, computer-based learning systems can be expected to better meet the expectations of the students with respect to the interpretation of the answers they type in the system. Having a full dialogue resolving semantic ambiguities is not generally to be seen in the near future, but the analysis of the input from the human side should account for every symbol entred and not just keywords.

Completely automated intelligent tutoring systems drawing on a knowledge database to bring a student from his current acquaintance with a subject to a level of proficiency measured against a cognitive model are still in the research domain and it is difficult to guess if their great promises will ever be fully realized. The literature shows that knowledge-based applications, modelled after the well-known examples of SCHOLAR developed by Carbonell in 1972 for tutoring in geography or GUIDON I (1979) and II (1983) using in teaching the expert knowledge present in MYCIN and NeoMYCIN, are applicable to very narrow domains of knowledge only. An excellent comprehensive review can be found in *Artificial Intelligence and Tutoring Systems* (Wenger, 1988).

A different source of expertise comes from teacher experience in a lifelong exposure to classroom situations. Many computer-based teaching systems try to transpose that expertise in a tutoring environment. In a few cases, a new fascination with computers, especially in the early stages of discovery, may blur the view of otherwise objective teachers regarding the difficulties related to their subject matter. Extracting expertise is always difficult and often iterative. It is to be expected that a number of cycles of design ➡ coding ➡ evaluation ➡ design might be necessary to arrive at an acceptable product. If modification of the original code or design are diffi- cult and costly, the chances of success are very limited.

The management of the production of software is a complex, difficult activity. The tools which can be used are closely related to the design activity since the progress of a program, properly decomposed in modules, with well defined interfaces, lends itself to supervision. Good code is easily readable and more is learned during code review sessions than when relying on estimates of the percentage of work accomplished at a given time (generally much too optimistic).

As the programs grow, the different phases of the scenarios imagined by the teachers undergo a number of tests by their coders and then by the whole project team when the integration of the final form of each single component into the final product is taking place. The real test, however, will happen when the product is put in the hands of external evaluators: a necessary condition since it reflects the real situation in which the product will work. Much more is being tested than just the code: there must be a user's manual or alternatively an audio guidance system (Vivier, 1989). If the system is to be used in a classroom, some teacher training must be foreseen. In order to gain valuable information from that first evaluation, a detailed protocol for gathering remarks and criticisms has to be agreed in advance. A point to be watched in particular is the independence of the teaching material vis-à-vis the operating system or, more generally, vis-à-vis the vast quantity of detailed chores which specialists perform without thinking but which leave naive users dumbfounded.

It is appropriate to raise these points during design without waiting for the evaluation phase, because they must be planned carefully and budgeted in the initial design of the pilot projects.

Production, distribution and maintenance

A fully packaged product including well tested software, a good description of the objectives, an installation guide – especially when using a network – and the proper documentation for learner and teacher can only be produced by a professional team. The most efficient way to achieve this result would be via a tender procedure, open to all interested parties (software houses, commercial publishers, etc.).

A central governmental institution awards contracts for the production of specific courseware packages on the basis of the product descriptions coming out of the pilot and design phases. This approach has been implemented in the Netherlands as the POCO project. The task of selecting products and managing the production process has been given to the Educational Computing Consortium (ECC), the former Centre for Education and Information Technology (COI) which helped prepare these policies. Since it is awarding the money,

> POCO will set standards for the production process as well as standards for the software itself; both of which will contribute to the 'user-friendliness' of the software (Henkens and van Deursen, 1988).

The Netherlands government hopes that, after the initial, subsidized years, courseware will be produced by the private sector without special government support. It must be noted, however, that the market is created by the large-scale introduction of micro-computers in the schools.

> 2,000 participating schools get a computer laboratory of nine 16-bit MS DOS computers in a network and two stand-alone computers (Henkens and van Deursen, 1988).

It is expected that the school system will budget the maintenance, extension and renewal of this starting base and allocate funds for the acquisition of new software.

An alternate strategy is found in other countries with a similar high degree of hardware penetration into the schools and a thriving software industry. Publishers of educational software are enticed to put products on the market that government agencies may recommend in the form of an approved list after a thorough evaluation. School boards across the nation will buy them in quantities large enough for the companies to show a profit. In the United States, where such a market exists, the system can work without governmental support but with the emergence of evaluation mechanisms, themselves turning into a profitable industry.

Even in the most advanced countries, three main problems stand in the way of quality educational software production. First of all, it is not perceived as a potentially high profit activity, although this could change if home computers are used in large quantities for out-of-school modes of education. In Geneva, where the state school system provides all teenagers with an initiation to the use of computers, this has spurred the interest of many parents in acquiring a home computer. It will be interesting to see if the sale of software follows a curve similar to the sale of hardware. The second problem, which seems to be worldwide, has to do with the practice of illegally copying programs, depriving the software publisher of any hope of profit making. Finally, the popularity of educational packages may have less to do with their pedagogical value than with some aspects of their presentation. Most teachers will favour models that lend a hand to their traditional approach to teaching, while students may be more attracted to game like lessons. Real innovation in education cannot take place without a strong governmental support to steer free market initiatives towards goals of lasting value.

Depending mostly on economic considerations, government action results in computers being placed either in a few schools involved in a pilot project or in all the schools of a given community. In addition, a certain number of computers are located in private homes, with or without organized support. In a few cases, particularly where distance learning is involved, tele-communication links will be part of the set up. There are many problems which are common to every situation, even if they find quite different solutions depending on the overall organization. Among these common problems are distribution and maintenance.

Without disputing the constant complaints from the teaching community about the lack of appropriate materials, there are thousands of quality computer-based learning products applying to different situations. Potentially useful and commercially available utility packages number by the hundreds. How will users know about them? When good software is produced by a development centre, how does one make it known to the outside world? Vendors will keep only the most profitable items in their inventories. Government agencies will restrict the list of approved products to manageable proportions. As a result, a great wealth of materials will never be seen outside the circles that produced it, unless it has the chance of becoming one of the few popular items everybody talks about.

If one agrees that in all cases, a certain amount of initiative must be left locally, it becomes necessary to create databases where well-tested and useful products could be registered, along with evaluations, reviews and teacher opinions regarding usefulness. Examples of such clearinghouses can be found in several countries. There should be at least one per region, exchanging data with a worldwide facility. Electronic access as well as other means of distributing the information must be found.

Advertising a product in the database means that there exists a way of getting the software on some acceptable form of support, under a commonly found operating system. It imposes some discipline on the software developers who must face the problem of packing their product properly, with clear installation instructions and documentation, before shipping. This is also true for software coming out of the development centres which, sometimes, ought to receive finishing touches from private software publishers.

Wise users beware of the maintainability of the products they buy. Hardware and operating systems evolve. A product not receiving the necessary updates will become unusable as time goes on. As an example, one could mention what is happening with the generalization of local area networks in educational setups. Many products do not run well in a network environment with a file server, and unless their distributor sends out a new networked version, they will stop being used.

University and government sponsored production centres must also be prepared to maintain their products and ensure their migration towards more modern environments. In doing so, they often want to introduce improvements in the original product, only to discover that the improvements cannot be retro-fitted in the old versions. While this is considered a gain in the commercial sector where a micro is often considered obsolete and expendable after three years, and very little consideration is given to past products, it may not be acceptable in a school setting where all versions of the same product are expected to behave in a similar way. Good pedagogical materials have the potential to outlive hardware and several versions of the current operating systems. Care should be taken to ensure maintainability.

Evaluation

Before buying learning material or selecting it for translation, adaptation and conversion, decision makers would like to base their decisions on a body of knowledge describing what is on the market and how it compares with current proposals. Software developers want to know the criteria used for judging their products. The authors of computer-based learning materials are eager to have an appraisal of the formative value of their product as well as a summative assessment of their effectiveness. Are the current procedures available today giving the kind of information needed to reach an informed decision?

The reviewing process associated with the selection of existing materials has been studied by a UNESCO programme on enhancing the quality of educational software and conducted by the International Council for Educational Media (ICEM). In his summary of the report, Tucker (1989) presents the following findings:

> The provision of information about what is on the market is obviously of major importance in a market such as the [United States]. Without this knowledge teachers will be hampered in their choice. Therefore many people demand, subscribe to and actively support evaluation services such as EPIE, MicroSIFT (p. 355).

He points out that often

> selection... is more likely to result from having seen a demonstration than from reading a review and that even where a review read, the general description carries more weight than the apparently more scientific evaluation table (p. 355).

The report also questions the adequacy of the instruments devised for the evaluation services.

> They purport to be scientific, and present their evidence as though it were objective. Yet most of these evaluation forms were evolved for the recording of both fact and personal judgement about drill and practice programs (p. 355).

The descriptive element of these reviews and of the corresponding journal articles have a major influence on the way in which teachers select software.

Ideally, programs should be evaluated with respect to their clearly stated pedagogical objectives. Although they are markedly more difficult to realize, programs that lead away from drill and practice, and towards development of creative problem-solving skills, should be encouraged. The Stanford/UNESCO Symposium pointed out that a great deal of research still needs to be done to help evaluators. Paramount among the open questions are issues related to pedagogical theory and particular design features of educational software.

Research on the motivational effects of computers on learning is even more limited than is research on its cognitive effects, although recent work suggest that several aspects of modern tutorial software, particularly the fantasy element, could make the subject matter intrinsically more interesting and hence could increase learning. This kind of evaluation must involve learners much more than teachers to yield fair results.

According to the Stanford/UNESCO report:

> ...most research studies have been undertaken at the micro level on small, limited experiments. A review of a number of these clearly suggests that the micro approach cannot answer questions at the macro level. [There is an] ...urgent need to launch research at the macro-level – research which should be both timely and developed with comparative methodologies, to enable decision-makers to use the results (Carnoy and Loop, 1986, p. i, para 3).

> Evaluation of the effects of computers on learning is needed to distinguish what may be classed as beliefs as opposed to well-founded experimental observations. Evaluation should involve both formative and summative methods and be carried out by independent researchers (Carnoy and Loop, 1986, p. 9, para 2.51).

To summarize, current evaluation methods of computer-based learning material give information about its availability, its user friendliness and some measure of its formative value. A collection of such reviews, in the database of a clearinghouse or with private organizations, can give precious indications on what to choose for a given purpose. However, decision makers need a body of research, best conducted internationally, to assess the real benefits acruing to the education system from the introduction of computers and to aim the development of national programmes where the largest benefits can be expected.

Transfer, adaptation and standardization

After selecting a strategy and a range of products to implement it, there may be a need to adapt existing software to different environments which can be different platforms, different cultures or different languages. The development cycle of good computer-based learning materials from initial conception through detailed design, programming, debugging, field testing, evaluation, revision and distribution is best measured in years, not weeks or months. Given the rapidly changing technical and economic basis of computers, such longevity is attainable only if such materials can be transported to new machines as they become available.

One way to ensure transferability of applications between systems would be to strictly enforce the rule that any publicly funded project adhere to accepted standards. In addition, public funds would not be allowed to buy non-standard systems. This looks fine on paper but is not applicable in practice because the world of standards is sometimes as strange as Alice's Wonderland.

A standard is usable only if there are available products that implement it. Unless one starts from scratch, these products must also offer a degree of compatibility with what is already in use and for which a large investment has been made. To take an example, the organization which would impose the Open System Interconnect (OSI) standards defined by the International Organization for Standardization (ISO) for all of its communications, would find it hard to find cheap solutions to link personal computers together and to mainframes. Many companies are committed to support OSI, but currently, there is no complete solution which is competitive with a number of proven, non standard products. The problems of standards are compounded by the so-called 'de facto industry standards'. The best known example is the class of machines called IBM PC compatible, which encompasses the IBM product itself and a large number of clones which would run the same programs with varying degrees of success. Sophisticated users get good bargains but many people are caught in a game where there are no written rules. The worst happens when there is hardware dependence, especially when buying a device which is to be plugged directly to the 'bus', like so many extension cards for graphics, scanners or network connections. It goes to show than there is more to compatibility than running a few demonstration programs.

A personal computer or a workstation is an industrial product. The 'standards' around it tend to protect the interests of its manufacturers. What can be defined by international conventions are interfaces, communication protocols, operating systems and programming languages. It takes a long time for standards to go through all the steps of getting the necessary approvals. The committee X3J3 has been struggling for the last ten years towards a new FORTRAN, not yet available. There are many vested interests in the definition of a new standard which explains these delays. It is sometimes argued that adhering to standards in a field changing so rapidly may stifle research efforts to break new ground. This may be true, but it should never be used as an excuse for not adhering to existing standards whenever possible. As users of informatics systems, members of the educational community should favour the use of standards when there are available and try to create their own 'de facto' ones when it is felt necessary.

Coming back to the production process, it must be recognized that there are many steps between a research idea and its successful implementation as a learning tool in general education. Doing research is fun. Sitting in front of an advanced development system, it is very stimulating to test ideas coming straight from artificial intelligence and to think of entirely new courseware material. For good measure, innovative interfaces involving multiple windows and multi-media communications can be thrown in. Whatever comes out will make an excellent show to promote the good work done at the lab, support doctoral dissertations and give rise to publications.

It is much less popular to try to adapt the same ideas for hardware which is readily available in a classroom. With a few remarkable exceptions, little or no effort has been made in this direction and there is no body of research that will give the pre-conditions necessary to adapt successfully an existing courseware to a different environment. Most often, the running program is taken as a specification and the software is rewritten for the new environment.

There are no easy solutions to the problem of producing and disseminating high quality courseware material. It seems reasonable to favour the adaptation of programs to different environments while preserving their intrinsic qualities. To allow for linguistic and cultural differences, modifications must be made locally. This ability to be locally modifiable without losing its qualities is also a condition of acceptability by local teachers who will feel as comfortable with computers as they are with books only when they can tailor their use to their own views and not to some strategies thought up elsewhere without their being consulted.

Possible problems of language and culture

It is unrealistic to assume that all users of computer learning materials must learn English prior to being allowed to experiment with them. Being able to modify the contents of the messages of a program without modifying its logical organization opens the door to transferring computer learning materials from one language to another (Franklin and Levrat, 1985). There are a certain number of technical problems which must be considered.

There must be keyboards with the local alphabet and the subsequent character representation must be supported by the operating system. After a number of years, the problem is solved on personal computers for most of the European Languages. It remains a major problem for the Arab world (Oualid, 1989) and much of the Russian Federation (Tchogovadze, 1989). Oualid states that

> the present state-of-the-art in research an development in data process-
> ing in the Arab countries focuses mainly on Arabization of software.
> However, the structure of Arabic writing is so fundamentally different
> from English, that it becomes the predominant task of software devel-
> opers in the Arab world to adapt existing packages to the Arab lan-
> guages.

The reference is made to generic packages and not to specific educational tools that would only come later.

If the data have been stored in messages which are directly addressable by the program regardless of their content, a translation of the data will allow the programs to be available in different languages. It would be highly cost-effective to apply that simple rule for all software that could be used internationally. Implementing it once the programs have already be written makes it more difficult. Straight translation of the messages to be displayed on the screen does not always give the best result since they are found to be loaded with cultural assumptions. Rephrasing them can be done with a simple editor, trying to keep the quality of the original dialogue. Surprising-ly, the analysis of student answers, using modern parsing techniques, can be easily transposed.

Translating computer-based learning material into a foreign language and making it work with a keyboard which is using the special characters of that language is no small accomplishment. To make it usable requires an understanding of the mentality of the students, of their cultural background and their current speech idiosyncrasies. The only way to carry material across several cultures is to engage actively in co-operative ventures, show-ing future users that the designers can offer an immediate response to their suggestions and criticisms.

The concern expressed at the Paris Congress 'about the domination of the computer field by the English language' is real, as is the inability of developing countries acutely short of financial and human resources to proceed with the large-scale introduction of computers in education. Both factors could increase cultural and technological dependence and widen the gap between the social stratas within countries as well as between de-veloped and developing countries (International Congress..., 1989c, p. 679).

In its final recommendations, the Paris Congress stated:

> The worldwide development, transfer, and adoption of technology based learning material and the exchange of information about the issues relating to it must be accelerated by setting up communication networks between regional or national centres and research institutes interested in such cooperation (International Congress ..., 1989*a*, p. 62).

In the face of the gigantic commercial pressure for the uniformization of the computer culture according to the American model, the plea for giving regions the means of progressing without having to abandon their culture must be heard.

The development of human resources

The education system is part of society and cannot deal in isolation with major changes occurring everywhere. At the same time as computers and related information technologies are affecting schools and universities, they are bringing the equivalent of the industrial revolution in the economically most advanced countries in the sense that they change the nature of work and what is expected from the work force. Many computer-related products are seen as labour saving and raise fears concerning the employment prospects of whole classes of workers.

Skills in computing are perceived as a key to competitiveness. Governments are prepared to invest in the introduction of computers in schools in order that their country will not be left out of the benefits promised by the new order of things. They want a properly educated labour force. They want their government agencies and their administrations to use the latest technologies, their army to use modern weaponry and their industries to be competitive. In every country there is an ever increasing need for system designers, communication specialists and programmers.

In this context, there is a tendency to consider the whole education system as a factory producing educated people according to the current needs of the market and to try to improve the efficiency of the process. The industrial way of dealing with that kind of problem is to try to computerize at least part of the tasks, eliminating jobs which are no longer needed and transforming others in such a way that they demand fewer skills and command a lower salary. In a nutshell, a few highly skilled specialists and a reduced number of qualified workers will do a more efficient job than before the introduction of the new information technologies.

Is the method applicable to the education system of a country as a whole? Is it going to dequalify teachers or put them out of their jobs? It is a very unlikely proposition because education is much more than teaching skills. There are social and cultural components to be transmitted, psychological adjustments to be made, and a sense of self-respect and of responsibility to be developed. The computer, which is such a wonderful instrument to store and retrieve information, and to compute and present models of the physical world or of human cognitive processes, is to become a third partner in education, helping learners and teachers in different if complementary ways.

The first goal the education system is asked to meet is training specialists in the different fields of information technologies. In all countries, higher education institutions offer now some kind of curriculum specializing in informatics, thus satisfying the most urgent needs. Their staff acquire the experience of dealing with a computer culture, largely United States dominated, even if more chips are produced in Japan and if many important innovations come from other nations. This culture has to be adapted to suit each country's specific characteristics. Those who went through the process of learning computer programming, who are familiar with the 'hype' so common with high technology, are the people who can reassure the teachers and, in co-operation with them, map a course of action for a successful introduction of computers into education system.

It is essential that any attempt in this direction be able to draw on the resources of high-level centres of competence, aware of the latest products and well-informed about the usual sources of problems and the main pitfalls. As soon as they get involved in a pilot project, an experiment or a global plan for introducing computers into their sphere of activity, teachers are eager to have contacts with people who are technically more qualified and willing to discuss the pedagogical issues involved. In no case should teachers be left with bits and pieces of hardware and software, with insufficient documentation and nobody they trust to turn to when things do not work as they should. There is a better understanding of the problem now than there was a few years ago simply because decision makers have become themselves micro-computer users and have experienced the joys and frustrations of discovering with great effort what their children seem to know intuitively.

Teachers at all levels are asked to participate in a vast action plan aimed at using computers in the educational system. It is, according to the British Association of Educational Communications and Technology, a complex integrating process involving people, procedures, ideas, devices and organizations, for analysing problems and devising, implementing, evaluating and managing solutions to these problems, in all aspects of human learning (Mallatratt, 1988).

Preparing teachers

According to the Stanford/UNESCO Symposium,

> Few countries seem to have taken the necessary steps to prepare teachers to use computers, even when hardware is installed in schools. There is also little agreement on how to prepare teachers beyond short-term courses (6-15 days)...that merely help understand how to use computers in the classroom. The problems of implementing even this type of training are apparently great. Those countries most committed to computer training for teachers (Sweden, the United Kingdom, France, Australia and Canada) have reached only about 25 per cent of their teaching force...Even though some countries have recently launched national teacher training programmes...,most are not willing to devote the necessary resources to training, but rather to purchasing hardware (Carnoy and Loop, 1986, p. 6, para. 2.15).

Furthermore,

> Symposium participants insisted that, since educational applications of computers depend on curriculum goals, effective training programmes have to be related to such goals. Longer training programmes [in computer science] to prepare teachers to develop educational software... are expensive, even though the 'pay-off' in terms of developing software [and training other teachers] may be large (Carnoy and Loop, 1986, p. 6).

PRE-SERVICE COURSES

Assuming that secondary school teachers have university degrees and that most future teachers go through a teacher-training school, tomorrow's educators are already in our institutions of higher learning. One must make sure that, regardless of the discipline and as long as these skills are not acquired before, every student receives an introduction to the basic principles of informatics. He or she will learn to use computers with their word processor, database and spreadsheet generic programs.

Equally important is the exploration of what computers can bring to a particular field of study. Besides the advantages that access to a network of computing resources – processing power, availability of data, telecommunications – brings to a research team, it will naturally permeate the way the discipline is explored and taught. Students exposed to these new approaches will want to reproduce them once they are themselves teaching, bringing to the school system an expertise which is difficult to instill to teachers already on the job, who have a strong tendency to stick to the approaches they experienced during their student days.

IN-SERVICE TEACHER TRAINING

When computers are brought into a school, a certain amount of training is obviously necessary for those who are going to use them. It is therefore logical to look at countries with a strong programme for introducing computers in schools to see how the problem has been solved. A look at the now historical steps taken in France, the United Kingdom, the Netherlands or any of the Scandinavian countries will provide a good model and give an idea of the difficulties to be overcome. However, the advent of micro-computers and their user-friendly generic packages has changed the scene so much that experiments prior to 1980 have lost some of their value.

The first level of training deals with introducing teachers to information and communication technologies. They must be prepared to operate a micro-computer and manage the distributed software. Where possible, they should also learn about networking and telecommunications. At a minimum, this initiation requires about forty hours of training which can be given either on a concentrated (two-week) period of time or spread over a year. It takes a considerable effort on the part of teachers and it cannot be assumed they will take the extra load on their vacation time or as an extra burden during the school year.

Still on the same level, to take into account the permanent transience of the technology, follow-up courses are expected to be organized, taking into account the new opportunities offered by the information technologies and answering questions about the changing role and needs of teachers. While there is general agreement on the desirability of improving the level of literacy in information technology, there is a dearth of teacher-trainers. If a certain number of teachers receive an in-depth formation, they can help with the initiation of their colleagues; however, it would be preferable to have staff with an informatics-related degree participating in the operation.

One way to improve the situation, especially with respect to the introduction of packages, would be to use computer-based self-learning packages or video tapes. With better communications, some form of open learning from a central institution could also be envisaged. The problem for the countries which face the hardships of getting started and which could benefit most from these techniques is that such material exists only in the languages of the industrialized countries producing them. The costs of a conversion keeping the quality of the original products are very high and so are the costs of updating them.

Such introductory training is insufficient for the most important component of a successful use of computers across the curriculum with computer-assisted learning packages and subject-specific applications. There is a second level to be considered: training teachers in the pedagogical uses of micro-computers. Since the type of training considered to be adequate would take far too much time, the 'cascade' model is favoured in this case: some teachers of each discipline receive in-depth training and in turn train their colleagues. This type of approach does not prepare the teaching staff to face such questions as what is learning, what are the cognitive processes involved that the computer can help with and how to change the presentation of current subjects to take full advantage of the introduction of new technologies in the curriculum.

It may be expected that teachers will start tackling these issues themselves, publishing and distributing newsletters, sometimes electronically, and serving as a forum to discuss current problems and policies. Although they may well be quite critical of the present situation and sometimes advocate the return to a classical approach without computers, all kinds of dialogues must be encouraged. They will give decision-makers both the opportunity to explain the basis of their options and welcome feedback on how things are working. It is not a substitute for research on the effectiveness of the new strategies but a way of making teacher experience known. Sometimes, it is quite comforting to realize that difficulties one experiences are not due to one's own inadequacies but exist everywhere and must be conquered.

IN-DEPTH EDUCATION OF SELECTED TEACHERS

For a variety of reasons – pump priming of the cascade model, ensuring teacher expertise in the choice of pedagogical material, associating teachers with the development process or staffing pilot projects with competent teachers – some specialists will be taken out of the field for extended periods of time, one to two years, to be given professional training related to the use of computers in schools. It is hoped that with their new knowledge, they will contribute to an increased teacher education as opposed to training. They are the ones who will think about the new roles of teachers, advise decision-makers on the best strategies and make them work in the school system.

There is little consensus on the content of courses these selected teachers will be offered. Since they lack a formal education in informatics, some computer science will be included, but the importance of actually programming algorithms in one of the computer languages has diminished over the years. Depending on whether these teachers are meant to help with the evaluation and development of new learning materials or to be the motors of massive introduction of computer learning in the schools, the emphasis of the courses will be entirely different.

Drawing on the experience of teaching for every student at the university level, one can identify six subject matters: *hardware:* principles of operation, main components of the system and common sources of breakdown or malfunction; hardware procurement and evaluation procedures; *operating systems functions and most important commands:* file handling, data management and archiving; *standard application programs:* word-processing, database systems, spreadsheet programs, communication software; *computer science concepts:* representation and manipulation of information; displaying data in a graphical form; structured programming approach to the resolution of problems; artificial intelligence, expert systems and their applications to education; *software development:* project management, programming languages and tools; authoring languages; tests and evaluation; and *computers and society:* cultural, social and economic impacts of the new information technologies.

There are more solutions than there are countries providing in-depth education for their teachers. To compensate for the lack of materials, a multi-media training package for teacher trainers has been produced as a regional initiative through UNESCO in the Pacific. The emphasis in such countries as Japan and Germany goes more to the cognitive sciences and the learning process than the purely technical aspects. Courses along these lines should be encouraged, leading to the formative and summative evaluations of the different strategies adopted for using the computer as a learning aid.

Emphasis on the purely technical side can be rather counter-productive in the sense that the trainees will identify more with highly specialized informatics experts than with the teacher population. Given the constant shortage in all the computer-related professions and the high salaries offered, there is a real danger that the costly programmes result in the loss of valuable teachers to the private sector. In the words of a Jamaican expert it can have serious long-term effects:

Currently, there is an inadequate supply of suitably qualified candidates offering themselves for teacher training and a steady loss of experienced classroom teachers in the developing world. This loss produces a positive feedback system whereby the devaluation of the profession yields fewer well-educated school leavers and adds to the need of the local private sector to recruit teachers (Nissen, 1989, p. 326).

Inspectors

The overall organization comprising high-level decision makers, competence centres, pilot projects and a plan for the introduction of computers in schools for uses across the curriculum is incomplete if it does not also look after its end users and how they cope with the new situations created.

There are many reasons to send qualified people into the field: advising local decision makers on global policies, evaluating the extent to which policies are effected, conducting research on the effectiveness of new approaches to learning, etc. It is argued here that such personnel is needed with a permanent mission of helping teachers locally, in their own classroom situation. The positions will hopefully be filled by people with the proper training coming either from the university research centres of from the body of teachers having mastered the in-depth formation.

Technicians for maintenance and repair

At a lower level, but just as important for the success of the introduction of computers in schools, is the infrastructure for maintenance and repair. Even in developed countries, where private firms offer maintenance contracts for school computers, some thought must be given to this kind of support activity. Breakdowns do occur and cannot be ignored. Maintenance contracts with immediate assistance are often too costly to be acceptable. Buying some spare machines to substitute for the ones needing repair while insuring a single contact point for the maintenance contractor can substantially reduce costs, even if it means hiring hardware technicians.

In addition, they serve another very useful function. In a complex but usual situation, where micro-computers are linked to a file server and a printer via a local area network, diagnosing the causes of a malfunction is not always easy. Causes may range from a pulled cable to an incompatibility between hardware and software products (PC compatible micros have several hidden switches and software packages are full of options). Even when the cause is identified, there are measures to be attempted to save valuable data; starting back up solutions with current versions of the programs just interrupted is not trivial.

In the case of a school system so decentralized that the intervention of a technician is not a practical alternative, some school staff members must be provided with a certain degree of competence in dealing with hardware problems. It is unrealistic to foresee that they can handle every type of situation but they can be provided with a 'hot line' to available help. The most frequent causes of trouble can also be publicized through the computer networks although they have a very limited utility in case of difficulties, communication being one of the first things to disappear.

Maintenance personnel can also educate the teaching staff to protect systems against increasingly costly and bothersome viruses. The game diskettes that students copy with little regard for copyright protection are infested with these hidden programs that play innocent pranks or erase a whole hard disk. There are programs that watch for and remove most of them before they do any harm, but the best protection is to impose a strict discipline.

Whatever happens, having people around with some experience in hardware and communication equipment reinforces the confidence of the teaching staff in the reliability of computers and related systems and makes it possible to try out alternate solutions or innovations such as connecting a new printer, a video-disk or a compact disk (CD ROM) full of data. If a school system can afford to hire them, train them, and above all, keep them, they are invaluable assets for the continued successful use of computers.

Teachers and the development of educational software

The Informatics Congress recommended that

> Education should not rely solely on industrial or commercial companies to produce educational software. Teachers and other specialists must become actively involved in the educational perspectives of software for their use in their classrooms (International Congress..., 1989a, p. 61, para. 21).

There is a variety of ways to accomplish it. Where central planning is the accepted method of working, priority areas will be identified and teachers will be associated with projects funded to provide educational material in these areas. Teachers have excellent ideas about how computers could be used in the teaching of their own discipline. Given such tools as authoring languages, or enough perseverance to learn programming, they will produce material they can use in their classroom and proudly show to their friends or to the local school authorities. These are of great value to their authors, much increasing their motivation and giving them new insights in the teaching of their own discipline. Unfortunately, their efforts will be lost unless they are the inspiration of a professional team working either for a software company specializing in education or for the national centre of one of the few nations that have such an institution. It is confirmed by the observation

> that criteria for the evaluation of programs during design and devel-
> opment are most likely to be found where educational institutions play
> a central role. The Scottish SMDP and the French software develop-
> ment linked to 'L'Informatique pour Tous' both show clearly the way
> in which proposals from teachers can be formulated within guidelines
> and against sets of standards. This ensures at least some of the aspects
> of the quality of the program before it is finally produced (Tucker, 1989,
> p. 353).

Teachers will also be involved in the testing and successive revisions of the material before it is sent to a software publisher for packaging and wide distribution. In the case of pilot projects, teachers associated with both the formative and the summative evaluation can bring special insight to the interpretation of the results. They can also describe their experiences to colleagues, thereby helping them to understand the goals and the extent to which they have been met.

Another approach is to provide limited funding and great freedom to teachers to experiment with any available software as a learning aid. Much will depend on the equipment and software available. The difficulty rests in collecting comparable data about the experiments and in convincing participating teachers that, the experiment being over, they must accept a solution different from the one they recommended. Evaluations are often too subjective and the issues rapidly take on an unwanted emotional dimension.

Part of the public domain software for learning is produced as a side activity by individuals on their own time (and sometimes using their own equipment). Most of it is badly designed and of poor quality. Furthermore, the amount of duplicated work is horrendous. Nevertheless some of the results are extremely good, and should be collected and made available on a much wider basis than a few colleagues and friends. One way of achieving this could be to set up contests with substantial prizes for educational software in selected educational areas.

Finally, it is worth mentioning that much development work is done locally to meet the needs of special education students with amazingly good results. Rolf Kristiansen speaks of the quantum leap in special education and the new perspective to disabled people. He says:

> The main challenge today has been documented as the selection and use of these new technologies in special education and rehabilitation, as a help and not a hindrance to disabled users. Examples have been presented showing the potential of the new equipment (Kristiansen, 1989, p. 113).

Efforts are needed to promote the dissemination of what already exists to those who need it most.

The use of informatics in planning and managing education systems

A clear distinction needs to be made between informatics as a management tool used in education and informatics as a tool or subject for teaching and learning. Every actor of the education system performs certain administrative tasks where the computer can help. Where networks link all the computing resources of an organization, the construction of interfaces between the administrative tasks performed by teachers within their daily educational settings and the computerized management system for the administrative personnel could result in a more efficient system with a significant reduction of paperwork and paper circulation.

Networked solutions and distributed databases are particularly attractive to those systems which are geographically distributed over a wide area with some central co-ordinating and financing authority but in which most decisions are made locally. The view given below is a bit futuristic, although it is being experimented with at various institutions with quite a variety of communication facilities ranging from the ubiquitous French Minitel to the fibre optics links connecting a number of very fast local area networks in universities. Since students, teachers and administrators use the same network, care must be taken to ensure the integrity and security of the consolidated database managed by the administration. Some discipline in the use of passwords and access rights will protect the system against the harmful actions of would-be 'hackers'.

Starting at the receiving end, students and parents are interested in facts concerning schedules, vacations, deadlines for registration and whom to contact for different problems. This information can be made available through an easily accessible database, updated as soon as a decision is taken. The same public wants to know about student progress and grades. In some systems, considerable freedom is given to students who are made responsible to for the completion of a number of credit courses chosen from a wide variety of possibilities. They can find out where they stand at all times by asking the computer to match their files against the schedule they have chosen. When a difficulty arises, they are presented with different courses of action.

Teachers are both providers and consumers of administrative information. If they are equipped with micro-processors on which they keep track of the work of their classes, a simplified procedure can be worked out for instance to enter the final grades in the system and to have the weekly or monthly student bulletin printed automatically. Such systems were already in operation long ago, when terminals connected to mini-computers were the only way to access computers in schools. Teachers are also interested in their status, salary, career plan, health insurance and other benefits, and they could query the administrative centre when they find it convenient instead of having to shuffle through stacks of outdated papers to find the relevant information.

Teachers are required to participate in numerous meetings; the computer can help in scheduling since it holds the timetable of everyone, saving secretarial work and many telephone calls. Teachers with administrative responsibilities, for instance school principals or the organizers of special events, will use the micro-computers and associated software packages they have in school to prepare budgets and schedules, and to compute interesting statistics. Although they will try to convince the school management to use the same tools to perform their tasks, it must be recognized that computerizing an administration is a job for professionals.

Spectacular progress has been observed in the level of productivity of administrative work and the quality of decisions taken as a result of the introduction of informatics into the management of the education system. It is not different from other administrations of the same size and there exists considerable experience in financial management, accounting, payroll and databases. Software choices depend on local constraints such as the human resources available, the type of organization and the structure of the management system. The development of specific software dependent on particular hardware should be avoided.

There is a problem specific to education which has now found a good solution: the establishment of a timetable. Commercially available programs find optimal solutions among the myriad of possibilities out of which only a few are compatible with all the constraints. Once the timetable is established, plans for room occupancy and individual teacher schedules are distributed.

Construction and maintenance programs for the variety of buildings that a school system must manage have also been successfully implemented up to different levels of details, including the consumption of fluids. In some cases, this has led to substantial savings.

Schools also operate libraries or, more generally, resource centres where many functions can be computerized. UNESCO, through its International Bureau of Education (IBE), puts at the disposal of countries which so desire the software package CDS-ISIS.

The introduction of computers in an administration results not in a reduction of costs, but rather in the performance of an increased number of tasks without a corresponding increase in staff.

The training of administrators

It is important to understand that applying informatics to the management of a school system is in no way different from the electronic data processing well known to other sectors of the economy. The same rules of specifying the objectives of the system, the sources and flow of information, the type and frequency of outputs, and the relationships between the different subsystems have to be followed. Work of lasting value requires professional staff to provide decision makers in charge of getting the system started with their basic training by including them in the team working out the specifications. The time needed to complete the process should not be underestimated: it is measured in months or years rather than in weeks.

The availability of properly prepared system analysts is crucial. If they are not present, the work of self-taught programmers will have to be supplemented by outside expertise. Using computers in the classroom either to teach programming or to teach other subjects is not an adequate preparation for setting up a computerized management system.

Secretaries, accountants and other staff usually attend courses of a few days duration to become familiar with the operation of the labour-saving tools found on personal computers: spreadsheets, word processor and small database systems. After that, since they are already knowledgeable about the operation of the keyboard, it will take only a few days to introduce them to the procedures of the integrated system. In the case of teachers and the simple tasks which are required of them, a few hours of explanations are quite sufficient.

Economic and financial constraints

It is relatively easy to assess the costs and potential gains of computerizing the school management system. A certain number of functions are to be accomplished; they translate into a number of working places to be equipped with keyboard and screen, and software packages to be bought and installed on a given hardware. Turn-key systems could be ordered from software companies if the local expertise is lacking.

The situation with education is much more complicated since so many factors must be taken into account. The single most important issue in general education is the equity problem. Any school system, after some time spent on pilot projects and experiments, must offer equal opportunities to all participants at a given level. This means that a programme aiming at computerizing all the schools in a given constituency will have to buy a slice of new equipment every year. Keeping up with technology, the falling price of micro-computer components and the new forms of technology developed in the advanced industrial economies, it is very likely that early acquisitions will require replacement before the whole programme has been completed. A parametre which is of the utmost importance but difficult to evaluate is the lifetime of current hardware. With the exception of the disks, the components of a personal computer are not fundamentally different from those of a television set with a lifetime of more than ten years. Yet, ten years ago, there were no personal computers! A survey of the literature for the Stanford/UNESCO Symposium (Carnoy et al., 1986) gives a somewhat arbitrary rule of amortizing purchases over a six year period.

A useful model would be the following: consider as investment the cost of infrastructure only and budget a constant sum in order to satisfy all the needs over a certain period of five to ten years, depending on the possibilities at hand. After the first few years, part of the budget would go to maintenance and part would buy new, more modern equipment, first to fill the remaining gaps and then to renew the oldest machines (not so much because they do not work any more but because they have become obsolete, their memory, processor and graphic screen being unable to support the new applications). With the decreasing price of hardware, such a model would allow the satisfaction of more and more needs as time goes on, provided the first users do not become greedy for fancier hardware as their expertise develops.

By contrast, a huge effort at one time creates problems of staff and teacher training which cannot be spread out over a longer period. It also results in some of the machines not being used at the beginning. The main drawback, however, is that all the machines age together and a renewal budget, comparable to the first one, will have to be requested every few years.

Any discussion on economic and financial constraints assumes that decisions to introduce informatics in schools have been or are about to be taken. In many countries, basic questions on the necessity or applicability of its introduction remain unanswered. Nevertheless, it is necessary to obtain costs in order to determine the set of economically feasible alternatives.

Evolution of investment and operational costs

In the following paragraphs, the emphasis will be on a unit laboratory to be installed with different configurations in a research unit, in a centre for teacher training or vocational training or directly in a school. For planning purposes, one can imagine that such a unit could be replicated as many times as necessary throughout the school system, with some economy of scale with purchase prices, support and maintenance.

HARDWARE

The unit lab to be considered will consist of one server with a hard disk of 30 to 200 Mbytes and ten to fifty desktop micro-computers linked to the server through a network. The server will have the necessary back-up facilities in the form of a cheap cassette tape. One quality printer and several cheap but robust impact printers should be part of the setup. Depending on the resources available and the requirements of the environment, the network can be realized inexpensively, with twisted pairs similar to telephone wires and special cards inside the personal computers. The price of the cards will depend on the kind of performance wanted: full Ethernet or Token Ring capabilities will increase the cost of both cabling and cards but offer a much better range of possibilities. The laser printer, which is expensive to operate, must be justified by handling office work and desktop publishing applications.

Single personal computers, with monochrome screens and a single diskette unit, approach the limit of $1,000 per unit. A colour monitor – preferred by many educators – will add a few hundred dollars. A mouse extension of about $100 could also be considered.

One initial investment that cannot be avoided is the provision for modern communication facilities. Buildings should allow the easy passing of cables. Proper access to telecommunication lines and, perhaps, to a satellite receiving station, must be present in the original planning.

It is often essential to provide a stabilized power supply which suppresses damaging surges and can compensate for short power outages of up to a few minutes ($1,000). It can even signal the server to safely shut itself off when the voltage is about to fall below the limit value guaranteed. Another kind of protection is the bolting of the equipment to the furniture so it is not stolen. Similarly, some provision for air-conditioning or at least a good ventilation is needed.

SOFTWARE

Good networking software comes at a price. For example, current versions of the *Novell* system, accommodating several protocols, cost about $5,000. Networked versions of a good word processor, spreadsheet, database system and the languages of the Turbo family (Pascal, C, Prolog) may cost another $5,000. Given the basic tools and a sufficient number of competent programmers, a school system may decide to rewrite some of these packages, especially if problems relating to language differences need to be incorporated. It is a sizable effort, especially considering that an adequate documentation has to be provided.

Should educational software be free? The argument is made that it will discourage the industrial production of software, but it has already been said that the private sector does little outside of government-funded programmes or the adaptation of already tested courseware coming from research centres. There are many free programs, but those using them must bear the cost of investigating what is available, adapting it to the local context and providing documentation.

The expenses associated with buying commercially available computer-based learning material depend very much on the subject and the availability of such material. There are many documented examples from France, the United Kingdom, the Netherlands and the United States. The system which seems to work best is to negotiate rights of use for a whole school system rather than buying single copies.

HUMAN RESOURCES

The unit lab mentioned earlier will require at least one co-ordinator with a reasonable training, some teaching aids for supporting students and an amount of administrative support throughout the year estimated at 20 per cent of the time of an administrator similar to a school principal. There is also the problem of securing proper maintenance services. Even with outside help, running the lab in a multi-function capability will require two full-time equivalent positions.

The big unknown is how much should be spent on teacher training and teacher support. For teaching informatics at the university level or for vocational schools, there are models involving the professional preparation for the teaching of a new subject, but for the introduction of computers in the classroom there is neither agreement on what should be done nor models to follow. The only constant answer from teachers to queries about such programmes is that they were insufficient or misdirected. Any country wishing to successfully introduce computers into the general school system either for computer literacy or for more ambitious computer-aided learning should be prepared to spend as much on teacher training and support as on hardware and software put together.

RESEARCH

Research costs are measured in terms of the number of positions which can be made available through grants or pilot projects. Regardless of whether they are aimed at following recent development in technology or at performing summative evaluations involving cognitive psychology, they must reach a critical mass and be supported by an infrastructure including an up-to-date library, electronic-mail, FAX and secretarial services.

A research team can use a slightly more sophisticated unit lab with the possibility of having a workstation replacing the server. It must be emphasized once more that a research group looking at computers in education cannot function properly without a good access to international electronic mail. The cost of that connection depends on the local telephone companies.

DEVELOPMENT

In some circumstances, the costs of development, that is of taking a bright idea, trying it out in the field, adapting and packaging it into a finished, usable product, will be borne by a software publisher. In most circumstances, however, those costs have to be borne by the regional development centre advocating the use of new computer-related methodologies. Costs involve field testing, adaptation, packaging, preparing and testing the documentation.

EVALUATION

Little is known about the impact of computers on the education system as their use spreads in a society. Where computer literacy is a goal, research into the differential benefits associated with alternative strategies for attaining specified objectives is needed. For computer-based learning, there are limited or no research findings available about the impact of computers on what is taught and how it is taught.

Except, perhaps, for the most advanced countries, these problems cannot be treated in isolation. Provisions should be made to have research teams active both nationally and internationally, with some norms agreed on to make the results coming from different nations easily comparable. At least one research team on the subject should exist in each country with sufficient funding and resources to conduct surveys and to attempt summative evaluations of all the pilot projects.

Cost-effectiveness and efficiency of the various projects and organizations

Cost-effectiveness is more usually applied to industrial, commercial or military organizations. The specific character of education – absorbing as it does a sizable part of its output as teachers and making no profits but rather producing pay-offs of long lasting value for a country's economy – makes it difficult to measure the effect on productivity of introducing information technologies.

It has been amply demonstrated that scattering hardware in the schools without proper teacher training is a complete waste. The only reasonable approach is to go through the phases of pilot projects to which some teachers are associated, then to proceed with extending the experiment to the whole education system, preparing teachers before imposing computers in their classrooms. Expanding from pilot project to full scale implementation requires caution. Some pilot experiences are not readily transferable where the full scale implementation does not fully replicate the pilot conditions.

Although there is an excellent chance that the advent of information technologies will increase the efficiency of the teaching process, scientific honesty admits that to date no compelling evidence of this has been demonstrated in controlled experiments. The vast effort required to meet the educational requirements has to be based on an act of faith.

It is not an excuse for ignoring the rules for successfully managing the introduction of computers in the education system. Many pitfalls have been pointed out in this chapter. But more important than any progress in hardware, software or methodology, the presence and dedication of teams of competent people during both pilot and full implementation phases is the key to successful projects. For reasons of morale, as well as constant updating of knowledge, members of these teams must never feel isolated from the international scientific community. In the light of the potential payoffs, the cost of a global communication network dedicated to education appears reasonable.

References

Bork, A. (1988) New Structures for Technology-Based Courses. *Education & Computing,* Vol. 4, No. 3, pp. 109–17.

Bricklin, D. and Frankston, R. (1986) Interviews. In: *Programmers at Work.* Redmond, Wash./Harmondsworth, Microsoft Press/Penguin Books, Ltd.

Carnoy, M., Daley, H., Devillar, R.A., Earthman, E.A. Herrmann, P., Loop, L., Misra, M. and Starbuck, J. (1986) *Education and Computers: Vision and Reality in the mid-1980's.* (Working paper 2.)

Carnoy, M. and Loop, L. (1986) *Computers and Education: Which Role for International Research. A Report on the Stanford/Unesco Symposium, 10-14 March 1986, Stanford University School of Education.* Paris: UNESCO.

Duguet, P. (1989) National Strategies and their Extension to the International Level. In: International Congress: Education and Informatics – Strengthening International Co-operation/Congrès international: Éducation et informatique – vers une coopération internationale renforcée, Paris, 1989, *Proceedings/Les Actes,* Vol. 1, pp. 283–90. Paris: UNESCO.

Franklin, S. and Levrat, B. (1985) Portability of Computer Based Learning Materials across Machines and across Natural Languages. In: *Computers in Education.* Amsterdam: Elsevier Science Publishers.

Hawkridge, D., Jaworski, J. and McMahon, H. (1990) *Computers in Third-World Schools: Examples, Experience and Issues.* London: The MacMillan Press Ltd.

Henkens, L. and van Deursen, K. (1988) Courseware Development in the Netherlands. In: F. Lovis and E. D. Tagg (eds.), *Computers in Education.* Amsterdam: Elsevier Science Publishers.

International Congress: Education and Informatics – Strengthening International Co-operation/Congrès international: Éducation et informatique – vers une coopération internationale renforcée, Paris, 1989. (1989*a*) *Final Report.* Paris: UNESCO.

– (1989*b*) *Proceedings/Les Actes,* Vol. 1, pp. 1–383, Paris: UNESCO.

– (1989*c*) *Proceedings/Les Actes,* Vol. 2, pp. 385–757, Paris: UNESCO.

Kristiansen, R. (1989) The Quantum Leap in Special Education. In: International Congress: Education and Informatics – Strengthening International Co-operation/Congrès international: Éducation et informatique – vers une coopération internationale renforcée, Paris, 1989. *Proceedings/Les Actes,* Vol. 1, pp. 84–113.

Mallatratt, J. (1988) Teacher Education and Teacher Training – The Identification of In-service Requirements to Support Computer Usage across the Curriculum. In: F. Lovis and E. D. Tagg (eds.), *Computers in Education*. Amsterdam: Elsevier Science Publishers.

Nissen, P. (1989) Training Teachers and Trainers. In: International Congress: Education and Informatics – Strengthening International Co-operation/Congrès international: Éducation et informatique – vers une coopération internationale renforcée, Paris, 1989. *Proceedings/Les Actes*, Vol.1, p. 326. Paris: UNESCO.

Oualid, A. (1989) Problems of Software Development in Developing Countries. In: G. X. Ritter (ed.), *Proceedings of the IFIP 11th World Congress*, San Francisco: Elsevier Science Publishers.

Southerton, A. (1989) OS/2 versus UNIX. *UnixWorld VI*, Vol. 12, No. 72.

Tchovagadze, G. (1989) The Age of Informatics. In: International Congress: Education and Informatics – Strengthening International Co-operation/Congrès international: Éducation et informatique – vers une coopération internationale renforcée, Paris, 1989. *Proceedings/Les Actes*, Vol. 2, pp. 658–69. Paris: UNESCO.

Tucker, R. (1989) A Summary of a 'Comparative Study on Criteria and Procedures for the Evaluation of Educational Software' undertaken for UNESCO. In: International Congress: Education and Informatics – Strengthening International Co-operation/Congrès international: Éducation et informatique – vers une coopération internationale renforcée, Paris, 1989. *Proceedings/Les Actes*, Vol. 1, pp. 35–17. Paris: UNESCO.

Vivier, G. (1989) Présentation du système d'auto-formation TELIMA (Télé-enseignement de l'informatique par Méthode audio-Active. In: International Congress: Education and Informatics – Strengthening International Co-operation/Congrès international: Éducation et informatique – vers une coopération internationale renforcée, Paris, 1989. *Proceedings/Les Actes*, Vol.2, pp. 494–502. Paris: UNESCO.

Wenger, E. (1988) *Artificial Intelligence and Tutoring Systems*. Los Altos, Calif.: Morgan Kaufman Publishers, Inc.

CHAPTER THREE

Applications

Alfred Bork, David Walker and André Poly

Introduction

The new information technologies can be used in a wide variety of educational environments. In many cases, we are, worldwide, only beginning to
explore the possible uses. In some levels of education, few applications are
available, but the potential for helping learning in all areas is great.

It seems appropriate to re-state some of the human and personal arguments for using computers and related technology in schools. In support of
learning the computer is seen as a valuable resource that can offer several
distinct advantages over other conventional classroom resources. The computer is capable of exhibiting endless patience, expressing no criticisms and
making no judgement on the learner's actions or performance. High motivation can be invoked where children can 'indulge in enjoyment' and
environments can be created to encourage group co-operative projects
where learners discuss actions and consequences, encouraging analysis and
planning. Learners can be placed in control of their own learning, working
independently of the teacher. The slowest learner may be able to experience
satisfying results having been released from the constraints of whole class
teaching. All learners may benefit from immediate responses and interactive
assessment techniques.

After the initial euphoria of novelty wears off, many countries take steps
to ensure that technology is not being allowed to drive education: learning
considerations should be given the opportunity to drive technology. So far,
substantial demands have been made on teachers by the introduction of
computers into the classroom. It has been necessary, particularly during
initial stages, for teachers to actively supervise the computer-related acti-

vities of pupils. This is going to change as more effective material is available.

Irrespective of the initial implementation workloads and constraints, there is a strong consensus that the new information technology, through innovative educational software and support materials, can lead to a significant contribution to education. Teaching strategies have already been enhanced by the new technologies* to enrich the experiences and increase the learning opportunities of pupils.

The best educational software available encourages the development of important cognitive skills rather than memorization of facts and processes, as the best teacher does in front of a sensible group of students.

Level of education

More details will be given of these applications in the last sections of this chapter, but let us introduce the discussion through the level of education.

Pre-school

Education of the young child often takes place primarily at home by parents, sisters or brothers, in kindergarten or by the nurse.

When a child is first born, that child already is an active learner. Some of the most difficult tasks in learning occur in the early years. Some educationalists maintain that it is best for the child to stimulate his or her reaction as early as possible, in order to ensure that knowledge is assimilated.

Thus, almost all children learn a complex spoken language, a learning activity of considerable difficulty for those beyond childhood. An English speaker who learns French at the age of 15 does not find this a simple task. Yet all 2-year-old children in France become proficient in French.

Another extremely important process for the pre-school child is the early development of mental capabilities. In this development, we can see signs of the computer being a useful device, although few current applications of this kind have been developed. There is some pre-school material in countries that do try to deal with the thinking patterns of very young children, following in some cases the psychologists who have worked in this area.

A further factor comes in with countries, such as Japan, that require children to take national examinations before they enter school. In Japan many parents show considerable interest in preparing their children for this

---

*   *New technologies include computers, networks, multimedia, telecommunication, in fact every device with an 'intelligent' chip inside.*

test. Not too surprisingly, there has arisen an industry to support this need. The examination in Japan determines whether children will be able to attend the best schools.

Since, effectively, the children are being prepared for taking an intelligence test, this material might be thought of as a mechanism for increasing human intelligence at a particularly critical stage in its development. Hence, even in countries that do not have such an exam system, such material could be extremely important.

Since young children cannot read and write, the written language can play no role in materials of this kind. However, high quality voice material can be supplied through laserdisc and compact disk attached to computer, as well as also iconic communication through 'touch screen' and/or 'concepts keyboards' which provide an opportunity to communicate concepts without words (but pay attention not to confuse concept and icon).

Primary School

In many countries of the world, formal school for children begins somewhere between 5 and 7 years old.

READING AND WRITING

Children write in most areas of the curriculum for many different purposes. This need begins in primary school and continues to all levels of education. There are two levels of difficulties. The first level is to write with a pen on paper: children have to learn at the same time what is a letter (a character), how to write a word, what meaning has the word they wrote and how to draw the shape of letters. Starting with a text processor gives them the opportunity to learn about letters and words and delay the difficulty of well drawing the text. The second level includes the ability to express something meaningful as well as an understanding that it is a process involving several stages. The ability to plan, compose and redraft are the main writing skills in the process approach to writing. These can be facilitated and enhanced by using the computer; it assists naturally with the creation, storage and manipulation of text.

Text processing can help children to understand the writing process, and to concentrate on the composing skills of writing in the knowledge that changes can be made in the redrafting process without re-writing, and it can improve children's attitudes to the processes of creating, drafting, editing and revising. Manipulating text in this way is central to the idea of text-processing. Other software such as inventive programs and idea organizers is important in this situation.

The Writing to Read programme in the United States (written by John Henry Martin) is a full course intended for students who are 5 and 6 years old. It is a phonetic approach to reading, using a simplified phonetic system related to the older Initial Teaching Alphabet in the United Kingdom. The beginning stages quickly try to get the students to type any word that they can say, using this phonetic basis. Then the student sees the word on the computer screen, and so learns to read it. A wide variety of media in addition to the computer is used.

MATHEMATICS

A second important intellectual component is the child's first detailed acquaintance with mathematical ideas. Here, current material, with and without the computer, is far too dependent on memory. Students memorize arithmetical facts and processes, but lag in developing problem-solving skills and intuition. We have good experience with the use of manipulatable material to help in increasing student's problem-solving skills and intuition. The computer could play a major role in helping with building these concepts of numbers and operations on numbers, and could introduce students to fundamental concepts of mathematical reasoning. But little material of this kind exists at present. Most existing computer material for arithmetic for young children stresses memory of arithmetical facts and processes. Some of the material in this area has been successful, as will be mentioned later.

SCIENCE

Science is also an important early component of education. Primary school education is often very weak in building notions of scientific process. Understanding at an early stage of the tactics of empirical sciences is a critical intellectual endeavour. Because of the computer's ability to provide a wide range of experiences in scientific reasoning to the student and to offer immediate and detailed personal assistance, tailored to the individual needs of each student, the prospects seem promising for contributing to a deep understanding of science at the primary level.

DATABASES

Finding, organizing and presenting information is an essential aspect of the curriculum in primary schools. Work with databases reinforces this by providing pupils with a highly motivating structure that also gives them an opportunity to develop a wide range of skills including discussion, decision-making, researching, recording, problem-solving and role-playing.

Computers and networks will provide opportunities to have access to graphical representation, databases by telephone and use of CD-ROM bases.

GEOGRAPHY AND HISTORY

Geography and history are seen by many educationalists to have a special role in primary school, encouraging understanding and appreciation beyond national boundaries.

General teaching objectives of history and geography should include showing how geographical and historical awareness can be developed out of popular topics, how a spatial framework can be used as a basis for developing this awareness, how skills can be developed at the same time as spatial concepts and how both skills and concepts can provide the basis for the development of sympathetic and empathetic attitudes toward people of different races.

ART AND DESIGN

Young children are encouraged to express themselves through art and design.

Educational programs encourage children to create: choosing shapes and drawing tools, rotation, enlarging, colouring, and so on. Such programs may appear simple, but the implementation of the learning strategy has to be given considerable attention.

Children are encouraged to make decisions from a range of simple shapes using felt or colored paper. Plasticine has been rolled out to show the effects of distortion. After such physical experiences, children can be introduced to a program and challenged to create a picture on one half of the screen to match the externally created shape.

Children have been encouraged to look at everyday objects such as cars, buildings and domestic appliances, and to analyse their form to produce a reconstructed picture.

COMMENTS

In some countries there has been a debate as to whether or not computers should be used with children this young. In some places the decision has been negative, at least not as the first priority in applications of computers to learning. But, as in many of the topics to be discussed, there is little reliable empirical evidence. One concern is that young children should have considerable human contact. But the computer can stimulate this contact, particularly with other pupils if pupils use the computer material in small groups.

It is also generally agreed that it is easier for a primary-school teacher, managing all the curriculum, to integrate NICT in a cross topics process and to be a more efficient integrator.

In Europe, some countries have now a compulsory course about NICT in their curriculum.

Secondary school

Perhaps the major area for the development of application of interactive technology for educational purposes has been, in a majority of countries at the secondary-school level. A great many different pieces of software have been developed for this level, although, surprisingly, no full courses as far as we are aware.

Historically, it was easy to create educational software according to rather modelled topics. In fact, it has appeared simpler to develop course-ware on subjects, *a priori*, more structured, more 'modelled', when semantics and intuition were much more present in primary education.

In some countries, the decision has been made to focus attention, at least initially, at the secondary-school level, but more and more (particularly, in 1991 in Europe) information technologies activities are carried out through the recommendations of the education authority or upon the initiatives of the schools themselves. Information technologies activities are compulsory in some countries which have recently renewed their curriculum.

Perhaps the most successful application at this level has been in the use of a variety of tools rather than specific tutorials. In particular, word-processing programs and other facilities for creating, storing, scanning, manipulating and displaying documents are being explored across the curriculum. The computer becomes a flexible and stimulating resource through which the creative powers of students can be released and their knowledge and understanding developed. Much material also exists in secondary-school science and mathematics, mostly in the form of small programs without much coherence and often fitting poorly in the standard curricula of a country.

Simulation has been a powerful teaching technique in use for many years before the introduction of computers. The computer has, however, made the technique available to a wider range of teachers and has enhanced some simulations, making them more realistic. Many examples exist in secondary education, where the situation is difficult or impossible to set up in real life

– too risky, too time-consuming, or too expensive, for instance historical events, analysis and decision-making in economics at the level of an office or at that of a country, physics and chemistry, biology and ecology. For example, a commonly used simulation deals with combating the effects of oil spillage at sea. The program has much to offer. Oil, blown by a variable wind, is threatening an area of coastline and the students have to decide how to deploy the resources at their disposal as effectively as possible. Information provided on the screen and in supporting documentation has to be interpreted.

A further example occurs in home economics where pupils analyse a range of diets. Before the computer, this exercise was carried out using pencil and paper, and many students found the calculations tedious and difficult. Programs are available that overcome the problem and, at the same time, provide students with the opportunities for investigative learning. Suggested diets can be analysed quickly and comparisons made. Students feel that the computer offers them anonymity and they tend to be more honest in recording details of their personal diet.

In modern languages, teachers use the word processor as a means of extending the range and quality of pupils' written work, strengthening language skills or providing remedial work. An area of great potentiality, but still very undeveloped, is that for learning languages. Interactive video would appear to be particularly useful in dealing with spoken language.

A rather new trend appears in the upper secondary level of some countries educational programme concerning vocational aspects of informatics, using more career-oriented programs, at least for some of the students.

Higher education

With higher education we begin with the universities, or in some countries such as France, with the *grandes écoles*. There are a variety of different types of higher education involved. In the United States there are the community colleges as well as the universities, and in the United Kingdom polytechnics as well as the universities. Often the community colleges and polytechnics overlap with the standard university programs, but offer also a variety of vocationally-oriented activities that are not available in the universities.

Again, this is an area that has received considerable attention with regard to computer uses in education. The university level population is typically much smaller than that of secondary school, and so the economic feasibility of large amounts of computer material at this level is less.

Many universities have special programmes set up to aid faculty members to use computers. In spite of this, the results in using technology in general education at the university level have been disappointing. Programmes that have cost large amounts of money have produced little in the way of results. It is fair to say that, at the university level, as with almost all other levels of education, the computer and its associated technology still plays a very minor role in the educational process. Only a small percentage of student's learning time in higher education is spent with computers.

However, specialized courses (informatics, programming, applied mathematics and physics, etc.) make extensive use of computers, while engineers devote over 20 per cent of their time to the use of computers.

Some of the phenomena we see at the secondary school level are also present here. Thus, the use of text-processing is increasing somewhat for taking notes, drafting reports, etc., and electronic dictionaries or databases are more and more present in university libraries.

Adult or community education and training

If we look at the full range of adult education, including training within companies, this might be the largest area of education. But these activities take place in so many different ways that it is difficult to fully account for all phases of adult education.

Training within companies, both for their own employees and for their customers, is a rapidly growing area. It has tended to make more use, proportionally, of interactive learning technology than do more formal school and university environments. Thus the bulk of the interactive video material that has been developed thus far is for training. But in training, as elsewhere, the bulk of the material in existing courses does not use the new technologies; lectures still dominate.

An important environment for informal adult learning activities is the public library; the major vehicle is the book. But we can expect libraries gradually to involve more media in learning activities. Brief experiences at the University of California, Irvine, with computers in public libraries, is encouraging. Material at this level needs to be entirely self-instructional, just as well-written books are. That is, the learning units must work without outside aid. Only limited help is possible in the library, and this is primarily devoted to assistance with accessing material.

Teacher training involves more and more the pedagogical use of new technologies and educational software, but there are still too few teachers dealing with them.

Types of applications

One way of classifying applications of interactive technology to learning is in terms of the *type of usage* of the technology. The computer, when looked at in educational situations, is not a monolithic device but rather one that can play a great variety of roles. In this discussion we classify those roles and discuss further applications.

We wish to make it clear that these various ways of using the computer are *not to be considered as alternatives*. Too much of the early literature and too many of the earlier approaches to computers seem to be based on the idea that some sort of competition is taking place between different uses of the computer. This attitude was often unfortunately stimulated by limited resources.

The aim of using the computer in learning is to *improve learning* and any aspect of computer use that helps with learning should be employed. We expect that in many areas a variety of modes of using the computer will be useful, and the selection of these modes will be a pedagogical issue, not based on some philosophical discussion about how computers 'should' be used in learning environments.

Five areas will be discussed in this section: *literacy* – the concern in this mode of using interactive technology is with helping students, at various levels of education, to become familiar with the computer; *informatics* – the computer can be the object of study and programming and other aspects of informatics can be considered; *curriculum* – in this mode of computer usage we move away from the computer as the focus to the computer as an aid in learning in many, perhaps all, of the courses and informal learning situations that the student is involved in; *testing* – testing using interactive technology has been explored for at least thirty years in using computers in education; and *management* – the computer can play an important role in the management of learning, both for the student and the teacher.

Literacy

There is no clear agreement as to how the term 'computer literacy' is to be used. Emphasis is put on the computer itself and on general issues relating to what computers can do and what effects they can produce.

AWARENESS

The simplest types of computer literacy applications assume that the critical thing is to teach people to handle the mechanics of the computer so the issues become where the off/on switch is, how the diskette is inserted into the machine, how it is removed and how a program already available is used.

Often vocabulary too plays a sizable role – students are expected to memorize definitions of various words associated with the computer, such as chip, memory board, central processor, memory, mother board and a whole host of other such useless words.

These mechanics of using computers are likely to vanish as computers become more common in society. Inserting diskettes could turn out to be more common in the future, or the technology may move in the opposite direction. Likewise, operating systems change and knowing how to start a program in a particular operating system may give one little clue about how to do it in another one.

TYPING

Another aspect of some computer literacy courses is what has come to be described as 'keyboarding'. This is a word that reflects a temporary situation at best. There are a few additional aspects of typing on computers but these do not need any special learning, as they can be learned through usage. Moreover, mouse devices and scrolling menus reduce the keyboard function simply to a means of controlling the computer and the programs that novices use.

COMPUTERPHOBIA

Another component of computer literacy that often receives stress is the notion that one needs to overcome 'fears' that the students may have about computers and that students should come to love the computer. There is little evidence, however, that children are afraid of computers. This might be more of a problem in dealing with adult education, but even here it does not appear to be serious.

Our culture talks so much about computers, in television and other ways, and there is so much talk about them in science fiction, that most people grow up expecting computers to do *everything*. The experiences of using computers in places such as public libraries indicate that children approach computers and use them completely freely, but that some adults have reservations. Teachers are more likely to have resistance to computers than students.

Part of the notion that computers create resistance is that a good deal of the software around today is not very user friendly. As we become more skilled in developing software and as software designers understand better the needs of the user, we can expect resistance to be less of a problem.

SIMPLE PROGRAMMING

Computer literacy courses often stress some simple programming. Some proponents of computer literacy argue that this is the most essential ingredient of literacy. Somehow, these people argue, the user must be able to 'control' the computer.

The issue of control is not a simple one. The question of who controls what is not absolute, but one that can have various levels. An office worker using a spreadsheet certainly has 'control' of what happens in that situation. Indeed, in a modern high-powered spreadsheet this control can be very important, on the condition that one does not have to be able to program computers to control them. Most people use most technology in ways that they want to, under their control, without understanding everything about the technology.

Furthermore, the simplistic introductions to programming usually provide the students with only a trivial amount of control, because the things that they can program themselves are likely to be at the trivial level. The issue of control is perhaps more of an emotional issue than a real issue. It seems likely that programming as we know it today will change greatly, and that fewer people will be involved in such activities.

USE OF SIMPLE TOOLS

Computer literacy courses in recent years have often focused on providing an introduction to a variety of commonly-used computer tools, for instance spreadsheets, word processors, drawing and painting programs, database programs, graphing programs and home finance programs.

We have already noted that the use of tools, such as word processors, can occur in subject-area courses. This approach is likely to be more valuable than a course in computer literacy, because learning occurs in a context in which the tools are useful.

COMPUTERS, SOCIETY AND ETHICS

These aspects unfortunately receive the least attention, probably because the necessary learning materials are the most difficult to create and employ. The issues involved are the ethical and moral issues concerning computers, and the issues concerning the positive and negative impacts on society due to the new information technology.

Existing moral codes have little to say about computers, while the rapid rise of computers has left us unprepared for the major social consequences. The teaching of these ethical and societal aspects of the new information technologies is not an easy process. Even university programmes often do not face this issue, although many departments try to, for instance one at the University of California, Irvine, which requires all seniors in computer science to take a course of this type. That course, like many such courses, is based on reading, writing and discussion. For example, to structure and fill a database concerning personal topics about each pupil or student may bring us to reflect on databases and personal freedom.

The type of education we are discussing is not something that can simply be handled at one point in the student's career. These ethical and moral issues, because they represent a long-term need versus short-term consequences of external technology of the computer, need attention at a variety of levels, probably starting with young children and continuing through adult life.

The issues themselves change as the computers evolve and the sophistication of the user plays a factor as to which issues are important. The typical approach in schools has been to get students to think of *information* as a possession, in the sense of intellectual property, and to apply to it the kinds of rules concerning stealing that might apply to other kinds of possessions, and also to dismantle mechanisms using computers and international network to obtain power through information.

This area of moral and social issues about the new information technologies requires more attention, on an international level, than it currently receives.

Informatics

Informatics is an interesting word, used primarily in Europe. In the United States and Canada, it has less use. A roughly similar expression in the United States is computer science. 'Informatics' de-emphasizes the hardware – the computer – and emphasizes a much more important element, the information.

UNIVERSITIES

Study of computers can happen at almost any level of education. Perhaps it is most developed in universities all over the world, at the undergraduate or graduate level. A university programme in computer science has a wide variety of courses, usually organized along functional areas, with different parts of computer science such as databases, artificial intelligence and software engineering as the topics. But in a few places one still finds an older organizational scheme, based on computer languages. Thus in this older type of course structure one might find a course in Pascal, in C, in Prolog and similar courses. Some of the courses will deal with hardware issues and some will deal with software issues.

A meeting on this topic was organized by the Working Group 3.2 of the International Federation of Information Processing (IFIP) in April 1990. Fifty people were invited; a publication is based on the meeting. There was lack of agreement on what informatics curricula of the 1990s should be like. Readers interested in the different positions should look at the publication.

SCHOOLS

Informatics within schools is often very different, as already mentioned. Here there is a much less developed history, at any level. Initially, informatics teaching concentrated on secondary school, but now many primary schools around the world also stress the subject and it has become compulsory in some European countries, particularly those which have recently renewed their curricula.

Much of the concentration in schools, however, is on one component – learning to program. Many of the courses are poor and therefore a waste of students' time.

Chiefly for expediency, many early programming efforts took place with BASIC as the programming language. Often little thought was given to this issue. This is strange in that most computer scientists believe that BASIC is either useless or actively harmful to many students; it frequently leads to bad programming habits which are difficult to overcome.

LOGO is also popular as an approach to informatics, although it is emphasized in other directions in school environments too. When LOGO is compared as a computing language to BASIC, it is superior. It stresses as an early stage the notion of procedure and so allows an approach to at least some components of modern structured programming. But LOGO is an old language and so does not meet many of the standards of the newer structured languages. Furthermore, the teaching of LOGO in practice today is perhaps 99 per cent relegated to Turtle geometry.

More recently, newer superior languages have appeared. But the emphasis in informatics courses in schools is still often on the grammatical aspects of the language, rather than on programming style.

Languages such as Prolog, although rarer in school environments, are present; there are several textbooks using Prolog. Prolog gives a very different view of the world of computers than an algorithmic language such as Pascal, so it enlarges the framework for students considerably.

Two superior informatics courses for schools deserve particular attention. *Martino the Robot* was developed in Italy, by Giorgo Olympo and his collaborators. The initial ideas of this course were based on an earlier product developed at Stanford University, *Karel the Robot*. But while *Karel* was simply a Pascal-based language, with added graphic capabilities, *Martino the Robot* is a full course, with all the types of student material and exercises, and all the types of teacher material, needed for a full course. Current work is extending the course to parallel processing. The second example is the informatics course developed at Moscow State University and the then USSR Academy of Sciences. While few computers were available in the then Soviet Union, this course shows that an imaginative curriculum design can be done in limited environments. It uses a structured language developed for the course and makes use of such computer science features as intelligent editors, thus reducing the emphasis on trivial grammatical details. It has interesting graphical interfaces for students, much more interesting than the limited type of graphics available from LOGO.

One can also raise the question of whether these languages should be taught at all in schools, or perhaps better, to what types of students should they be taught. A related question is that of age, that is, should programming be introduced to very young students, or should it be reserved for later in the student's career? These issues, like many issues in computing, should be decided empirically, but almost no adequate empirical information exists today.

Curriculum

The major use of the computer is the *curriculum* use, that is, as a learning device within courses, at many different levels and in many different ways. Sometimes the distinction is made between learning *about* computers, and learning *with* computers. The first two areas we looked at, literacy and informatics, are learning *about* computers. In this section we consider learning *with* computers (and through informatics).

The use of interactive technology to assist learning is a rapidly changing area, so readers should be cautioned that if they are reading this material well into the 1990s, there may be better examples, and even new strategies. Furthermore, any classification such as the one presented in this discussion is arbitrary; some modules may therefore be difficult to classify.

An important distinction for the future concerns how much material of a given type is available. Much of the early material was in the form of isolated programs, relative small chunks of code representing only a small amount of student time. In contrast to this we have a few extensive developments, much larger collections of programs and related learning material in other media.

A small amount of material cannot be expected to make major improvements in education, no matter how excellent that material is. It can at best be a small perturbation on an existing course, not involving any fundamental changes in the course content, structure, or learning modes. Hence we can expect development of large components of courses to be increasingly important in the future.

The following classification scheme is used in reviewing applications within courses: drill and practice, tutorial interaction, simulations, tools, programming for problem-solving, computer-based laboratories and hypertext.

DRILL AND PRACTICE

Perhaps the oldest use of computers within the teaching of subject areas that are not directly associated with the computer is the drill and practice material. There are many early examples of this. The programs that established this domain were the materials developed at Stanford University by Patrick Suppes and Robert Atkinson, beginning about twenty-five years ago. These materials were fundamentally very simple, based on a set of problem generators, each generator producing a set of problems of a given class. Thus the class of problems generated might be the addition of two 2-digit numbers. Students are presented with a problem of this type generated randomly and then allowed to enter an answer. The answers are either right or wrong, and no additional help or assistance is given. Students stay with a type of problem until it is mastered. Teachers are typically informed of students experiencing difficulties. Material is sequenced through a series of 'strands', covering various aspects of the subject area (such as arithmetic in this example).

Since these materials have probably been used by more students than any other technology-based learning modules, the experimental information relating to them is better than almost anything else with computers. Not only have the materials been marketed in the United States by Suppes himself, through Computer Curriculum Corporation (now part of Paramount), but a dozen other companies have produced and marketed similar or related materials. Similar material is available almost everywhere. So perhaps millions of students have used programs of this type, in all parts of the world. Some of the best experimental studies anywhere in education, such as the longitudinal study made by Educational Testing Service in Los Angeles, have involved these materials.

The results of the studies are positive. Drill and practice, used in school environments as they occur today, increases student capability, particularly in the case of students who are behind. Most of these studies have been conducted with either arithmetic or reading material.

Nevertheless, drill and practice is often criticized. Much philosophical discussion in the literature of computer-based learning denounces the use of the computer for drill and practice, regarding this as a low level of activity. This is, perhaps, unfair. As long as school and university courses make extensive use of drill and practice, without computer, then the computer is a reasonable alternative. Most campuses all over the world do such teaching, and much of the international testing in science and writing is done at this level. Students can receive far more problems and get far more direct feedback, particularly in large class environments, than they can with other modes of handling drill and practice.

It should be emphasized that the use of drill and practice in conventional courses, with and without computers, is not restricted to the elementary level that Suppes material might suggest. For example, if one examines calculus courses all over the world, the major component of these courses almost everywhere is the large amount of drill and practice in differentiation and integration. This is *the student* viewpoint. The professor often views the course as conceptual and may lecture on that level, but what the student is asked to do, in most situations, both in homework and tests, is to differentiate and integrate.

The drill and practice can be given at a variety of pedagogical levels. As indicated, the original Suppes material – and much of what exists today – offers little feedback to the student except correct and incorrect. But it can be very much improved by paying more attention to just what the student is doing. Thus it is often possible to recognize a particular student problem, a 'but', and give immediate assistance with that problem. This feedback is almost impossible in conventional classes, so drill and practice can begin to turn towards the tutorial material discussed in the next section and towards combined testing and learning.

This is not to say that we should be emphasizing drill and practice in learning. Whether drill and practice should be used as extensively as it is, with or without computers, is a different question. Much of the use of drill and practice is related to memory, either of facts or processes, and there is far too much stress on memory in our courses as they exist today. Serious consideration should be given to other types of computer materials as well.

The process of putting less emphasis on memory should receive far more attention than it does at present. This is *not* a technology question.

This interaction, between the nature of the curriculum itself and the type of technology-based learning materials present, is a very important one underlying all the uses of computers and courses. Computers used in learning environments may be introduced strictly within the framework of existing courses, or they may imply major differences in courses, in content, in learning strategies, in the role of the teacher and in course organization.

Drill and practice in its pure form is not involved with the initial learning of the material. The typical situation is to use it after the material has been introduced, perhaps with some other learning mode, simply to be assured that the students can perform the necessary operations. This is to be contrasted with the material to be discussed next, tutorial modules.

TUTORIAL INTERACTION

The image brought to mind by the term tutorial before the computer existed, is that of one person working with a very small group of individuals, perhaps just one as is the case of Oxford and Cambridge, where typically a tutor worked with a single individual at a time. Thus, Maxwell studied with Hopkins at Cambridge, as did almost every other prominent physicist of the nineteenth century in England.

The tutorial mode is to be contrasted, as a learning activity, with the lecture mode. In the lecture mode the teacher talks for long periods of time, with only a slight amount of participation on the part of the students, if any at all. The tutorial mode is very different in that the student plays a much more active role. A tutoring environment, for instance, is what can happen with a very good teacher if there are only two or three students in the teacher's office. Under these circumstances, most teachers will not lecture, as lecture does not seem to be the most appropriate mode. The session might proceed as an interactive conversation, with both the teacher and the students talking frequently.

One example of the tutorial mode is the Socratic dialogue, as seen in Plato's descriptions of how Socrates taught. The tutor, Socrates, primarily *asked questions*. The aim of the Socratic tutor is not to convey information, as many lecturers seem to attempt, but to get the students themselves to come up with the information and the critical ideas, through a careful continuing set of questions. The hope is that students can *create* the knowledge, through their own efforts.

Other tutorial approaches are possible. One mode frequently used with graduate students in universities is for the graduate student working with a teacher assistant to reply to questions framed by a student. Or, better, the graduate student can react to student questions with other questions, leading the students themselves to answer the questions they have raised in the Socratic tradition. Laboratory experience can also be tutorial.

The model for tutorial interaction for computer units might be a conversation between two human beings, where one or both are attempting to learn something. The characteristics of such a conversation need to be noted. First each of the people tends to speak *briefly*; if there are long speeches, the interaction ceases to be conversational in nature. Even more critical, it is important that each person pay attention to what the other is saying, and that each new utterance should be based not only on what has just been said previously, but on the entire conversation, or perhaps even details of earlier conversations. We must *listen carefully* to what the other person says. Such a conversation is completely impossible without a common language. One can hardly communicate fully with another person simply by *pointing*, a fact that seems to escape some recent developers of interactive technology-based learning materials.

The discussion so far does not depend on whether the computer exists or not. At first glance, it might seem that tutorial activities of the type just described on the computer are not possible. The computer cannot now compete with a very good teacher, and perhaps this will never be possible.*

But we have extremely few very good teachers in the world! The question is not whether the computer can be as effective a tutor as Socrates, but whether the level of learning as it occurs in most schools in most parts of the world can be raised with computer tutors. This has already been fully demonstrated to be the case, on the basis of available material. This type of computer material is sometimes called a *dialogue.*

A tutorial situation is not necessarily a one-to-one situation. Socrates seldom worked with one student, but usually had several students following him around Athens. Likewise in computer tutorial situations having several students work together is often superior to having a single student. The advantages of co-operative learning in groups, peer learning, becomes a major factor when several students at a display are interacting with a tutorial dialogue. That is, students assist each other, in a very effective and highly individualized fashion. As examples of tutorial materials, two pro-

---

* *Remember the definition of an 'Intelligent System': a system will be defined as intelligent if the answers given to some questions cannot be attributed to a human expert or to the system.*

grams from the Scientific Reasoning Series are described. The purpose of the full series, ten programs, is to assist students to think and reason like scientists, to solve problems as a scientist might.

Heat is a tutorial program concerned with the introduction of new concepts in science. The concept to be invented by the student is heat. It is assumed that the student is already familiar with a thermometer as a way of measuring temperature. The aim of the early 'conversation' in this student-requested dialogue is to get the student to review and reconsider what he or she already knows about thermometers. This information is the basis for the rest of the program.

After the title page, the dialogue begins immediately with a question – how do you measure your own body temperature? Note that no text precedes this question. The program is immediately interactive, unlike a book or lecture. Note too that the interaction is in the student's native language; both the question and the student reply are in English. (Other languages are possible.) A question a few moments later asks the student what procedure is necessary to get a reasonable reading for temperature. The program expects replies such as 'keep it in my mouth for several minutes'. Again, the program is flexible in processing reasonable answers. The tone of the interaction is conversational. As with the next example, this description stresses only a very small part of heat. An interactive program can only be roughly described in print.

The next example, *Families,* is concerned with the development of a scientific theory, as a scientist might do it. Here the theory to be discovered by each student is genetics. The student gathers experimental information directly at the computer, forms tentative hypotheses tests experimental predictions based on these, modifies the hypotheses and gathers new data. All this is interactive, like a conversation. A typical student will require over two hours to succeed. But because of individualized assistance, almost all students will succeed in this non-trivial task. Students learn about the processes of science by being directly involved in them in this interactive way.

SIMULATIONS

We have already presented some examples of simulations. The word simulation presents us with some difficulty. The other titles that we are using in the discussion of curriculum applications of computers are mostly based on pedagogical considerations. The notion of simulation is a technical term from the computer field, referring to a type of computer program. But the term simulation is commonly used in education, and so we use it as the title for this section.

A simulation is a program, or a segment of a program, that models or simulates some aspect of the world, real or imaginary. It is usually a calculation-based program. Within the sciences many of the programs developed for professional research are simulations, so this is a common type of computer program. Hence, it is not surprising that it began to be used in learning environments. Scientific theories are also models. Thus the genetics program described above has an embedded simulation, a very small part of the total program.

One early simulation, done in many locations, involved landing a rocket ship on earth. The user usually had control of the engine. That is, the user could fire the engine whenever desired. The ship was descending, and the problem was to land the ship with a very small velocity, so that the landing was smooth. A further refinement was to land with a minimum expenditure of fuel; in many cases this was partially built into the program, because the user was allowed only a limited amount of fuel. Reports on the fuel, as well as reports on position and velocity, were given to the user. In more elaborate variants this information was visual, or the situation was two-dimensional.

Simulations are also widely used in industrial training environments, particularly where very expensive equipment is available, or in situations where there is danger involved. Thus airline pilots today in all parts of the world are trained on elaborate simulators involving computers and video; the pilot behaves almost as if in an actual plane. Since a plane is complicated, these simulations are expensive; they must include elaborate video and computer graphics, for example, if the prospective pilot is to develop full capabilities in a realistic environment. The situation must look and feel like a real landing if the pilot is to learn to land a Boeing 747.

Simulations developed strictly for learning purposes can be specific and task oriented, such as the airplane simulation just indicated, or they can reflect vague purposes on the part of the designers. Some situations appeal only to the designers; with such simulations it is very difficult to establish a pedagogical role, although academics are often excellent at doing this after the fact.

Simulations, used reasonably, can play an important pedagogical role. Perhaps the most important role that they tend to play is that of developing student's *insight* or *intuition*. In courses it is usually simple to teach the principles of the course, or to get students to work out restricted types of problems. To develop greater capabilities and to extend student intuition is highly desirable but difficult pedagogically. Simulations are often in use in this situation, creating a range of student-controllable experiences. The names controllable world or microworld are frequently used to describe such programs.

A simulation in classical mechanics allows the student to experience Newtonian laws of motion far beyond the experiences obtainable on earth, where gravity and friction are almost always the dominant forces. Students in such environments as that developed at the University of California (Irvine) can 'play' with mechanical worlds, changing initial conditions, force laws and important variables such as masses. Simulations can let students plot anything they want, in addition to seeing actual motion. So, for example, the abstract spaces of physics, such as phase-space, can become real to the student, since the students can observe many different phenomena in phase-space.

The effectiveness of simulations in learning situations varies greatly. Often simulations are unfortunately of much more interest to the developer than to typical users. There are several important problems. First, how does the student learn to use the simulation? This is a more critical issue than may appear at first glance, because the simulations are often difficult to use. The typical way of presenting large amounts of textual information, either on paper or on the screen, will often not work with contemporary students, put off by large volumes of non-interactive text. A better strategy is to use interactive techniques, allowing the student to learn the simulation by using it, with the computer watching to see that success is being obtained and offering help if necessary. Second, is the student *learning* anything from the simulation? It is common knowledge that one can observe phenomena, even simulated phenomena, and not derive any of the benefits intended by the developers of the material. An effective learning simulation should be constantly checking to determine what the student knows. Third, what is to be done about the student who is not progressing? Students may not realize whether they are learning anything or not in a simulation environment. The question of what is to be learned, since building insight is difficult to describe, is not likely to be conveyed directly to the student. Explicit help may be necessary. Finally, a student may enjoy a simulation, have fun using it, may use it for hours on end and may yet find it has no cognitive effect. This is all too common!

These problems can be alleviated, particularly if the simulation is combined with tutorial material. Such material can try to find out just what the student does know or understand, at a given point, and can prejudice future actions to assist with the problems the student is having. If there is an excellent teacher present, that teacher may play this role too. But, alas, in many situations there is not an excellent teacher present, and even if there is, the teacher is unlikely to have the time to work in an individual fashion with each student using the simulation. The use of the computer in ways that increase teachers' difficulties in class, giving them more to do without removing previous tasks, is not likely to be viable worldwide, although it may work well with a few excellent teachers.

TOOLS

Simulations tend to overlap into the category to be discussed now, tools. That is, certain types of programs are called either simulations or tools. The mechanics simulation mentioned is referred to as a tool by some developers and users.

Tools, however, have a broader conception, going beyond simulations to include many other types of programs. The general notion of a tool is clear – it does not have a single function but rather does a variety of different things. However, there may be a single dominant function. Tools may be though of as *enhancers* of one type or another. Early tools enhanced physical power, while tools using the computer enhance intellectual or memory powers. In this sense we might think of every use of the computer as tool-like, but this would be broadening the concept beyond its usefulness.

Undoubtedly the most widely known computer tools and the best-selling computer programs are tools for business, rather than learning environments. The three most common tools in this category are word processors, spreadsheets and databased facilities. Vendors of *Lotus 1-2-3*, *Word Perfect* and *D-Base III* have sold millions of copies. Those tools account for more computer use than any other single way the computer is used, in terms of people time. In the personal computer market, such business tools are almost dominant.

In what sense is a word processor a tool? A word processor is designed to help one aspect of the process of writing, be it for informal purposes, short documents or formal purposes. A document might include within it various types of visual information, too, in which case the boundary line between word processors and desk-top publishing becomes indistinct. Facilities may differ from one word processor to another, but full-scale word processors will almost certainly have spelling checkers, thesauruses, facilities for multi-column text and for footnotes, multiple choices of font styles, and many other capabilities. As this market is competitive, with three or four products near the top and many others striving to reach higher positions, new capabilities are added frequently; we often see new versions of the word processings tools available.

The reader will note that little has been said about *education* in the last few paragraphs. Most prominent examples of tools are from the business world. But these tools have had a powerful effect on education. With some people this effect extends to the belief that only tools are useful. We do not accept this point of view, but we do believe that they can be useful in some learning situations, along with all the other types of uses of technology discussed.

Most of tool use in education involves business tools. It could be said that education is 'picking up the crumbs of the business table'. These programs were not developed for education and are not necessarily the best for educational purposes. Word processors were initially developed for use primarily by secretaries in business offices. They can be very powerful in assisting students in the process of writing, an important component of many types of courses, while not necessarily being the best possible tools for the purpose.

If someone decided to design a series of writing tools particularly appropriate to science students aged 12, the tools might differ significantly from word processors already available. This has not happened, however. Either education uses the word processors that are available from business, or, worse, develops inferior copies of these. Part of this reflects the fact that schools may not use the same computers as those commonly used in the business world, and so the more elegant business software may be unavailable to them. This is particularly a problem in the United States and in the United Kingdom, where the Apple II and the BBC computers are widely present in schools but not in the business world.

The situation with regard to tools in the writing process is beginning to improve. We now have packages that contain both drafting and editing aids (such as hyphenation and spelling checkers), as well as the writing aids themselves. But this area still needs further attention, particularly at the level of curriculum. We have to the best of our knowledge, no full scale courses in writing based on interactive technology. Often *only* an elementary word-processor is available to students.

A tool useful in business may not be useful in education. Although spreadsheets have been used in educational environments, these uses have been minor. This is not to say that they may not be used more extensively. We can see promise in using spreadsheets in understanding modeling. But each tool needs to be considered in each pedagogical situation.

Tools for learning present us with some of the same problems already mentioned with regard to simulations. The first problem, and often a major problem in learning environments, is *how* does the student learn the tool? If the student is in a course in writing, learning to use a complex word processor may be a non-trivial task. Furthermore, the teacher may not be too familiar with the tool. Lecturing about word processing takes valuable time away from writing and offers a passive learning mode. As the number of tools in education increases, this is almost certainly to be more and more the case, because these tools will typically have been developed after teachers completed their initial learning cycles. It is not desirable to take large amounts of class time away from learning the subject area, learning to write, and devoting it to the mechanisms of how word processors work.

We need tools that are *self-instructional,* tools that help the student, starting where the student is and only slowly introducing the capabilities of the tool as the needs of the student increase. We do *not* have in mind the usual manuals, on or off the screen, obtained from computers at a particular point by requesting help. Having pages of text to read on the screen, or in a book, perhaps not even appropriate to what the student needs, is *not* the best way to learn. Rather, we need the same tactics as in good tutorial material: the problem of helping people to learn how to use a tool is the same as the learning problem approached in tutorials generally.

These self-instructional tools need to be sensitive to the level of the student, perhaps by keeping records internally as to what students have and have not done, with regard to the capabilities of the tool, and with regard to the student's cognitive structure. But few examples of such built-in learning sequences have so far been constructed. The importance goes far beyond education, since the problem of learning how to use tools exists not only in the classroom, but also in all other places in which the tool is used.

PROGRAMMING FOR PROBLEM-SOLVING

We previously discussed the notion of teaching programming, either in the situation of literacy or in the study of informatics. But programming can also occur within subjects and classes, particularly science and mathematics classes, as part of the instructional material of those classes. Even language classes, or humanities classes, might require programming, using *Prolog* or other languages.

Under these circumstances programming has a different purpose. It is no longer teaching about the computer and how it can be instructed that is the primary focus. Rather, programming is used to enable students to learn in the subject field, such as physics or chemistry.

One typical use in this regard is to allow the students to tackle more difficult problems than those possible without the use of programming. Thus, the structure of a physics course can bypass some of the mathematical limitations of the student. The student may not know how to handle differential equations in a science or mathematics class, because that is to come at a later stage of education. But numerical solutions of differential equations on the computer are understandable by students at an early stage and so problems demanding the solutions of differential equations can be presented much sooner in the student's career.

This means that the 'delaying action' often necessary in science courses to allow the student's mathematical background to evolve is no longer necessary. As a result, powerful ideas can be introduced earlier in the student's career and there is less marking time while the student's mathematical background is built up. Many applications of this kind could be described as problem-solving within the subject area. The problems can be more important than those usually dealt with.

It is reasonable that the use of programming is likely to be mainly restricted to courses of a more mathematics-based nature, such as mathematics and science. There are, however, applications in other areas as well, although often these are further away from the student's needs and may best be handled by tools. The possibility of building databases using *Prolog* or similar facilities is intriguing.

The problem mentioned with simulations and tools also occurs in this situation. How does the student learn to use the programming language? But here the problem is more complicated, because a programming language is more complicated than a simulation or a tool. One solution could be to require students to learn programming before the course begins, perhaps by taking an informatics course of the type already described earlier or perhaps learning programme in a course within a particular subject area.

There is still considerable disagreement about where programming should be taught within curricula both in secondary schools and in universities. Some believe that, in the interests of conserving resources and of building a sounder attitude toward programming, the teaching of programming should be left to specialists with background in informatics; others argue that the needs of programming are different in different fields, and so programming should be taught within the subject matter discipline.

It should be emphasized that learning to program is more than simply acquiring the grammar of the language; issues of styles are much more important in programming today than are issues of grammar. Furthermore, the use of such tools as intelligent editors and CASE can reduce the student's dependence on grammatical details and enable them to use programming more quickly for its intended problem-solving purposes. These tools, however, are little used in subject-matter areas.

Programming is not the only thing that must be learned. Programs must be entered into the machine, and this typically assumes that an editor will be needed too. Furthermore, there may be debugging tools also. All these present similar problems. Integrated programming environments, such as *Turbo Pascal* or *Quick Pascal,* can ease the problem, but these multiple learning tasks are still present. It is possible that some of the tools can have their own built-in instructional material in the sense described in the discussion of self-instructional tools, but this is almost never the practice at present. However, only minimal capabilities are needed with such tools as editors, at least at the beginning stages, so the task is not as difficult as might appear at first glance; the student does not need to learn everything about the editors.

This use of programming languages within courses to assist problem-solving is perhaps the earliest educational application of computers, dating back to the 1950s, within physics courses. But, due to the lack of a coherent history in this area, it is constantly getting rediscovered, usually with a new programming language. New groups tend to ignore the history of computers in education and are often unaware of similar previous work.

COMPUTER-BASED LABORATORIES

A new type of computer use in learning environments has arisen recently, particularly associated with the learning of science. This usage attaches equipment directly to the computer and uses the computer to record the results of measurements. Usually these measurements will be presented graphically, a graph showing one variable versus function of time.

The equipment attached to the computers, unlike actual scientific equipment, is likely to be very simple. The attachments are often called probes. Thus a typical probe is a temperature probe, a device that reads temperature continuously and sends the information to the computer electronically on a moment by moment basis. A program determines the sampling interval, so the graph with such a probe would be a plot of temperature versus time. The user may have choice as to time scale, so this could be looking at a microscopic situation, or a situation where the probe is sampled only once every minute.

In addition to being able to see the data, often graphically, the student may be able to see other information derived from the observed data. Thus, a common probe is a sonar probe, showing the distance of an object from the probe. The object can be moving back and forth, and so a graph of distance versus time is a standard display. It is easy to compute graphs of velocity versus time and acceleration versus time, and display these to the student as part of the same facility. Problems can be assigned, based on this equipment.

The student could be asked to move so that certain conditions are satisfied (constant velocity, for example). A chemistry example is the investigation of the rate of reaction of an acid and carbonate by placing the chemicals in a vessel on a balance that is interfaced to a computer. The weight of the mixture decreases as carbon dioxide is liberated and the resultant weight of the reactants is measured by the balance and logged by the computer. A graph of weight against time is displayed and, by examining the gradient of this graph, the rate of reaction can be determined at different points during the chemical reaction. The automatic logging of data allows the small changes in weight to be continuously monitored and the graphical display of results permits identification of the important principles underlying this experiment without the students being distracted by plotting graphs.

Technical education courses in some schools now contain units on interfacing and control. In one, students in groups design a robot, construct it, interface the device to the computer and devise programs for controlling it.

The repeated problem of how the teachers and the students learn to use this equipment, and how it fits into the more general pedagogical situation becomes important again. The aim presumably is not just to get the student to make measurements, but to use these as some way of understanding something about the empirical nature of science. This is a broader task than simply getting pretty graphs on the screen, both more important and more difficult. Curriculum material based on interactive approaches using tutorials is needed if this approach is to be useful with all students.

HYPERTEXT

Since 1991, it has become important to give a place to the emergence of *Hypertext* in education.

Hypercard (Apple) has been used for a few years by very young pupils (8 years old) but some other *Hypersoft* is now offered to teachers.

A recent congress 'Hypertexts et Apprentissages' (Paris, October 1991) focused on the new way offered by this type of approach to structure a complex situation and provide facilities of presentation. The new tools, which are not expensive and use both graphics and colour with access to CD-ROM, may give a new style of tutorial design.

COMMENTS

We have discussed many different ways in which the computer can be used within the learning of subjects other than informatics. This list is not exhaustive, nor is the classification a perfect one. Thus it may be difficult to classify a particular program and it may seem to have aspects of several of these types.

Good material often involves a *combination* of types, as we have already mentioned several times. The aim is not to use the computer in one way or another, but rather to improve learning environments. Hence decisions need to be made on a pedagogical basis, rather than on some philosophical argument about which is 'best'.

A common theme, it will be noted, is the question of how the material fits into the classroom context or into the more general learning environment in which the student is immersed if there is no classroom. Curriculum material must have a context, an environment in which it works. Thus an isolated program, no matter how wonderful, must be fitted into the overall learning experience in some reasonable fashion if it is to be pedagogically valuable.

A second common feature, present in many of the issues discussed, is the issue of how the teacher and the student learn to cope with the software involved. This raises not only issues of teacher training but also of how the students can most easily, and with least expenditure of time, learn to use the computer programs.

It seems likely that the tutorial mode for computer uses in education will increase, and perhaps, combined with some of the other modes to be suggested, even become the dominant mode. The advantages of being able to learn in a highly interactive and highly individualized fashion, to be further discussed later, are perhaps best seen in the use of tutorial materials. The problem with using tutorial materials widely in education without computers is simply that we do not have enough excellent teachers to, or enough funds, to allow all education to proceed in this way. The computer offers us a major opportunity to make education more interactive and more individualized for almost all students in the world. But little good tutorial material now exists. We must develop large quantities of tutorial programs before we can fully realize the benefits of this mode.

TESTING

Testing via computers has distinct advantages. First, the computer can be responsible for both the correcting, and the recording activity. The records can be as simple (perhaps an overall score, or just a pass/fail) or as complex (information about each problem) as the designer or the teacher desires. This information can be selectively available to the student, to the teachers, to the administrator and to the parents; privacy can nevertheless be maintained where essential or desirable.

Another aspect of computer-based testing is that the material can be programmed to offer various forms of direct pedagogical aid to the student, either while the student is taking the test or immediately after. Thus the notion of the word 'test' expands in this environment considerably over its pre-computer use. At each question the machine can be instructed to tell the result of that question or, and this applies in all the other situations described here, it can be instructed not to tell students the result of their responses to the question. The computer can be directed to give detailed assistance to students after each question, specifically assisting with precisely the problem that the student had in discovering the answer, or it can reserve such help until several questions have been asked, or perhaps until the whole test has been completed, in order to build up a more detailed view of just what is happening. It can repeat a question the student has missed, the same question or another of a similar type, later in the program.

In these situations, the student does not answer an item on a test and then wait for days or weeks to find out whether all the thought processes involved were correct or not, as with conventional testing. Rather we have the advantage of immediate feedback, immediate aid to the student. The computer can therefore be used to give a *different* type of test than is currently available without computers.

These last considerations suggest that a technology-based test can play a very different role than that played by a test given in a non-computer environment. Typically, testing in courses as they exist today is intended for *assessment*, usually for assigning a grade. With technology, the role of the test can be entirely different. The test can be a critical part of the learning material of the course, very focused learning material since the student receives assistance only if it is directly applicable to whatever problem the student is having. So the test is for diagnosis and help, not necessarily grading.

The results of an on-line test can be used to determine what learning sequences the students should see next, immediately after the test or after some delay. Tests can thus structure the learning sequence individually for each individual.

Although it is common for teachers to say that taking a test is a learning experience, most students do not view it this way. In the computer environment it can be made true, in the sense that it is factually true and that all students will agree.

Computer testing can avoid some of the poor testing forms characteristic of much older testing, particularly when it must be done with large groups of students, either within one school, or in a wider geographical area. One form of testing that has become common, unfortunately, is the use of multiple choice. The student is presented with a collection of (usually) four or five possible correct answers and asked to choose one correct response. This is an inferior form of testing, for many reasons. First, multiple-choice questions promote guessing. Second, multiple-choice questions promote a way of taking tests that puts more emphasis on the test-taking process (eliminate the likely wrong answers, etc.) than it does on the learning material itself. The vast literature for students on how to take tests strongly supports this viewpoint. Much of this literature could be described as telling students how they can do well on multiple-choice tests without understanding the subject matter! Third, this mode of testing does not correspond to actions in the real world and so students are not prepared for actual situations. In most situations, there are far more than the four or five possibilities that are presented as multiple-choice answers. Fourth, multiple-choice tests frequently reward an incorrect answer. The typical strategy for building such tests is to put in likely incorrect items as distractors. So a person who works a problem incorrectly, but in a way that is known to be commonly incorrect, will often find his or her answer in the choices. The incorrect strategy used is reinforced from the student point of view. In some multiple-choice situations the student may know that the answer was wrong, usually after some period of time, but may have completely forgotten what the reasoning process was that lead them to the wrong answer. But, particularly in regional or national testing, the student never receives information about the results of a particular question, so the immediate incorrect reinforcement is never counteracted, even in principle.

We can ask why such a weak mechanism as multiple choice has become common in computer-based testing. We suspect that this is due to two reasons. First, testing of this kind had been done before, without computers, and new developers are often imitators of older strategies. They do not reconsider the possibilities. Second, it is somewhat easier to program such material, in that templates can easily be constructed to handle multiple choice. While the difference between programming multiple choice and programming free response is not tremendous, it does represent some difference; the use of multiple choice probably reflects to some degree laziness or lack of resources or knowledge on the part of the developer.

One possibility present in computer-based testing – but not in pre-computer testing – is that the test may vary from user to user. The principle mechanism for doing this is that results of earlier questions affect later questions. Thus, a student doing well in earlier parts of a test may be shifted toward more difficult questions, or given a much shorter form of the test. But a student who is having considerable problems may move in the opposite direction.

This strategy of adapting the test to the individual user, tailoring the test, can be done in a variety of ways.

The most obvious way to create tests that adapt to the student is an informal method and can be done directly by the developers themselves. In the development of the test, information can be gathered on student performance on each question. Then decisions can be made during the design process based on that evidence as what to do next with each student. These decisions can occur at many points along the way, making the resulting test different for each student.

A second strategy is to work with a mapping of the conceptual structure of the area. This may be what is implicitly done by the developers in the first category, but now this mapping becomes explicit. The test may start with different questions that cover a variety of concepts known to the developers. If these present troubles, then the ideas tested can be broken down into smaller pieces until the precise difficulty that the student is having can be located. Work in Italy by Giorgio Olympo is a good example of this strategy. This approach may be particularly useful in mathematics and science because of the logical structure of these areas.

The final strategy to be mentioned is tailored testing. Here the test is usually one that is trying to establish level, for example a student's reading level. Work of this kind was done extensively within Educational Testing Service, based on mathematical approaches developed by Frederick Lord. In each case considerable data are available to the computer for each question. The choice of the next question to be presented to the student is made on the basis of an algorithm that depends on how the student has performed on each of the previous questions and on the data stored for each question. The basic idea is to use the information about student performance and the information about the questions to pick a new question that yields *maximum new information* about the student's level. So far, fewer questions should be needed. Unfortunately most of the work in this direction so far has been based on multiple-choice questions.

Thus we can argue that computer tests can be much richer than conventional tests. The computer opens up a whole new range of testing possibilities. But, so far, existing material does not make extensive use of these possibilities.

We can think of going much further than we have so far. For example, it is possible to construct an *entire course based on tests*. This differs very much from the usual courses, where testing is an infrequent activity interspersed with long didactic sections of the course. With the approach suggested the test, or quiz, becomes the main focus of the course. Tests are given frequently.

The beginning introductory level physics course developed at the University of California, Irvine, in the late 1970s was of this type. Students starting a new unit typically began with tests on that unit. These tests never used multiple choice. The tests had within them *all* the learning material of the course, but as already suggested, this material was not presented to a student until a need for that material was demonstrated by student performance on the test up to that point.

Management

The next application of the computer in learning that will receive consideration is that using the computer as *a tool for management* of learning. Management can mean a variety of things in this context. It can refer to school management, where the emphasis may be on preparing the kinds of information about student attendance and other aspects of learning that are required by the governments, or by administrators; it may refer to management in the sense of curriculum management – providing the teacher with information about the progress and problems of students, and storing grades or progress reports on the student; and it may be intended directly to aid students in learning, by offering students a stream of advice about where they are in the learning process, and what resources might be appropriate to the problems that they are facing.

SCHOOL MANAGEMENT

One of the oldest uses of computers in education is in school management. For several reasons, educational institutions need information about the school. One type of information needed is attendance – data on who is in school at a particular time. In some places, such as some of the states in the

United States, the average daily attendance affects school revenue. Such attendance is also necessary because of the custodial role of the school, taking care of the student when the student is not at home. It may also be necessary in order to determine how many lunches the school restaurant needs to prepare (in France for instance). The school may need to know where the students are at all times and may need to check with home if the student is not present. Or there may be dire consequences if the student is not in class. In all these situations requiring student tracking, keeping attendance, the computer can, in a routine way, be of considerable help. The computer involved might be a simple batch computer in the administrative offices, or in a wider domain it might be a timesharing computer with terminals in each class; it might be individual personal computers exchanging information via diskettes, or it might be networked personal computers, with on-line electronic card-readers (in entrances, libraries, and so on). In addition to attendance records, other information might be useful for school administrators, such as the ability to spot students in academic or social difficulty.

Another aspect of school management helped by the computer is class scheduling, particularly in comprehensive secondary schools. A wide variety of classes must be planned, and one hopes that as many students as possible will be able to attend these classes, so finding a schedule that will satisfy both the student demands and the teacher preferences as to when to teach particular courses, is a sizable activity. Computers have been very useful for many years in such situations, even if they never solved the question of large time-table overloading the curriculum when the classrooms are not adequate for the students.

CURRICULUM MANAGEMENT

As we have commented, the curriculum in schools is often determined by state and federal guidelines, and, more particularly, by the curriculum materials available. These could include textbooks, teacher guides, video, computer programs, and other similar information of assistance to the students in learning the subject area. The record-keeping problem for such material is partially logistic – who has what material at a given time? But the computer facilities for accounting for such material can go further than this. Using the database of curriculum material, a teacher should be able to find what units would be particularly valuable for a student needing special attention.

The ability to inform teachers and administrators about a wide range of curriculum material can make an important difference to the way schools are structured. Often classes are very limited by the amount of curriculum material available. As long as the teacher is the primary deliverer of information, as in most schools at present, this is not a problem. But as the teacher moves more to the role of facilitator, a person aiding the learning of each student, then the ability to access the best curriculum material for this situation becomes a more and more important task. Hence the computer and electronic telecommunications become very important. For example, a particular help is provided to students and teachers through the French network MINITEL giving access to databases on educational software with guidelines, advice and so on.

STUDENT INFORMATION

Management systems can supply information directly to the students. Thus a student can be allowed to check the accuracy of the school's records concerning himself or herself.

Another important possibility is direct feedback to the student on progress in a course. An example is seen in the Camelot system for teaching composition, developed at Miami-Dade Community College. In this system, each student receives a weekly individualized letter reporting on his or her progress and suggesting further study. These letters, based on the teachers' assessment of the writing of the student, done in a structured fashion, all come from a central computer.

It is also possible (and compulsory for some French examinations or registrations) to use a network and electronic mail just to have access to the timetable, results of examinations, corrections of tests and so on.

Special education

Students with a physical impairment may require alternative means of gaining access to the computer that will allow them to take part in the normal work of the class or to communicate when they come back home. Visually-impaired learners may require spoken feedback from the computer. A child with severe attentional problems may require carefully tailored software to capture interest. The severely communication-impaired child may require a personal communication aid.

For normal classwork, the 'standard' classroom computer has proved adequate. When individual needs are considered, however, the picture is different. By their very nature individual needs require individual treatment and it is rarely the case that the same provision can satisfy the needs of more than a handful of special users.

INFORMATION TECHNOLOGY FOR THE DEAF AND THE BLIND

Deaf people do not have one disability but two, the physical disability of deafness and, by far the more serious, the communications disability.

By the nature of their disability the deaf are barred from certain areas of employment and social communication because of the reliance on the telephone. With the increasing use of information technology in the mass media deaf people should be experiencing newly-found freedom. The widespread use of electronic mail for the deaf and, at the same time, voice synthesizers for the blind (with a Braille keyboard) seem to extend the communication between disabled students inside their home life.

Interactive video has meant the combination of two powerful educational technologies – computers and video. With computer control the interactive video delivery system can open up a significant range of possibilities in all areas of education. One important feature of interactive video is its ability to create controllable worlds or 'microworlds', a world within the computer with which a student is able to interact. Deaf children must be exposed to a series of microworlds enabling them to interact directly, from which they can extract meaning.

Deaf people need to refer to a dictionary far more frequently than do those who are not deaf. This can be demotivating in their 'enjoyment' of reading! However, interactive video may provide a powerful, dynamic, interactive video dictionary to make reading a joy.

Deaf-blindness is a deceptive term. It is not simply a problem of deafness plus blindness, nor is it solely one of communication or perception. The deaf-blind are multi-sensory deprived; they are unable to use their distance senses of vision and hearing to receive non-distorted information.

The term deaf-blind does not automatically imply the absence of all vision and hearing, although this can sometimes be the case. More often, a student will have some residual use of one or both of these senses and it is in the stimulation of these that the computer may be seen to be of most benefit.

Programs may offer us the possibility of teaching a variety of skills, concepts and tasks. The computer can often be paired with other teaching devices and aids or used to reinforce work done in other areas.

For the less able students, perhaps those with poor vision use or concentration problems, the computer can first be used to increase their awareness and attention skills. Later the student can progress to programs specifically designed to help vision training.

INFORMATION TECHNOLOGY FOR REHABILITATION AND THERAPY

Research has been carried out into applications of computers in the rehabilitation of and therapy for the disabled. Work on communication aids for the deaf has concentrated on speech transcription systems that, perhaps with the help of a shorthand machine operator, can transcribe speech into a written form and display it on a computer screen for deaf people to read.

A speech-impaired person with intact language can use either a computer screen or a speech synthesizer to communicate. However, a major problem is the slowness with which such a person can operate a keyboard. The most severely disabled have limited muscular control. For example, some are only able to suck and blow down a tube to select letters of the alphabet; not only is this an excruciatingly slow means of communication but it can also mean that such people may have great difficulty in conducting a conversation.

Several ways are being examined for improving the speed at which a disabled person can communicate. One system is based on a high speed keyboard to control a speech synthesizer. For the physically disabled ways are being investigated to allow a computer to be programmed to predict the words or sentences a disabled person may intend to say.

Advances in medicine, increased awareness and legislation requiring equal opportunities for all students have presented exciting challenges to educators. Consequently, school systems have an opportunity to provide access to educational services for an increasing variety of children with special needs.

Pilot projects are underway designed to link housebound students with a school in their community. The students are considered as members of specific classes within their schools. The telecommunications component of the project allows scheduled interaction with teachers and classmates, thus providing educational and social enrichment.

Media

Various technologies can be involved in interactive learning today. The root technology is the computer, which can have auxiliary devices adding sound, still pictures, moving pictures, measurement devices, telecommunication facilities, robotics, etc.

The choice of particular technologies should be a pedagogical decision. The computer is the basic medium for information learning, but the decision as to whether video disks, compact disks or other media are required for a particular application should depend on the learning situation and on the decisions of the design group. Decisions that say in advance that the program must run in interactive video, for example, are not the best decisions to make. The pedagogical role of the application should determine the medium.

Computers

The digital computer is the *major new technology* of the twentieth century, and perhaps even of the twenty-first. It is a new technology that has developed very rapidly, with important consequences for many aspects of our society. This development is still continuing and the applications of the computer are continuing to grow. Education is no exception.

The following is not an attempt at a complete discussion of the nature of the computer, simply an outline of the major functions of the computer. First, the computer is capable of very rapid, and very accurate, mathematical and logical decisions. Typical time for execution of instructions in contemporary computers is one to four million – and more – instructions per second. The individual instructions are simplistic (add two numbers, compare two numbers, look for this collection of letters within that collection of letters), but the fact that instructions can be executed so rapidly and that the program can depend on the result of previous action, gives the computer its major potentials for education. Later the critical issues of interaction and individualization will be discussed. These are possible only because of the ability of the computer to make decisions rapidly and to choose different paths of the program based on student performance up to that time.

The second major characteristic of the computer is memory, the ability to store data internally. Stored data can be accessed rapidly, even if stored in other computers in other parts of the world. Memory, as with other components of the computer, has continued to grow cheaper and smaller. Now it is possible to obtain major textual works available on the computer. One current computer comes with the complete works of Shakespeare! The complete French *Grand Robert* dictionary is available in a computer-readable form; access is provided phonetically; synonyms and quotations by the main authors are found in word processing software, etc. Alternately the computer can store a very sizable amount of information concerning interaction with the student, the basis for the interactive learning decisions.

Several types of memory are available on computer. First there is the fast memory, very rapidly accessible. Even a personal computer today is likely to have 4 million bytes (characters) of fast memory, in the developed countries. But slower memory attached to the computer and some of the devices to be described in a moment allow much greater storage with longer access time. Almost all modern computers have several types of memory.

One often needs to be able to carry away from the computer the programs and results, and this requires that some memory should be portable. Thus a student working on a word processor in school may want to take an electronically readable copy of the composition for use on his or her home computer; certain types of storage such as diskettes makes this practical (when the computer is not portable itself).

Of particular importance for school and university use of computers for education has been the development of the personal computer, or micro-computer, a small compact machine that can sit on top of a desk and allow individual users to access it. The cost of personal computers has not declined as much as one might think, given the data on the cost for computers suggested above. Vendors of machines offer, for education and other uses, increasingly sophisticated machines, with faster processors and with more memory. Hence, the price of the computer has been stable, but the capa-bilities have increased, surprising users and specialists year after year.

The development of operating systems on personal computers has also been spectacular.

Started by Apple on the Macintosh, followed with WINDOWS on DOS, it has become easier to manipulate modern software with less training.

Mouse, scrolling 'menus', windows presentation (and, for the profes-sionals, quick touch functions) give a real fluent interactivity which, too often, consigns computers or operating systems to the museum, after two or three years.

Networking

Early educational experiments generally involved large computers. Many users at individual terminals shared the computer. Since only one computer was involved, the users could share information and communicate with each other.

Initially with personal computers such sharing and communicating was not possible, but a new technology, networking, has grown allowing even greater possibilities than those available with the large computers. Net-working is a mechanism for connecting computers, either a group of local computers in the same building or computers vast distances apart. As with many other uses of the computer, much of this development was not looking towards education; networking grew up for scientific and business uses of computers. Nevertheless, networks have great promise for education. Several significant networking projects link schools in many countries. These projects have taken many forms including direct linking school to school, block linking or bulletin board format.

More and more, the link between computers is done by telecom networks, independent distance, according to the cost/quantity ratio, the speed of transmission and the status of the users. Recent personal computers may include a modem which can be directly connected with the local telecommunication network, enabling delivery access throughout the world.

ELECTRONIC MAIL

One use of networks is electronic mail, the exchange of messages through the computer. Students can communicate electronically with students nearby, or great distances away. Many pedagogical possibilities present themselves. Students can focus on a common problem, combining their capabilities and resources through electronic mail.

One recent project involved schools in the United States and fifty schools in Europe. An educational framework was prepared to help selected schools start interactive dialogue and to assess whether such exercises are meaningful and benefit educational objectives. It was decided not to 'direct' subjects for discussion or to dictate style, although 'starter' questions were suggested. Schools were free to explore the technology and experiment with all types of discussion over areas of interest of their choice. Some schools became involved in a transatlantic newspaper.

The use of electronic mail for cross-cultural stimulation is perhaps an obvious use of electronic communication. Students can explore their societies, contrasting their own with others. This is very often the starting point for real work towards enlarging mutual understanding.

A less ambitious use is to permit students and parents to communicate during periods when students are far away or between students and their teachers.

Distance learning (or distance assistance) is also a large user of electronic mail given its rapid response rate (one day) at a lower cost than the telephone.

LOCAL NETWORK

A local network inside a school or a university also changes the way in which computers are used by teachers.

The old 'computer lab syndrome' is dying out. It is now quite common to see some computers in a lab, one in a geography class and one or two in the library with a CD-ROM 'jukebox'.

A student working on a text is able to have access to the *Collins Dictionary* for translation, to load geographical software and a satellite picture coming from the libraries, or to deposit a message of absence in the headmaster's mailbox.

Connection with the personal computer at home is now possible in some countries at very little cost.

BULLETIN BOARDS AND CONFERENCING SYSTEMS

One variant to electronic mail is the Bulletin Board. It might be considered as a group mail system, where an entire group communicates. All the messages are available to everyone in the group.

One use of this has occurred in college courses in which the use of a bulletin board replaces, perhaps on a periodic basis, a discussion-based class. Instead of the students coming together in a single physical location to conduct the discussion, they communicate through a bulletin board. All students read what the other students have to say and all send messages to the bulletin board. Typically the discussion is based on a set of reading assignments.

A further development is in a conferencing system environment. Here in addition to communication, other capabilities such as voting are provided. Few such systems have been used in education.

OTHER USES OF NETWORKING

Another use of networking is the sharing of data. Students can have access to large databases, perhaps physically far away. Thus a group of students, in different locations, could jointly study the problems of world hunger and starvation, using major databases related to this problem. The use of data is combined with a joint problem-solving activity, another plus made possible with networks.

A well-known example of such joint sharing, the National Geographic Society's material on acid rain, involves many students using similar tactics to gather information about acid rain. Through the network, all the data go to a central computer. The processed data then go back to each of the schools. Other similar activities are also available for networks.

Such electronic communications are also used for local, regional and national examination registration, announcements of results, descriptions of schools and curriculum, and many kinds of updated information that students, parents and teachers need to know quickly.

The network can also be the main delivery system for learning, working in a distance-learning environment. Students can be scattered over a large geographical area, as in other distance-learning situations. Experimental programmes have offered such courses, and full degrees have also be awarded this way. We can expect this type of application to increase in the future.

Video

An auxiliary media that the computer can control is video. This is possible in a variety of forms, including ordinary video tape recorders, controllable by the computer. But there are some severe handicaps with computer-controlled videotape players; a video sequence to be accessed may be a long way away, not close on the tape to material just shown. Since tape can be moved only slowly, the access time may be too long in a learning environment.

A better solution for most educational uses including interactive video is the videodisc player. Here a television picture or sound is stored on a laser-read disk. Several formats are in use. The format most practical for computer control stores a single picture on a single track on the disk, storing about 54,000 pictures on one side of the disk (half an hour of video material).

The tracks have individual numbers associated with them; the program can tell the player to go to such-and-such track and show the picture there, as a still picture or it can tell the player to go to such-and-such track and play, at normal speed, with the sound turned on, until one gets to another numbered track. Speed of playing and the presence of sound, pictures or both can also be controlled. A bit of additional software is needed for the computer to do these things, but the writing of the software is trivial.

Since video also stores sound, the addition of a videodisc player to a system, plus suitable control hardware and software, sound, still pictures and moving pictures to be added to the computer program. These can be under the control of the program. Thus one can choose to show a particular video sequence over again, or a piece of the sequence, if the student has not learned whatever was to be learned with that sequence. The combination of computer and laser-read videodisc player is often called interactive video. Newer hardware allows full software control of the video image; the software can specify where the picture appears on the screen, and the part of the picture to show.

Perhaps the major problem in the use of interactive video system so far in education has been that the standards for interaction, to be described in the next section, have been low for many of the existing materials. Since video up until this time was a completely linear medium with no chance of interaction, video producers were often satisfied with very weak interaction, since it was much greater than they had been able to achieve before. As a result, many video disk programs do not achieve the full power of a combination of computer and video disk.

An educational example of interactive video material with reasonable interaction is a project producing modules to help English-speakers learn to recognize spoken Japanese. The units are tutorial. Both video sequences (some made particularly for this project) and sound are on the videodisc. Students are queried about what they see and hear, and additional help is available when needed. The programs have several different learning tracks in order to accommodate students of widely different abilities.

Compact disk

A newer medium is the compact disk. This medium was initially developed for music, and indeed has become an extremely important aspect of home music systems very quickly worldwide. Sales are rapidly increasing in this application.

Storage on a compact disk, unlike storage on a video disk, is digital, like storage within computers. It is possible to store digitally everything that can be stored in the analog methods used in the videodisc. Thus pictures and sound can be stored on compact disks. Since storage is digital, fidelity, which increases with sampling rate, and disk space are tradeoffs.

The typical compact disk has less space than the video disk. It is usually capable of storing, 500 million characters. This is an enormous amount of information, compared with computer storage in the past. But the use of video quickly uses up this space, so video is still restricted in using the compact disk.

Various tactics have been developed and proposed for the compact disk so far. The initial one in use is CD-ROM, based on the notion of read-only memory. What is now available educationally with this medium is almost entirely text material, with some access capabilities. Thus we mentioned the French *Grand Robert* dictionary as one example.

Several newer formats for compact disk have been proposed. One of these, Compact Disk Interactive (CDI), was proposed by Philips and Sony, initially for the home market. This home equipment is not available as yet, but some programs in the CDI format have been developed and others are underway. An industrial unit is available. The advantage of this equipment is, since it is intended for home use, that it will be cheap. Home units are expected, with considerable memory and computer power, to cost about

$1000. But initial plans for the home market do not include a keyboard, and so limit somewhat the possibilities. Later this technology may well become important in educational environments other than the home.

As indicated, one of the problems with the compact disk is the question of how much video (moving images) can be stored on the disk. This has led to considerable research following the approaches of computer graphics in compacting images and so storing images in less space but with some reduction in image quality. Several strategies in this direction have been pursued. Perhaps the one that has obtained the most publicity is the DVI strategy, now being followed by Intel and IBM.

In both the compact disk and laserdisc approaches, at present, there often is not full control of the video image through software, as already mentioned: changes in where a video picture is to be seen on the screen must be done by video techniques and so cannot easily be altered after the disks have been pressed. Newer techniques allow more versatility and include the possibility of having many images, all from full frame video on the disk, displayed simultaneously on the screen.

The interactive use of laserdisc/compact disk is so far minimal in educational environments, as described, except for video disks in training. But this situation can expect to change when equipment and experience in production are more readily available.

Since 1990, all French *lycées* have been equipped with a CD-ROM reader connected with the local network of PC computers and all students are able to access about 12 CD-ROM concerning French literacy, economics data, dictionaries, historical actualities, etc. in the school's documentation centre.

Other hardware developments
Several other hardware developments may eventually become important in education. Perhaps the most important will be the use of voice input. Although much voice research has occurred in the laboratory, it is difficult to assess how close we are to practical applications of these tactics. The problem is a complex pattern recognition problem, one that should be amenable to computer solution as hardware capabilities increase.

The use of pointing devices should also be mentioned. These are practical today in a variety of different styles – arrow keys, mouse, joy stick and touch screens. Some videodisc systems have given particular attention to this, using touch screens as a pointing input device. But the type of material that relies entirely on pointing is limited; one misses the full richness of a natural language with such a limited set of choices.

Other developments include digitizing tablets which deliver the screen image on an overhead projector and allow the teachers to display on a large screen what is running on his personal computer and scanners which digitize any picture or text, so that they will be directly integrated in graphics or, after a character recognition, in text processing.

As an example, a prototype copying machine in 1991, providing an English version of a French text (six cross languages).

If we look further into the future, we can begin to see other possibilities. Thus the possibility of brain wave analysis, communicating with the computer entirely by thought, does not seem inconceivable. Some of the technical problems are similar to the technical problems of dealing with spoken input, because they involve complex pattern recognition processes. A limited form of brain wave input has been described in a book on future education systems, *Education and Ecstasy* (Leonard, 1987). Here the attempt is not to obtain full brain wave input, but only a limited variety that indicates at a given point in the program 'I understand', or the opposite. It is difficult to know when these techniques will be practical, if ever.

The effect of informatics on learning

This section looks at overall possibilities for technology in learning environments, an important component of any consideration about what applications should be designed. The computer and its associated equipment such as videodisc and compact disk are not the same as other learning media. Rather they have unique capabilities of their own, capabilities we are only slowly beginning to understand.

Individualization of learning

Almost all humans believe that they are unique, different from all other humans. In education it has long been believed that each learner is different, with different learning styles, different backgrounds, different memories, different interests and different desires.

Yet in much of the history of education we have had, under the pressures of numbers of people to educate and limited resources, great difficulty in treating people as individuals in the learning process. In a classroom with thirty students, typical of schools in developed countries, the amount of time a teacher can spend working with each individual, is of necessity, small. In universities classes are typically larger. Fewer teachers are available in many countries, so class sizes are often large. Teachers may be uncomfortable with an individualized approach and prefer an approach where they are dealing with the class as a whole. Hence, individualization seldom occurs within current education systems, in spite of our belief that it is desirable to treat each person as a distinct and unique individual.

Some individualized education, however, has always taken place. We mentioned Socrates in our discussion of tutorial material. The wealthy are, in many countries, able to afford tutors on an individual basis for their children. Expensive universities and private schools too are often able to have more teachers per student. But this type of individualization only goes to increase the differences between the haves and the have-nots in society, because it offers a superior education to those already at an advantage. Individualization has simply been too expensive for education to afford, except on a very limited scale, for most students.

Today's new interactive technology brings to learning the possibility that we can radically alter this situation. The primary characteristic of the computer, as a learning device, is that it can be highly interactive, with the student answering meaningful questions every few seconds. This type of interaction begins to resemble a human conversation, where each person plays a dynamical and active role.

Because of the frequent interaction possible with the new information technologies, we can individualize the learning experience. Each time the student answers a question, the program can pay careful attention to that answer and build a picture, or model, of the student learning progress. The most valuable aspect of this model is that we can determine what the student does not know. This is a critical ingredient in individualizing the educational process. For each student, the question of what is known and what is not known, at a given moment in learning, will be different. The knowledge of what a student does not know, or cannot do at a given point in learning is very important in determining the next learning sequence; this may be different for each student, in good interactive material.

The computer will not make all the decisions at this point that an extremely good teacher can make. Although this may eventually be more possible than today, if some of the promises of artificial intelligence turn out to be reality, it does not seem likely that computer interactive teaching will approach teaching involving a very good teacher.

But we should not find this discouraging. Remember that the current situation, classrooms as just described, is that very little individualization and interaction occurs. There are a number of problems. Not all of our teachers are good teachers. But even more important, there is not enough time for the teacher to work in detail with each student.

Even today, without the use of techniques of artificial intelligence, we can do a credible job of individualizing the educational process, increasing individualization for almost all students far beyond what is obtained today. No new technology is needed; we already have this capability. But we need the curriculum material based on the capability. Little such material is currently available, so the technology today seldom leads to individualized learning.

INDIVIDUALIZATION AND MOTIVATION

Individualization has some very important consequences. A student who interacts frequently with the computer and who finds that what the computer does matches his or her needs is much more likely to stay with the material. Such a student is highly motivated to increase time-on-task, and quality time-on-task is one of the major positive variables determining effectiveness of learning.

So good interactive learning material is likely to be intrinsically motivating. We need not rely on gimmicks to keep users interested in difficult computer-based learning tasks.

INDIVIDUAL STUDENT PACING

A second consequence of technology-based individualization is that each student can move at his or her own pace. Thus it is not necessary to have the lock-step strategies – all students moving at the same pace – that almost completely dominate most education systems at present. The whole conception of grade levels could vanish in a system that makes considerable use of individualization, because different students would be in different locations within the learning sequences for different subjects.

When students work individually with tutors, they do not all move at the same pace. So it is reasonable to assume that a highly individualized system making extensive use of computers in the tutorial mode would also find that students do not progress uniformly. In a full technology-based learning system, students themselves can have some choice in just how far they progress in particular areas.

INDIVIDUALIZATION AND MASTERY

There is another possible consequence of individualization, if the materials are constructed appropriately. We can keep a student within a given learning area until that student demonstrates full and complete knowledge of that area. Thus all students will learn the material fully, will *master* the material.

This applies to all aspects of learning, including higher cognitive skills. In current education systems, mastery is obtained only for a small percentage of the students, those who typically make excellent grades. In an individualized education system using technology reasonably, it should be possible to obtain mastery for everyone. Learning environments would be greatly improved.

It is difficult to overestimate the possibilities of all students learning to master. This alone would be a major change and enhancement of our learning systems.

Interactive learning

The importance of learning interactively, with the student playing an active role in the learning activity, has received attention in this chapter. Learning is better if the student is active, creating the knowledge rather than receiving it passively.

The new interactive learning technologies give us the best chance we have had in thousands of years for a fully interactive system for all students. But we may not realize this possibility. Again it depends on the development of effective material.

Changes in the curriculum

The use of new interactive technologies in learning environments can also lead to changes in the curriculum. A variety of possible changes are discussed below.

INDIVIDUAL STUDENT CHOICE

In current education, students seldom have much to say about the educational process. A student may be able to choose the topic of a paper, within limits, or choose courses in secondary school or university, but the overall structure of almost all courses, at all levels of education, is specified by teachers, or perhaps more accurately, by the curriculum developers and authors of books and other learning materials.

A technology-based environment allows us to present the students with choices of content, within limits specified by the designers. That is, at various points along the way the students can be offered alternatives along with enough information to make the choice meaningful. Students can, to a great extent, be given control of content within courses. This can include various ways of learning the same content, very useful in assuring mastery learning when students have different learning styles.

These choices should not encourage the student to wander randomly through the material, as seems to have happened in some of the earlier experiences with hypercourses, based on hypermedia. Rather, they can be combined with the ideas expressed in the last section, particularly the ideas of mastery learning.

Another possibility of student choice has already been mentioned, that of adjusting pace to individual student need. Most education at present follows fixed paces, with all students moving through the material at the same rate. This is no longer necessary when the new information technologies are used.

CHANGES DUE TO EVOLVING SOCIETY

Another possible curriculum change comes about because society is changing. The world evolves much more rapidly today than it did in the past, because of increasing numbers of people and because of increasing skills in transportation and communication. The rise of modern science has also been an important factor stimulating change in society. This acceleration should be reflected in education systems.

This implies that the curriculum needs to be examined continuously, to see what is applicable at a given time and what is not applicable. The *content* of courses should change to meet these needs. Since computer material can be highly modular and is always changeable, it is particularly able to react to these changing requirements.

Some of the changes are brought about by the computer itself. Thus the issue of what a student needs by way of rote information in mathematics is coming under active consideration in many parts of the world. While most students today learn the process of long division, around the age of 10, fewer and fewer people in society do long division on paper. The presence of calculators and computers, and their rapid spread in many parts of the world, has lead to their being the principle device used for long division. So the question can be raised about whether long division should still be taught in the conventional fashion. A considerable time in the child's life is spent on the long division process, so we can raise the question of whether that time may well be better spent in other ways, for a child who will spend most of his or her life in the twenty-first century. Similar comments can be made about addition and multiplication of fractions, and other processes learned in arithmetic.

This question is not limited to children. Very similar comments can be made about the present courses in calculus in all parts of the world, in secondary schools, in colleges and in universities. Almost all calculus courses are involved with drill and practice in the operations of symbolic differentiation and integration. But these processes can both be done by computer, or by hand. Differentiation by computer has long been easy and theorems discovered about fifteen years ago at Cambridge University make integration an algorithmic process also. In the developed countries, software for this purpose, even running on small computers, is available. So we can question what the future content of the calculus course should be, given the capabilities of interactive technology.

These examples, from elementary arithmetic and from calculus, are only intended to illustrate possibilities inherent in reconsidering the content of courses. They furnish reasonable examples of how the computer itself effects the curriculum. But we could look at many other areas, including areas dealing with thinking skills, writing skills and information access.

RESEARCH-INSPIRED CHANGES

Another area where changes in the learning material can come about and that can be computer-assisted is based on research in learning. While we have much to learn about how students learn, research projects in many countries are exploring these issues. One interesting example comes from the research in science education. It has been found by many observers that students do not come into a science course, such as a beginning physics course, with a mental blank slate. They already have intuitive *models* of what happens in the world, based on their experiences up to that time. These models are not learned in school, but rather are developed through students' everyday activities and experiences; research reveals that they are often very deep seated, and not articulated consciously; they are not easy to change.

One such intuitive model, for example, is that of how bodies move, the typical beginning topic in physics. The general belief students have is that objects need a force to keep them in motion – their everyday experiences with motion fully support this model. So students presented with Newton's laws of motion will often implicitly reject these laws as not corresponding to experience. This rejection is even a healthy mental process, because we expect students to rely on experience in science. Experimental efforts, many involving the computer, have shown that these problems can be overcome, primarily by providing the student with a variety of alternate experiences, perhaps generated by computer programs, that challenge the experiences that they already have and thus challenge their everyday theories.

Our point is that we learn something about the learning process and this too can lead to changes in the curriculum. Computer-based curricula, as noted, allow the flexibility to make such changes easily.

Changes in the role of the teacher

Another area in which the new information technology may lead to changes in teacher roles.

TEACHERS TODAY

The role of the teacher is not identical in classrooms today. As we examine classrooms in various parts of the world, we can see different strategies in use. But by far the most common teacher role today might be called the textbook-lecture learning mode. Here the teacher spends much of the time talking to students, or alternately, examining students.

Teachers often also play a role in determining the content of the course, but less than might be expected. Most of the pedagogical decisions are made when the textbook is chosen, because few courses depart extensively from the textbooks used.

Teachers often have difficulty in coping with large classes. It is not infrequent for teachers to resort to threats of various types, particularly about the grades that students may be receiving. Some teachers today believe that these threats are essential in keeping students in the learning path.

There is nothing sacred, however, about the role that the teacher plays in the class. It is determined by the situation obtaining today and existing learning technologies. The teacher must cope with large numbers of students in classes, and common strategies are all oriented around that view; a technology-based system might imply very different roles for the teacher.

TEACHERS TOMORROW

Technology opens a whole new range of possibilities for teachers in learning environments. If students are working on an individualized basis, perhaps in small groups, the teacher no longer needs to be in the role of a lecturer. The assessment role can also be considerably assisted by technology.

In an environment using the new educational technology the teacher can have very different roles. Students learn directly with use of the technology, without the teacher playing an active role. The teacher can organize the learning resources available to students. The teacher can serve as an *adviser* to the students, suggesting what they work on next. The teacher can offer individualized aid to students who are not learning despite the learning resources available, the 'supermarket' of resources that characterizes the course. Thus the teacher's efforts are focused where they are most valuable. Finally the teacher becomes more of a friend of the students. This makes the job more pleasant for the teacher and inspires creative effort on their part.

Some of today's teachers might not like this role, but other individuals would find it a very desirable environment.

Changes in assessment

The assignment of grades, assessment, is a major activity in current education, both in individual classes and in countries. We have already considered some aspects of that activity. As with the other factors mentioned here, the situation could be very different in a technology-based learning environment.

Currently assessment is based on examinations. A class will typically spend a sizable amount of time on didactic material, perhaps weeks, and then will be presented with an examination. Typically all students take the examination at the same time. The process of assigning grades is often given great importance by the teachers, by the students and by the parents. The importance of grades in later life is often grossly exaggerated.

It is characteristic of today's system that there is a firm and distinct difference between when the student is learning, and when the student is being tested. Examinations may be internal, developed by the teacher, or external, even nationally based. Some education systems require all students to take certain examinations at certain times, fixed by the school or national schedules.

This situation can change drastically in a computer-based environment. The computer allows testing and learning to be combined within the same situation. The computer allows assessment to be a continuous, almost moment by moment, process. Good computer-based learning material can continually probe the student to identify problems, thereby making assessments at all stages of the learning process rather than at fixed intervals. Furthermore, knowing the student's weaknesses, the computer can select the appropriate learning sequence to be presented next. Again, this can be done on a continuous basis.

In the mastery learning environment, assessment assumes a different role in the learning process. Here the primary use of assessment is to determine which learning materials will be presented next to the student. Students will be kept in an area until mastery is demonstrated in on-line assessment. A variety of learning materials are needed in this environment. Suppose the student is found to have problems in a given area, has been presented with a learning sequence and is still found to have problems. Then the program should present that student with a different learning sequence, one that will better match the way that student can best learn.

In such an environment, grades are no longer an important part of the process, because it is assumed that all students will learn everything to the mastery level. So the purpose of assessment is also altered in a computer-based mastery learning environment.

Changes in classroom structure

The new information technologies also have major consequences for class structure, changing it radically both for the student and the teacher. Different classroom structures may imply different school organizations.

The CHILD project in Florida presents an example of such a change. This is an elementary school project, partially implemented in several school districts. CHILD schools have four special classrooms, two for language and two for arithmetic, divided by levels. The classroom has a series of learning stations around the room. It is not organized with the student sitting at desks, facing the teacher. Pupils work in small co-operative groups at each of the learning stations. Several learning stations involve computers and possibly other technology-based medium. One station might be devoted to video, one might have reading material, one might have objects that enable a student to gain experience, as for example with rods in a mathematics course, and one might have computers.

Students, in groups of two or three, work on an activity at a given station until it is satisfactorily completed. Then they move to another station. They may spend several days working at one station, or a shorter period of time. The teacher works with these individual groups when they are in need of some direct human assistance not furnished by the material at the learning station itself. A management system controls movement of the students through the material.

Quite different ways of organizing classes may come in connection with technology-based material. Perhaps the classroom will vanish. Different curriculum developments may specify both differences in the role of the teacher and in classroom structure. Thus it is not necessary that all classes be organized in exactly the same fashion for all subject areas, given the flexibility inherent in modern interactive learning technology.

Changes in course structure

Typically, education systems all over the world are organized in courses. But a technology-based system might be very different. Even the name 'course' may no longer be appropriate.

COURSE LENGTH

Currently most courses in a given institution are of the same fixed length. This is primarily because in the previous non-computer record-keeping systems it was difficult to manage any other structure.

But there is nothing magical about a given period of time for a course. In most universities in the United States, for example, a typical course is ten or fifteen weeks. But this length is not dictated by the subject-matter.

Why should we, ideally, have courses at all? Learning should be a continuous process, from birth to death. Divisions into courses are artificial, particularly in technology-based environments.

COURSE STRUCTURE

Whether we use the word 'course' or not, we can expect great changes in the structure of the learning experiences. Some of these new structures have already been mentioned in this report, while others are new. Several of these organizations may be present in a single course.

Traditional organization, with computers. The course follows the traditional pattern, but much of the instructional burden is shifted to the computer. This pattern is not surprising, as it is a natural easy evolution from current courses.

Mastery-based organization. All students should learn everything to the mastery level. The computer keeps students working on a topic or skill until mastery is attained. Various learning materials are provided, as different students may require different materials.

Quiz-based organization. This is a variant of mastery learning. The students' activities are primarily quizzes, with the learning material appearing only when the quizzes indicate student problems.

Hypercourses. Hyperstructures allow more student choice in the learning materials, including choice of content. The teacher may be allowed to determine some of the paths to be followed. In more advanced hypercourses the ideas of mastery learning can also be incorporated.

Changes in classroom management

Classroom management has a variety of meanings, as previously noted. First, the teacher typically keeps records of what is happening with each student, sometimes only records of results on examinations, but sometimes more detailed records of student performance and behaviour. Some of these records, such as attendance, may be required by administrative groups in the school system, but many are associated with grading.

This process is made much easier if the classroom is *networked,* so that information about student progress can be stored in a file server accessed by each computer through the network. While such systems are not in all educational environments, their presence is increasing, so for the future it seems reasonable to think about networked classrooms and networked schools. The networks can form a hierarchy of increasingly far reaching communication capabilities.

In such a system detailed information is available at every moment to the teacher; helpful information can also be made available to all students. The teacher can be warned about student problems. Thus the management system can be part of the individualization of education, allowing the teacher to give direct assistance to those students most in need of it at the moment.

Distance learning with technology

Finally, we can expect the increased use of interactive learning technologies to change the nature of distance learning. Computers and associated technology are not tied to a particular physical location, so they lend themselves naturally to use anywhere. But, as with many other educational applications of technology, we are still in early stages of development.

Reference

Leonard, G. 1987. *Education and Ecstasy.* Berkeley, California: North Atlantic Books.

CHAPTER FOUR

Current restraints and prospects: regional examples

Europe and North America

Peter Gorny, Dentcho Batanov and Robert Lewis

Across Europe a key factor determining the use of information technologies in education and training is the degree of central government intervention.

The Europe Region is far from homogeneous with regard to education systems and their underlying policies, and to the introduction of informatics into education. We shall discuss both the extremes of this process: informatics as a subject (teaching and learning about information technology) and information technology as a tool or medium for the teaching/learning process. We shall not limit ourselves to the general school system but will also take industrial training into account.

In none of the countries of the region has the introduction of informatics into the education system reached a state which might be considered as stable: indeed, within only a few months, new concepts may both be proposed and introduced experimentally into some schools, as a result of changes in the attitude of the policy-making bodies of the country or local initiatives. This rapid change forces a reviewer to refrain from the attempt to draw a complete and detailed picture, and rather to be content with taking some snapshots and highlighting some situations which go a certain way to characterize the overall development.

However, in certain parts of the region, some similarities do arise. For example, in countries in the east of Europe the fact that there are no major differences between their education systems has only served to improve their co-ordination. Notably, alongside the fundamental school disciplines these countries have in the past twelve years or so been paying increasing attention to career orientation and training, geared mainly to the growing

demand for personnel capable of servicing and developing the new information technologies. But while national strategies and policies in this respect have not differed greatly, there have been certain differences in terms
of specific achievements and the rates thereof. Despite these differences,
there is one common denominator: the emphasis these countries place on
the introduction and application of computers in education, with less attention to communication systems and the relevant distribution of information.
As a result, most of these countries have replaced the term 'new information
technologies' with 'computerization' in/of education. On the whole, it has
been a predictable and natural process, for four reasons. First, since the
mid-1960s, countries in the east of Europe have been manufacturing their
own computer technology. Second, the rapid orientation of these countries
towards the development and manufacturing of microcomputers enabled
them to achieve a relatively massive introduction of micros into the education system. Third, the Russian Federation (then the USSR) (in the mid-
1950s) and subsequently Bulgaria, Hungary, Czechoslovakia and other
countries, acquired and evolved practical experience in the use of CAL-sys-
tems (COURSEWRITER and SPOK in the Russian Federation and Bulgaria,
PLATO in Bulgaria, etc.). Fourth, a late-1970s and early-1980s analysis of the
experience accumulated elsewhere in the world pointed to the existence of
the same trends in such developed western countries as the United States,
France, Germany and Japan.

Changing educational approaches

The introduction of information technology into the education system has
its roots in different implicit political goals for school systems. Following
the phrasing of Papagiannis and Milton (1987), we can distinguish among
the goals of 'computer literacy as employment preparation', 'computer
literacy as informatics' and 'computer literacy as productivity enhancement'.

The term computer literacy is used by these authors to cover all different
approaches for introducing information technologies into education. The
goals do not exclude each other and none of the countries in the Europe
Region has implemented only one of them in its educational policy, though
the weight of the three issues may differ and change through time.

A good example of rapid changes can be found in the didactical approaches to teaching informatics and in applying it in teaching/learning.
Being aware of the fact that the term 'didactics' has a great variety of
definitions, we stress that in this chapter it will be used as an umbrella

expression for all the psychological, pedagogical, methodological and organizational concerns of introducing information technology into teaching and learning.

It seems to be a rule that during technological development, education systems always follow the same pattern: in a situation with few computers in schools and a small number of qualified and experienced teachers, the policy is to stress informatics as a school subject. The didactical approach is more or less what might be called algorithm-oriented or (in the early stages of development) hardware-oriented. This implies that the main objective is programming, sometimes even on the basis of logical circuits. In the Europe Region, only a few countries...or regions within countries – are still pursuing this approach. The programming languages used vary from any dialect of BASIC to PASCAL or LOGO. A clear dependency between the age group in which informatics is introduced and the adopted programming language can be observed: LOGO (and little more than its turtle graphics) for primary schools, BASIC-like languages for lower secondary and PASCAL-like languages for upper secondary schools in those countries where 16-bit machines have become common place.

Typically, investment has been channelled chiefly into secondary education – most higher education establishments are already well equipped or have their own sources of financing. The finances have been allocated on the basis of the following priority: hardware (computers and peripherals); personnel training and retraining; and research and development (including software).

Different programmes in various parts of the region have been pursuing the following six essential objectives, listed by order of priority: acquiring 'computer literacy' by as many young people as possible, and by adults as well (with the aid of television); introducing a specialist subject into both secondary and higher education; accelerated training for teachers not specialized in computer technology to use that technology as a teaching tool; meeting young people's growing interest in computers by a variety of extracurricular forms of work (clubs, workshops, training courses, etc.); direct use of computers as an educational tool, with software developed, as a rule, by teachers of the different school subjects; and formulation of applied research assignments related to the computerization of education and formation of research teams to deal with them.

A detailed analysis of the national programmes in the east of Europe and the current state of their implementation, of the priorities and the relevant appropriations yields three conclusions. First, the new information technologies have been narrowed down to and transformed chiefly into computerization of education. Second, the dominant desire for rapid and effective results is not adequately supplemented by serious and deep-reaching scientific preparation for the materialization of that process. Finally, the material base is developing too quickly for its users to catch up with its growing potential.

These largely negative inferences notwithstanding – and they are due mainly to insufficient experience and a lack of streamlined organization – the national programmes have been playing a definitely positive role, both as political documents and as practical guidelines for the transfer of a large portion of the new information technologies into education systems.

With a growing penetration of information technology into society and (slightly delayed) into the schools, the didactical approach is moving to application-orientation. The concern shifts from the mapping process of 'algorithms ⟹ developments computer languages' to analysing real world systems, in order to formalize a well-defined part of, for example, human work, so that a program can be designed to support or substitute for this work. This approach can be developed to the extent that the students do not really program any more in one of the computer languages, but learn to use application software, thus stressing the employment preparation and vocational training. Another variant of the application-oriented approach focuses, from a societal viewpoint, on the problems connected with the introduction of computers into industry and administration. Besides the introduction of various application software systems, the main elements of the content in these computer awareness programmes are: technologically-induced unemployment; change of qualification demands on the labour force; design of ergonomic work places at computer workstations; equality of access to information; security and privacy of information; integrity of data themselves; and changes in private life caused by information technology (including communication technology).

A special approach which focuses on problem-solving abilities has to be mentioned here: the children learn to build 'microworlds' in order to investigate some selected mechanisms from the real world or from a fictitious world. If this approach is applied in higher education, problem analysis and program design are the central points. (We shall not investigate the fact that in many employment areas, the overall goal of general education and the special demands for programming skills complement one another.) This category of approaches includes 'tinkering' with LOGO, Boxer, STELLA, or similar systems supporting the modelling process – often with the help of powerful visualization tools on the computer system. These approaches can be found at lower secondary level in the United States, Canada, the United Kingdom and France, while in Scandinavia and Central Europe, the pedagogical objectives connected with this approach seem to be somewhat weaker. This type of approach, however, is not dominant in any part of the region.

The most recent development deserves the name of culture-oriented approach. It can be found in quite a number of the countries of the region, though mostly only as a future concept to be pursued after a transition period with one of the application-oriented approaches. In some places, experimental schools work with this concept and in at least one subregion it has been declared the official policy. Its main idea is that knowledge about information technology itself is not more important than, for example, knowledge about the physics of an electrical engine. Instead, a sensible and balanced attitude to the technology should be stressed, so that it can be responsibly applied in all conceivable situations, both in vocational surroundings and in private life, thus becoming an extension of the 'three Rs' as a new fundamental cultural skill. The approach is not only culture-oriented but, in contrast to the concepts mentioned above, it is centred on the student and not on the teaching process.

The Canadian Province of Ontario started the implementation of this approach in 1987, with its Ministry of Education Memorandum No. 91, which states, inter alia:

> 1. All students in Ontario schools shall have the opportunity, to the full extent of their abilities, to become knowledgeable and creative in their use of computers as personal tools.

> 2. Students should be given opportunities to use computers in a variety of activities, such as drawing, writing, composing, exploring, calculating, analyzing, role-playing and accessing information resources. This can be accomplished through the use of word processors, simulation programs, graphics editors, sound editors, spreadsheets, database managers, and telecommunication media. Students should explore the ways in which network configurations can provide a medium of communication and collaboration between peers and teachers both within and outside the school. Students should come to see the computer as a self-help tool of everyday life.

The recently introduced National Curriculum in England and Wales has similar objectives.

Information technologies in schools

It is obvious that the policy described in this memorandum has very far reaching consequences for school organization and teacher education. In practice, every single teacher in the schools involved has to be trained for this concept, which gives most attention to the goal of enhancement for personal development. All schools will need corresponding equipment and software in practically all classrooms, accessible by the students throughout the full schoolday. These conditions can only be created with a far-reaching and generously financed long-term programme.

Therefore, many of the countries of our region have not yet declared such extensive goals, but have restricted their ambitions. This often means that the use of computers as tools for teaching in many school subjects is the main objective, necessitating an appropriate in-service teacher training and a broad development of educational software. The French 'L'Informatique Pour Tous' and the German 'Informationstechnische Grundbildung' are representatives of this more cautious and teacher-centred attitude; they have been followed by similar programmes in other countries which seldom go further in the Ontario direction. In Germany, for example, only the state of Lower Saxony has chosen a culture-oriented approach, but in a teacher-centred way and without the necessary budgetary and organizational backing.

While in North America, the United Kingdom, France and Southern Europe, many courses are already offered to primary school children, there seems to be a wide agreement in Switzerland, Austria, Germany, the Netherlands and the Scandinavian countries not to start the courses before the fifth school year (age 10–11). In these countries, only a small number of younger children use the computer in experimental classes. This is also true in other European countries which may have goals such as: overcoming the psychological barrier in the encounter with the new kind of technology; creating an interest in computers and the enrichment of the play environment with suitable didactic games (which also pursue definite pedagogical objectives); and using computer games to introduce mathematics, the mother tongue, music, etc. In this age group in particular, there is a shortage of in-depth psycho-pedagogical and methodological research to define the requirements for a proper and efficient use of computers.

As mentioned above, access to equipment and teacher education are major hurdles in the realization of information technologies use in schools. Policies such as those in England and Wales and in Ontario require huge investments, with teacher education by far the greatest. In Portugal the

Minerva project has so far been only in (self-) selected schools, which has enabled the regional centres to support schools in training and hardware to a high degree.

Teacher training and retraining

In the east of Europe quite a lot of attention and money have been devoted to this area. In Bulgaria, for instance, more than 17,000 secondary school teachers have gone through a week's course (36 hours) in computer application; another 2400 have completed a month's training; 750 have finished a three-month course, and 450 have undergone a year's training. Practically all those involved in the management of secondary education have received some training. Since 1985, the Department of Informatics at the Kliment Ohridski University (Sofia) has been turning out teachers in that subject. Meanwhile, Hungary has trained about 2500 teachers for special informatics classes. The Russian Federation, Poland, the former German Democratic Republic, Romania and Czechoslovakia have done likewise. As far as the higher educational establishments are concerned, thanks to a much earlier start, practically all their faculty members are now capable of using computer technology.

Material facilities

In many countries, particularly those early in field, the advances in technology have brought on major problems of reinvestment. In the countries in the east of Europe, 8-bit micros are used on a massive scale to provide rudimentary computer literacy in and outside the general secondary schools, while vocational secondary schools and the higher educational establishments find the 16-bit machines more suitable to their purposes.

While Bulgaria has joined the Russian Federation and Germany in working on the development of a micro tailored to education's special needs, other countries have been using production-line micros with a specialized configuration and software. This diversity of hardware has been a serious obstacle to the exchange of software and to co-ordinated efforts along this line. Some of the difficulties are also due to the continuing high cost of the hardware manufactured by the respective countries. One positive development, nevertheless, has been the relatively equal distribution of micros among the different schools. For the present, it is seen as suitable to install a special computer laboratory with fifteen to eighteen micros in each school. In that respect, Bulgaria, with more than 20,000 computers spread out among its 1000-odd secondary schools, offers a good example. The situation is similar in Hungary (an average of five to fifteen microcomputers in each school) and Czechoslovakia. Recently, there has been a tendency to link the machines in each laboratory into a local network, thereby increasing the reliability and efficiency with which they are used.

In introducing computers into secondary education, considerable effort has been concentrated on the development and proliferation of educational software. Approaches vary from single learning programmes in any of the programming languages (usually in BASIC) to structurally complex and very user-friendly authoring languages which have proved especially suitable for use by non-professionals in the area of computer technology. Some countries have developed specialized computerized environments for various subjects, such as Bulgaria's Plane Geometry Environment and the Russian Federation's Foreign Language Environment. Reference was made earlier to problem-solving and modelling environments. The training and retraining of teachers in many countries in the region has resulted in a significant domain of educational software for practically all school subjects.

Three main problems remain. There is practically no exchange of software among the different countries, due to the difference in hardware, poor organization and methodological differences among the education systems. In terms of methodology, the quality of educational software is low; in most cases, the new technology applies an old educational technology mechanically. Finally, there is no efficient system for evaluating software quality and for its rapid dissemination.

Specialized secondary education and training

The main aim of this branch of education – to give students a specific professional orientation and training – determines the existence of differences in the contents of the special subjects. The idea is to equip the laboratory facilities with modern numerical-control machines, laser generators, industrial robots, etc. Bulgaria, for example, is currently introducing into technical secondary schools a computerized environment called Mechanics, and a similar approach is to be found in the United Kingdom following the Technical Vocational Education Initiative (TVEI) of the Department of Employment.

Countries in the east of Europe have been paying particular attention to extracurricular work with young people, aimed at deepening and channelling their interests in the area of the new information technologies. Broad networks of computer clubs function in all countries; workshops are a very popular form of computer use; specialized books have large print runs. The Russian Federation, Bulgaria and Hungary are among the regular organizers of national summer training camps in informatics; for the past several years, the Russian Federation and Bulgaria have also run bilateral and international camps of this sort. Within the International Programme 'Children in the Information Age', Bulgaria organized a Programming Olympiad for children who had won awards in their national competitions. This Olympiat was the precursor of the International Olympiad in Informatics, the fourth of which was held in Bonn, July 1992.

The training of young industrial and office workers and specialists uses similar methods and forms. Here, alongside the clubs, courses and individual activities, much use is being made of television's potential as an educational medium. Hungary, Bulgaria and the Russian Federation are the leaders in this area.

Higher education

The longest traditions and the most significant results with respect to the introduction of the new information technologies in the countries in the east of Europe are in higher education. The adoption of the new curricula and syllabuses at the beginning of the 1980s made it possible for computers, communications and CAD/CAM technology, and systems to arrive not only as elements, but as the core of practically all subjects. The basics of programming and computer application, data structuring, database and knowledge base structuring and use, and the methods of process and system management, provided the corner stone over which the superstructure of the special subjects was erected. The technology of computer use itself changed, with the machines now being used chiefly in an interactive mode. A large number of fine and diverse software packages and systems were accumulated, thanks largely to the efforts of the higher technical establishments in the Russian Federation, Bulgaria, Czechoslovakia and Hungary where conditions were conducive to the rapid introduction of modern CAD/CAM systems, industrial robotics configurations and computer-aided management systems for teaching and learning. The higher education establishments, particularly the technical ones, pioneered within the education system the testing and launching of video and video-computer systems (Bulgaria and Czechoslovakia), closed-circuit television (Bulgaria) and local computer networks (Bulgaria and Hungary). This has shown the way for the transfer to education of the new information technologies, in the full sense of this term.

In the United Kingdom, the Computer Board for Universities and Poly-technics (the main government funding body for hardware in higher education) has invested in the Computers in Teaching Initiative programme, aimed at increasing the use of computers in all undergraduate courses.

The trend in higher education in the region is to expect all students to be able to access information resources via the computer and to use the computer as a professional tool to organize their own academic work, including text processing and the visualization of scientific data. In many colleges, introductory courses to informatics are obligatory. In some colleges, especially in the United States, students are only admitted if they can certify that they have access to a personal computer, while others try to supply the students with personal computers or give them access to personal computer clusters or pools. While in the United States these investments are normally organized on the basis of local initiatives, resulting in great inequities between the institutions, in the European countries and in Canada, state programmes attempt to realize the same concept more centrally though at a slower pace. For example, at the universities and *Fachhoch-schulen* (colleges) in Germany, approximately 1 computer workstation per 100 students is at present publicly accessible (not counting mainframe computer terminals): the official goal is the ratio of 1:10. In the other Northern and Western European countries, the situation is estimated to be similar: in the rest of Europe, it is not quite as positive. In North America, the ratio is 1:10 in a few leading universities, but it otherwise varies widely, depending on the economic situation of the particular area.

In many countries, the higher education curricula are being or have just been revised in order to integrate obligatory introductory informatics courses for certain study lines, or even for all students. Normally, the focus is directed at first towards those subjects where professional qualifications in computer handling skills are demanded; once these needs have been satisfied, the focus turns towards the other subjects.

The concepts for the courses range from skills in handling application software to programming courses with an algorithm-oriented approach and courses with an informatics-oriented approach which focuses on the more permanent principles of this science and derives from them the quickly outdated skills necessary for the manipulation of application systems (Gorny, 1989; 1991). It has to be stated, though, that in none of the countries of our region have these compulsory introductory courses yet been implemented for all students.

Fig. 4.1 Taxonomy of educational software
(presented in the order of prevailing learner-orientation or teacher support)

Regional Assessments

(1) Open learning support:

    (a) Problem-solving tools ('tools for thinking with'):
        programming systems (such as LOGO, Prolog, Boxer and GARDEN),
        dynamic modelling systems (such as STELLA, DYNAMIS),

    (b) Tools for structuring knowledge by organizing data:
        text processing and document preparation,
        hypertext systems,
        drafting and design,
        databases,
        spreadsheets,

    (c) Communication systems,

    (d) Information retrieval, including hypermedia

(2) Guided discovery learning:

    (a) Simulation systems,

    (b) Computer-assisted (educational) games,

    (c) Process and robot control,

    (d) Intelligent tutor systems.

(3) Resources for teaching and learning:

    (a) Electronic blackboard, etc., including multimedia,

    (b) Tutorials,

    (c) Drill and practice.

    (4) Aids for educational management and school administration

Changing technology and diversification of application areas

Applying the taxonomy of educational software, we shall find that most of the software used in general schools supports the organization of data with text and graphics processors, databases, spreadsheets, hypertext systems, etc. (1b), or guided discovery learning (2).

The use of tutorial and drill and practice software (3b, 3c) has decreased considerably since its peak several years ago, but it is still used to supply individual coaching for pupils and students with learning deficiencies or cultural deprivations. An average student is probably exposed to this kind of software for not more than a few minutes per week – even in highly equipped American schools and colleges. In the future, we might find an increasing use of this software category, once more progress has been made in the development of knowledge-based ('intelligent') tutor systems (2d) which allow more context-sensitive advice to be given to the learner, especially in error situations. To date, very few of these systems are to be found in schools, owing to high development costs and expensive hardware.

A new educational application is electronic communication (1c). There are numerous electronic mail, electronic conferencing or bulletin board systems based on scientific community networks or commercial mailbox systems used to support communication between students, between students and teachers, or between teachers.

In contrast to the situation in general education, drill and practice and tutorial systems have a growing market for on-the-job training in many professions. Obviously, certain pedagogic concerns are considered as less important when training adults rather than children, so many companies apply tutorial software when introducing new methods or techniques to their staff. Most authoring systems developed during recent years aim at this market and have proved that computer-supported tutoring is an efficient means for training.

The newest tutoring systems are based on hypermedia technology and combine access to pictorial material on video discs and CD-ROM with retrieval from databases and communication technology, including satellite-based video conferencing in distant learning.

Apparently the more expensive educational software systems, such as hypermedia or multimedia applications and knowledge-based tutor systems, are finding their domain primarily in industry and commerce; primary and secondary schools will have to wait some years for them. This trend results in a widening gap between two groups – one concerned with school software, the other with industrial training software – both developing their own terminology, methodology and sequence of conferences.

Tertiary education has its place between the extremes of general education and industry mentioned above. Numerous experimental hypermedia and multimedia systems, and several 'intelligent' tutor systems are in use in colleges and universities of the region.

An important trend, which is considered likely to overturn the present educational software market, can be observed in practically every country and all subject areas: the increasing use of visualization concepts. These begin with direct manipulation and the desk top metaphor of XEROX and Apple, whose ideas have found an entry into a great variety of window and user interface management systems, and end with visual languages for graphically representing states and transitions, data and processes, and messages and objects, on a procedural, descriptive, functional, logical or object-oriented basis, thus offering alternatives with high pedagogical advantages, compared with conventional data base definitions, programming and modelling concepts. It is predicted that text-oriented, command-driven or menu-driven educational software, lacking the possibility of visualizing input and output data pictorially or schematically, will disappear as suitable hardware becomes available in the schools.

International co-operation

Within the region

Bilateral agreements and seminars are a traditional form of co-operation which continues to involve practically all countries of the region. At the day-to-day level, this co-operation is usually between two universities, two institutes, two schools, etc., yet the tasks it tackles are of national importance. In more recent times, bilateral seminars have tended to become multilateral and are seen as one of the keys to co-ordinated action in strategic industries.

Initiatives are also taken in parts of the region, often based on political or economic groupings. For example, the countries in the east of Europe are co-operating in the area of the new information technologies in education. The Programme for the Improvement of the Education System through the Use of Computer Technology, adopted in 1986 by Council for Mutual Economic Assistance (CMEA) member countries, covers the period to the year 2000. The detailed subprogramme for the period to the end of 1990 contained three sections, with ten projects in general secondary education, thirteen in secondary technical and vocational education and nineteen in higher education. There is an international team involved in each of these projects. A co-ordination meeting is held once a year for each of the three sections, along with several working meetings on the various projects.

Similarly, the members of the EEC, also with EFTA partners, have recently started the Third Framework Programme covering many aspects of advanced technology applications with the aim of stimulating economic growth. Of particular interest is the Developing European Learning through Technological Advance (DELTA) Programme. Whilst DELTA, under DG XIII is concerned with training and higher education, DG V has had some projects in the compulsory education sector.

Although not specifically related in information technologies in education and training, the EEC also has collaborative projects on courseware development and university/industrial training collaboration and, more recently a programme to stimulate collaboration with the countries in the east of Europe.

The Council of Europe also contributes to co-operation in this field. In addition to a series of conferences for policy-makers and those in higher education, it has teachers' workshops with information technologies in schools as their theme.

The Scandinavian countries collaborate through the Nordic Council of Ministers with Europe-wide programmes and involvement in the EEC programmes. The twinning of European towns and cities also provides a framework for links between schools. It is now common for electronic mail interactions to take place with examples of collaborative inter-school projects on topics such as languages, culture and the environment. Such collaboration also takes place with schools and colleges outside the region.

Another important contribution has been made by series of advanced research workshops held by the North Atlantic Treaty Organization (NATO) which have included topics on the application of informatics to education and training.

At the research level, in addition to bilateral collaboration between national research councils, the European Science Foundation includes cognitive science in its field of initiatives.

Beyond the region

UNESCO is the organization which provides the main platform for worldwide collaboration in this field. Much support has been given to countries in the east of Europe, for example, the international programme 'Children in the Information Age' (Lyudmila Zhivkova Institute, n.d.), launched and organized by the Bulgarian Government, UNESCO, the International Institute of Applied and System Analysis (IIASA) and the World Health Organization (WHO). The three international conferences hosted by Bulgaria under this programme pointed to a steadily growing interest in the problems accompanying the use of the new information technologies in the upbringing and education of children.

Under the UNESCO programme for co-operation, adopted by the fourth consultative meeting of the CODIESEE co-ordinating group in Sofia (1984), Bulgaria has been the co-ordinator of the Member States on the 'Development of the Students' Creative Abilities'. Results were reported at a seminar, and at a meeting of experts, in Sofia, on 'Didactic Computer Games for the Purposes of Education, Rearing and Developing the Creative Abilities of Students'. Bulgaria is also co-ordinator of co-operation on 'National Strategies in the Use of Computers in Education'.

Within the International Informatics Programme (IIP), two international projects have been proposed for the development of new approaches, methods and means for the applications of the new information technologies in education, and for the establishment of a consultancy centre for the developing countries. Yugoslavia and the United Kingdom organized a four-week summer school in the uses of information technologies in education for twenty teacher educators from developing countries (Lewis, 1990).

The Organisation for Economic Co-operation and Development (OECD) is also important and influential. Several international and regional conferences and workshops have been held with many publications of great value, particularly at the level of policy-making.

Technical Committee 3 (Education) of the International Federation for Information Processing (IFIP) has not only organized five World Conferences on Computers in Education (at four-yearly intervals since 1970; the fifth, WCCE 90, met in Sydney in 1990); its working groups cover the whole field; they run seminars and conferences two or three times each year. Its publications make an important contribution to the international literature (for example Lovis and Tagg, 1988).

An important though selective contribution to knowledge exchange is also made by the World Bank where its programme with China has priorities in education and includes the uses of information technologies.

Looking to the future

Certain trends can be observed, particularly in the most favoured parts of the region: first, in general and higher education, towards the use of information technology as a self-help tool in everyday life; second, to introduce information technology to children earlier in their school life; third, in vocational and higher education, towards hypermedia and multimedia systems and 'intelligent' tutor systems; fourth, towards a growing separation of the development of methodology and software for industrial training, and for general education in the school system; and fifth, towards a preference for educational software with highly interactive visual user interfaces. These trends are interconnected and will develop with a broad palette of variants, depending upon the different cultural conditions in the region.

There are well-defined needs which many countries identify. A qualitatively new – in terms of content – curriculum and syllabus should be developed in all school subjects on the basis of the needs of informatics (algorithmic approach, data analysis, modelling, optimization, etc.). The new educational technology means not only adding new technological tools to the old technology, but requires, first of all, new theory and new scientifically-determined methods for the assessment of the correct place and role of these tools in the processes of education.

We must achieve a transition from databases to knowledge bases, with the aim of developing expert systems for the different areas of knowledge within education, including the processes of teaching and learning.

The creation and development of a real information environment for every student, school and country, and for the region as a whole, implies that local networks become ubiquitous. Access must be ensured to an intercontinental information network. Electronic mail, books, libraries and other similar techniques should become the main means for the use, dispatch and distribution of information.

To underpin these developments, much can be gained within and beyond the region by international and bilateral programmes of basic research. The time has come when much valuable pragmatic experience on the use of informatics in education and training exists. This allows practitioners, policy-makers and researchers to come together to formulate key questions which require careful, sometimes long-term study. Whilst some aspect of the necessary research are context and culture specific, much would be gained from an internationally stimulated initiative to move all countries closer to gaining more benefit from information technology used to support learning.

Asia and the Pacific

Mike Lally and Neil Hall

Most nations in this region have at one time or another been colonies of European powers. This colonization left considerable influence on the administrative structures of these countries, an influence that has diminished considerably over the last twenty years. Many of the smaller nations have at various times provided a secondary-school education aimed at qualifying students for further study oversees, and so they follow foreign curricula. However, this influence of external examinations seems to be decreasing over recent times (Barrington, 1989), though it exists still in some parts of the region. There are instances of systems where education is modelled very closely on education in the former colonial power. In New Caledonia, for example, the structure and function of the education system is based on the state-controlled school system of metropolitan France (Wacquant, 1989).

Although the region contains many developing countries, some with very large populations, over recent years there has been an active interest in the use of informatics within general education. One of the first comprehensive outlines of the use of informatics in the education sector of countries of this region was presented in a UNESCO publication (*Computers in Education. An Outline...*, 1985). This led to the publication of some guidelines and issues relevant to developing informatics in the countries of the region (Anderson et al., 1986), together with an inventory of regional training institutions, publications and societies (*Computers in Education: Inventory of...*, 1986).

Current situation and regional characteristics

In 1987, a regional workshop was held to begin the development of a multi-media package for training teachers in informatics for education. This package was completed and guidelines for its use were developed during a sub-regional workshop in December 1988. During 1989 and 1990, a guidebook for developing educational software was produced (UNESCO Principal Regional Office for Asia and the Pacific, 1990), together with a set of guidelines for developing informatics policy and examining possible support structures necessary for informatics teachers.

The situation among countries varies enormously, but a few examples will suffice to give an indication of the different directions and the outcomes which have been achieved.

Almost every school in Australia has at least one computer (largely funded by the federal government from 1984 to 1986), the average number in primary schools being two or three and in secondary schools, about fifteen (Fasano, Hall and Cook, 1988; Fitzgerald, Hattie and Hughes, 1986). It is already apparent that the cessation of federal funding has slowed down the rate of growth of information technologies in classrooms (Fasano et al., 1988). It is also clear that computer-based technologies in Australian class-rooms are moving beyond the one stand-alone computer system.

Computers are used in all New Zealand secondary schools and in about half the primary schools. These machines have been largely funded through parent contribution and there is little likelihood that government funds will become available for such purchases (Frampton, 1989).

Australia's National Computer Education Program had as its goal a raising of the country's skill base, through the development of knowledge-intensive industries, in order to make Australia less reliant on the fluctua-tions associated with exporting commodities. This objective was accompanied by statements related to equity – for example, access to computer technologies for girls and disadvantaged groups – and to the need for education to move towards higher retention rates, a commitment to education beyond the compulsory school years and a view that education in science and technology should be extended. Computer-based techno-logies are widely used in Australian and New Zealand schools (Hall, 1982).

Although computers did not have a large presence in Japanese general schools in the 1980s, the situation has changed radically in the last few years, following considerable research in schools associated with higher education institutions. (A similar research situation still can be found in China.) On the other hand, even in the 1980s there were examples of large and im-pressive uses of informatics in vocational schools of commerce (Regional Seminar on Computer Educational Software..., 1988).

In Japan, there have also been research initiatives from universities and private enterprise. An example of the former is an attempt to develop a portable operating system (LAPLAS), which will allow different educa-tional software to be used on different machines. The Centre for Educational Computing in Tokyo is co-ordinating the development of an educational computer, with input from computer manufacturers, software houses, school textbook publishers, and relevant industry and educational organiz-ations.

Countries with large populations, notably China, India and Indonesia, have also begun to implement informatics education, although the very large number of participants requires a selective implementation. India launched a pilot project (CLASS) in 1984, and in 1986 China discussed a draft general policy for informatics.

The approach to utilizing informatics in education within the Republic of Korea is somewhat different from that discussed above. While other countries have largely focused on a mixture of computer literacy, programming and applications, the 1987 Korean plan called for the Korean Educational Development Institute to produce a collection of CAI materials which was to be used for improving the teaching/learning process. The resulting software is closely linked to the prevailing theoretical approach to teaching and learning.

In many of the countries of Asia, changes are taking place regarding the content of the informatics curriculum. There is a move away from teaching only programming to one of investigating a range of application packages. Examples of countries which are re-examining their curricula are Malaysia and Thailand.

General constraints

The developing countries of the region all place high values on education, generally for much the same reasons as in most developed countries: economic growth, efficiency of production at local and national levels, and continuation of the nation's culture. At the same time, universal primary education is not always achieved in these nations and resources for teaching are almost always limited. The importance of information technologies in the classroom does not seem to fit well with the present levels of economic development in all countries. In some, such as Nepal, Papua New Guinea and the Philippines, informatics education exists in the wealthy and independent international schools rather than in government and community-supported schools. There is a lack of scientific and technological development in some cultures of the region, often there is no suitable industrial base, many countries have few resources that could lead to manufacturing, many lack the funds necessary for any major capital development, and there is a shortage of suitably qualified and experienced people. In some, teachers have low levels of general education, have difficulty with subject content and teach in traditional teacher-centred ways. There are few textbooks and few teaching resources (Laws and Horsley, 1988). Yet these teachers are well respected and have a wide role in the community, as is common elsewhere in small communities.

Countries of the region wishing to advance in science and technology face a number of cultural factors that may impede progress. Few of the population have high levels of experience or competence with computer-based technologies. This situation is made more difficult if the culture discourages argumentative debate and encourages teachers to be widely involved members of the community, thus leaving them with little time for professional development (Owens and Phillips, 1987), and if the system ignores the linguistic and cultural diversity of its users (Wacquant, 1989). Contemporary computer-based technologies are unlikely to have a place in schools where the majority of families lead a subsistence horticultural life and where the status of the old colonial order continues to thrive, or where there is ethnic and class domination (Wacquant, 1989). Finally, where teachers are minimally trained, they are likely to have difficulty coping with unstructured curriculum innovations (Guthrie, 1983).

There is the example of Kiribati, a very poor country measured in terms of gross national product (GNP) or average income, but one in which the people maintain a reasonable standard of living and are relatively self-sufficient (Hindson, 1985). Kiribati has schools on twenty-four islands, all teaching the same syllabus, with 3500 kilometres between the two most distant schools. The schools are largely based on Western models of education, are poorly equipped with little furniture and few books, and generally have large classes. Almost all 6 to 14 year-olds attend school; they are taught by teachers who have travelled outside Kiribati and who generally hold at least two-year teacher-education diplomas. Today, many countries have still to solve the problem of universal primary education and there seems little chance of increased government funding for education (Guthrie, 1985).

Specific constraints

A shortage of available hardware is common to all countries of the region. In some countries (China, Malaysia, Sri Lanka and Viet Nam) only pilot schools have had access to informatics, while in others (Nepal, the Islamic Republic of Iran and the Lao People's Democratic Republic) an informatics programme in schools is yet to begin.

Most countries in the region have a centralized education system. This would indicate that the introduction of informatics should begin by policy decisions at the central level. Such policy decisions would be based on clearly defined objectives, either from the manpower planning approach or from a view of general education for attaining higher goals. Most informatics and education policies in countries of Asia and the Pacific are of the former type and have been responsible for the prominence of the teaching of programming languages.

Educators in countries such as Australia, China, India and Malaysia have become concerned about the dominance of a technology-based approach and argue the benefits of using informatics to improve the teaching/learning process. A major constraint to the systematic implementation of informatics education in most countries of this region is the lack of a clearly-defined set of objectives, with a policy statement and accompanying implementation plan. India and Malaysia are examples of countries where policies and implementation strategies have been clearly developed at an early stage.

The implementation and use of informatics continues to suffer from the lack of systematic training of and support to teachers. Most decision-makers continue to see informatics as activities which will work by simply putting computers into schools. The importance and difficulty of providing support for teacher development is not perceived. Current training of teachers is mainly of the in-service type and is usually directed at science and mathematics teachers. This can happen as a formal directive (China, Nepal and Viet Nam) or informally (Thailand and Indonesia). Some countries (for instance, India) require teachers to have specific academic qualifications, while others (such as Nepal and Malaysia) insist that teachers undergo a specific centrally controlled training program.

Limitations to the training of informatics teachers include lack of skilled teacher trainers and training materials, language barriers (especially for those countries with non-roman alphabets), a bias towards science and mathematics teachers, and lack of local software.

Software

In nearly all countries it is generally agreed that different types of software could be better used if targeted at different subjects within the curriculum (Regional Seminar on Computer Educational Software..., 1988). Several countries, including Sri Lanka, Pakistan, Thailand and Indonesia, have suggested that the use of content-free software in the classroom is currently inappropriate to their curriculum needs. For example, drill and practice programs are seen as having more value if used in mathematics courses or English grammar and vocabulary courses, while simulations might be better used for courses in natural sciences. There is agreement that specific software could be used for formal and informal education, as well as in self-study and group learning activities. Both Malaysia and Japan indicated that while earlier and current approaches stressed a more individualized education approach, they were in fact moving towards more of a group learning approach. Thailand and Indonesia indicated that their experiences showed that both individualized and group learning techniques were valuable, given specific situations.

An often debated issue concerns the value of adapting existing foreign software to local requirements, as opposed to creating original software to local specifications. The majority view is that in most cases it would be more appropriate to create new software specific to individual curriculum and cultural needs, since the reality is that any educational software development needs to reflect the directions and emphasis of current general curricula, which differ across countries.

Co-operative activities

The sharing of educational software was considered to be of critical importance to the implementation of informatics in countries of the region. The mechanism for such collaboration was one of the major topics for discussion in Tokyo at the Japan Council of Educational Technology Centres/UNESCO Regional Seminar on Computer Educational Software Development, Evaluation and Dissemination (1988). One of the major issues raised during the seminar concerned the implications of software development with regard to differing languages and cultures. Different languages do affect the ease with which software can be adapted. For non-Roman based scripts, there are additional problems concerned with developing an appropriate user interface. An alternative solution to this incompatibility is to design software in such a way as to minimize the amount of re-coding when translating from one national language to another. However, further co-operation is needed to develop such guidelines.

Differences in cultural background were considered to be a more serious barrier to the exchange and conversion of software. Content which may be suitable for one culture may be completely inappropriate for another. Such cultural differences indicate that a network for the sharing of software in the curriculum areas of history, social studies, English, etc., is likely to be difficult and therefore of limited value. On the other hand, mathematics and science education are curriculum areas which are more neutral and have greater similarity in content and sequence across the various countries of the region. However, cultural values and influences are changing over time and so the exchange of software which has a bias in culture should not necessarily be excluded from some form of sharing network. On the other hand, differences in culture and language should be considered when designing software with the intention of sharing this among different countries. A mechanism for such sharing needs to be developed.

There is a consensus that teacher input is vital for software development; however, a question arises as to whether teachers should be asked to implement the software itself, since they are already burdened with their daily teaching load and may not really give maximum effort towards software implementation. Furthermore, teachers may not have enough programming skills to give the software the technical excellence it deserves. There is a need to identify possible powerful authoring systems which may be useful for lesson generation. In such cases, it might be easier to train teachers in the use of such tools, together with the principles and procedures involved in courseware generation. Further work needs to be carried out, along the lines of the Japanese initiatives mentioned earlier.

Conclusions

Some of the countries of the region are struggling to provide universal primary education and basic literacy. The major difficulty in many of the countries is to argue the position that informatics education is a priority. Other constraints such as high illiteracy rates, shortage of teachers and lack of running water make it difficult to convince decision-makers of this, even though informatics education will be of undoubted benefit to these countries in the longer term. There is the question of changes in lifestyle brought about by accepting modern computer technologies; moreover, it is not certain that technological developments in schools fit in with the existing overall educational goals of these countries. It is not at all clear that Pacific island nations will benefit from a stronger emphasis on information technologies in their schools.

Co-operation does exist at political and cultural levels, as well as in more specific aid programmes. All the same, it needs to be recognized that co-operative ventures in information technologies are difficult, especially among countries that vary in population, language and culture. There is a high degree of agreement with the notion that no one country in the region has the resources needed to incorporate fully and independently informatics into general education. Different countries wish, for a large number of non-educational reasons, to pursue the question of hardware provision independently. However, there is a strong desire to co-operate in the fields of software development and teacher training. This co-operation may occur at a regional level, but subregional grouping is highly important This importance comes from a sharing of common scripts, cultural contexts and languages. It seems necessary to begin to analyse what is the most appropriate level of co-operation at these different levels.

Africa

Fatima Seye-Sylla

Throughout the world, both in developing and in more advanced countries, computers are used within the framework of research projects to develop new kinds of activities and materials. Some such experiments are being undertaken in Africa. One can cite the Logo project in Senegal on the introduction of computers into the primary school as the first of this kind, while the Aga Khan Foundation project in Kenya uses the computer to facilitate the teaching of various subjects in the secondary school.

At university and vocational school level, computer science is taught as a subject in such a way that the students become programmers or analysts or engineers. Within the Africa region, such countries as Côte d'Ivoire, Nigeria, Cameroon, Senegal, Kenya and Gabon have already set up computer science courses in schools. For such countries as the Central African Republic, the possibility of introducing informatics into education is a very new issue which has yet to be studied.

Whichever level of the school system is considered, African countries, no matter what their geographical situation, have encountered similar problems, whether they are Portugese-, French- or English-speaking. These problems can be analysed under two headings: the economical and the socio-cultural aspects.

Economic aspects

Financial considerations do not allow African countries to face up to the crucial problems which are linked to the introduction of computers into education. These problems are discussed below.

Lack of developed human resources

In general, there are very few computer specialists in Africa. At university level, the whole Africa region suffers from a shortage of teachers of computer science, for several reasons.

The brain-drain, because of the poor environment. Students go to Western countries with high expectations of being useful once they return to their own countries. However, upon returning, there is the shocking realization that there is no one for these bright thinkers to talk with regarding their work and aspirations. If we look at how scientists (or experts within any domain) really work, we find that they do not operate in a vacuum. A scientist operates within a rich network which is comprised both of other scientists and of the technologies on which each scientist relies. For these reasons, specialists go back to Europe or the United States, for a richer environment and better earning.

Poor pay. Teaching itself does not provide much money compared to working in a private company. For this reason, computer specialists might prefer to make more money outside teaching.

Computer science specialists are not teacher-oriented. Rather, they are work-oriented because, as noted above, African universities and vocational schools prepare high level technicians (programmers, analysts and engineers) who are ready to operate on computers full time, but who are not necessarily ready to communicate with people.

Scarcity of computer science courses. Many students cannot have access to computer science courses because of the severe educational requirements (high score in mathematics, difficult entrance tests in universities and public vocational schools, and high tuition fees in the private schools). At the primary and secondary levels, teacher resistance to the use of computers in schools remains a serious problem. It therefore becomes very difficult to convince them about the value of using computers in education. It is even more difficult to train them on a regular basis, if incentives are not provided to stimulate them. As in many countries throughout the world, teachers are indifferent to any kind of change in schools due to the fact that they are not involved in the making of the change; they are not the decision-makers, but merely the agents to carry out the change, whether they like it or not.

The lack of computer specialists able to conceive and design computer software and/or hardware is also a problem, as existing materials do not suit the region's needs; they do not take into account the African physical conditions – heat, dust, shortage of electricity and sand – all of which increase the cost of maintenance.

Maintenance is expensive. In the schools which use computers, it is very unusual to have an expert in computer maintenance and thus an expensive maintenance contract has to be signed with private companies to ensure that the computers work properly. Furthermore, spare parts to repair computers and peripherals are not easily accessible to African countries. Because they are imported from abroad, they remain very expensive.

Lack of financial resources

All the problems mentioned above are largely related to the lack of financial resources. With sufficient financial resources, more people could be trained in computer science, either abroad or on the spot by using visiting lecturers.

The problems related to teacher training would be resolved easily if one could satisfy the teachers' aspirations, mainly involving promotion after training.

At primary and secondary levels, African countries do not have enough classrooms. Thus, there are too many children in one class. This makes it even more difficult to use computers in schools. Maintenance costs usually go beyond the original estimate (10 per cent of the purchase cost) because of the physical conditions mentioned above.

If the means were available, one could create sophisticated environments appropriate for the computer, with air conditioning, isolation from heat, dust and sand, provision of regulated electricity and supply of enough spare parts for computer maintenance and repair.

Socio-cultural aspect

Software is not adapted to the African social context. Because it is conceived and designed abroad, it does not take into account indigenous thinking, beliefs and feelings. For example, in some educational software, mostly interactive, the computer reactions to the users' answers can be very discouraging to an extent; some teachers are unwilling to pursue the work because they feel some kind of frustration. Examples of this problem can be found within the exercises built into the software itself. Educational software dealing with rockets, snowmen and other Western features will be easily understood by Western children, who might even improve the learning environment by adding other related examples. The African child will have to spend much more time trying to understand this novel environment. The reverse would also be true – a computer micro-world made by African specialists would be troublesome to foreign children.

For many people, computers are seen as a way of getting a job after school. Because of the financial problems mentioned above, the use of computers in schools is so selective in African countries that parents who do not have the financial resources to send their children to the schools (mainly private) which are already equipped with computers, react negatively to the partial introduction of computers into the education system. They are not ready to accept the idea of following the different steps (pilot projects, extension and generalization) which are considered to be the right way to introduce a new tool or subject in any sector. Within the Senegalese Logo project, many parents came to complain about the choice of the pilot schools because their own children did not have access to computers.

The Aga Khan Foundation's project, which introduced the micro-computer to enhance teaching in their Kenyan secondary schools is the first major project of this type in East Africa. Since the early 1970s, the University of Nairobi has co-operated with other Nairobi schools to teach informatics. According to one specialist involved, because Kenya inherited the British exam-oriented school system, parents give much more value to academic education than to technical and agricultural education. Thus, even though the specialist was prepared to help teachers to use the computer to promote thinking among the students, she had instead to help teachers and students to use the computer to master the syllabus. Thus the computer was used to master a specific type of subject and not to create a stimulating learning environment, or to be taught as a subject itself (Dr. Mubina Kirmani, personal communication).

Prospects

The prospects for African countries are not yet well defined. Pilot projects do exist (Kenya, Gabon and the Côte d'Ivoire) but few countries have a national policy for the introduction of informatics into education. Senegal's policy really started in 1988 with the creation of an Informatics Department within the government. The Senegalese policy has to take into account the results of the ongoing pilot project 'Computers in Education', which started in 1982 at the primary school level. The plan is to introduce computers into the entire education system progressively, from the primary school to university. Even though computer science is already being taught at the university and vocational schools levels, the problems indicated above have to be addressed with the participation of the relevant departments.

The following suggestions are made in view of the economical situation of Africa, the evolution of technology and the author's experience in the field of computers in education, during six years in Africa and in the United States. The suggestions or solutions to the problems are mainly based on research, training, the raising of consciousness and the creation of a learning body to promote co-operation at different levels.

At the regional and sub-regional levels

The shortage of developed human resources can be solved through regional and sub-regional co-operation. The first step will be to set up a database on existing specialists at national level. Data collection is sometimes a difficult task. At the university level, it is possible to make a list of the teaching staff with their specifications. A complementary issue will be to select a body of young students (say 50 to 100) at schools abroad, with the specific mandate of building an infrastructure upon their return to their own country. One can guard against) litism by choosing students who are academically qualified (rich or poor, male or female), as well as students who are willing to collaborate with their peers. Such a body of students will have an ambitious mandate – to shape the future of their country. This commitment to their country should take a variety of forms. Some graduates will find themselves in the universities, others in business or in government. What they must share is the desire to serve their mother country in a capacity in which they feel they can provide the most productive service. This body of students will interact with the specialists already listed in the universities and research centres. This collection of data will feed the national database, which should be computerized and permanently updated.

The second step will be to build a network linking the national databases to help create a learning body to promote the exchange of information and experiences among countries at sub-regional and regional levels. Each specialist would be able to profit from the others' experiences.

There is a computer science school at the sub-regional level in Gabon (for Burkina Faso, the Central African Republic, Chad, Côte d'Ivoire, Gabon, Mauritania, Mauritius, Niger and Senegal). A teacher-training programme to train teachers and to strengthen the school's capacity could be introduced by providing the necessary funds to build the required infrastructures.

At the national level

In addition to the computerized database of present and future specialists, it is very important to set up a research laboratory at national level, with a core of researchers of different competencies (computer scientists, psychologists, specialists in linguistics and sociology, and teachers of various subjects) and equipped with computers of different makes. The laboratory team will be in charge of testing educational software and hardware, evaluating them and making recommendations to schools. The team of researchers will produce a standardization guide to be followed by the producers of computer materials and a users' manual for the materials (software and hardware) which they judge adequate for the country, with or without modification.

A laboratory for the maintenance of computers and peripherals should be set up with high level technicians and the necessary equipment. The training of these technicians should be undertaken by computer manufacturers or by their representatives in the country.

It would be of great help if an assembling factory could be implemented for at least each sub-region to construct computers using spare parts imported from abroad. This would provide jobs and cut down the cost of computers in the long run.

At university level, African governments should agree to release funds to send students abroad for the specific goal of being future university teachers in computer science, with enough incentives to avoid the brain-drain. Planning for this kind of training should be established. Here is a suggestion: for five successive years, the countries which already have graduates in computer science can send five engineers to a specialized computer-science teacher-training school each year. The press should help to educate the lay people on the use and utility of computers, using national languages to show that computers are only tools to achieve a goal and do not necessarily provide a job. Citizens must be made aware of the necessity of introducing computers into schools if Africa is not to lag behind the rest of the world.

Conclusion

Computers are still expensive for developing countries and one might argue that instead of acquiring computers, these countries should build more schools, acquire more textbooks, set up a family-planning policy to control population growth, invest more in the rural area to promote self- sufficiency, find a way to release women from their daily workload to favor their enrolment in schools, increase women's participation in the development process and plan for the eradication of illiteracy.

But can Africa remain indifferent to this technology revolution? Should Africa follow, one by one, the steps of the developed countries? This would be the best way to remain the slave of the tool, rather than its master. Ready-made computer hardware and software would then be used just as they are imported from abroad.

Can Africa be isolated from the other continents which are already computerized? As mentioned earlier, the African region sends students abroad. In almost all the universities in Europe and the United States, students work with computers; they master the computer, either as simple users or as specialists. Will these students come back to their home countries and not use the skills they have learned, or will they prefer to stay abroad and be able to do what they want and communicate with their peers? I think this will lead to a waste of money, time and energy. Is Africa going to deny the efficiency of computers and not use them and profit from them, because it is poor? Since we are poor in natural resources, I think the best way to improve the economy is to develop and use human resources. Why cannot Africa use computers to increase productivity, to set up computerized databases on specialists and institutions in order to facilitate networking and the exchange of information and experiences? By managing and sensitizing the few developed human resources we have, it is possible to build a very powerful infrastructure that would help to develop Africa.

Even though the Africa Region is poor, objectives can be achieved if the political will exists. In any kind of activity, priorities have to be established within a nation, a region and a sub-region. If African countries want to develop the human resources through education, which is a factor of sustainable economic and social development, they will have to put their maximum efforts together to achieve this goal.

Arab States

Samir Qasim Fakhro

One of the most important challenges in development is that of manpower development. In informatics, training qualified man-power in sufficient numbers has proved to be essential to its development. Hence the strong relationship established between informatics and education since the early stages of this new field.

The Arab States have already initiated numerous programmes to introduce informatics into several spheres of services and activities. Some have also proceeded to explore the introduction of informatics at university level and in some institutions of middle and higher learning. Extensive work has been done to provide means for developing such low skilled manpower as junior programmers, operators and support personnel. Nevertheless, the need for manpower remains far greater than the supply (UNESCO, 1986).

The visions of the various Arab States on how to proceed with this vital matter diverge considerably. Each state has a different orientation as to where to place the resources, what language to use, what software to be developed and used, and who will train the teachers and with what. The need for research and development in the areas of Arabic linguistics and informatic adds an extra factor of divergence to the decisions of these countries. We shall focus below on the use of informatics in the second level of the education system of the Arab States. There are two reasons for this. First, very little effort has been made to introduce informatics into the primary education of the Arab states (for example, Iraq and Morocco). Second, the majority of Arab universities have followed international trends while developing their computer science and engineering programmes, and while introducing introductory computer courses into the curricula of their various teaching disciplines. This tendency can be attributed to the desire of these universities to obtain recognition by international evaluating bodies. In addition, the great majority of Arab universities are currently using either English or French as their language of insruction.

Thus, the use of informatics in the majority of Arab universities is similar in many ways to its use in universities in the other regions of the world.

It must, however, be mentioned here that during the last few years, universities in several Arab states have launched educational and training programmes, as well as research and consultancy projects, in order to help enhance the use of informatics in the educational systems of these countries.

Typical trends and situations in the use of informatics in education

The discussions below are based on the reports published by UNESCO and other regional organizations (Chamma'a et al., 1986; Mandurah and Rehab, 1989; Al-Kasimi and Rida, 1987; Gheith et al., 1987.), as well as the proceedings of several regional and subregional conferences which were held recently in the Arab Region (*Experiences of...*, 1989; Fakhro, 1989). The findings can be summarized as follows.

First, although some fourteen Arab states have recently started to use informatics in secondary education in accordance with high-level policy decisions made by their respective governments, it is quite noticeable from reports of member states of the Islamic Educational, Scientific and Cultural Organization (ISESCO) that only a few of these states actually possess national plans for the introduction of informatics into their educational systems.

Second, all fourteen Arab states teach informatics as a subject; almost all use BASIC as a programming language; a few also teach Arabized LOGO (for example, Morocco). Iraq has adopted the ALKHAWARIZMI Arabized language. Countries such as Iraq, Jordan, Egypt, Saudi Arabia and Kuwait have also prepared teaching manuals.

Third, concerning teacher training in informatics, a number of points were made. Very few states were able to recruit teachers who had already undergone sound training in informatics (for example, Bahrain). Other states have opted for opening teacher education programmes in informatics at their colleges of education (for example, Saudi Arabia). The majority of Arab states provided the teachers of other subjects (for example, mathematics and physics) with training sessions varying between one month and two years in length, after which they were asked to teach informatics (for example, Iraq, Jordan, Egypt and Tunis).

Fourth, concerning equipment and relevant facilities, all of the countries teaching about informatics provide premises especially fitted for computer use and these same premises are used for computing practice. For example, such countries as Algeria, Iraq and Egypt have already invested considerably in computer hardware, purchasing a variety of compatible hardware in bulk quantities. There is also a great variation in the amount of computer hardware per country. However, only a few countries have facilities for connecting computers within a local network at the level of school (for example, Kuwait, the United Arab Emirates and Egypt). Several Arab states have established computer clubs for students' hobbies and projects (for example, Jordan, Bahrain, Morocco, Tunisia and Kuwait).

Finally, almost no Arab state is currently using informatics as a tool for teaching or learning on a significant scale.

Restraints and prospects for introducing and using informatics in education

Use of informatics as educational tool

It is apparent that the use of computers as educational tools is very limited in the Arab states. In order to overcome this acute problem, it is recommended that regional or sub-regional centres are established to address the problems discussed below (Dress et al., 1987.).

Hardware. Measures will have to be taken to limit the effects of the problems entailed by the use of disparate hardware, both in countries already using equipment as well as those in the process of acquiring the necessary hardware. In any case, a flexible system (with a sufficient amount of compatible hardware) will have to be installed in order to provide sufficient assisted learning and training facilities for students and teachers alike.

Teacher training on the use of informatics in education. Training should be provided for informatics teachers as well as for teachers of various subjects who need to use informatics as an instructional tool. Both categories of teachers need adequate initial training and complementary training in order to be able to participate in teams entrusted with producing and/or evaluating educational software.

Software development and production. Along with the training system, it is necessary to create a system that will promote the development and use of educational software. It would be quite improper to use the computer for programming purposes only, although this temptation is understandable when good software is rare. Such software should therefore be produced as soon as possible. The teams entrusted with this task might consist of computer professionals, educators and teachers of the relevant subjects in the school curricula.

The problem of dissemination and documentation of Arabic software (including educational software) is real and always hard to solve. Particular attention must be paid to this difficulty as it necessarily affects the efficiency of the work of users of informatics in schools (either students or teachers of the various subjects).

Given the scope of the software problems, it would be advisable to organize exchange programmes among Arab states, as well as between these states and developed countries in other regions.

Research work. Educational research work is usually carried out early in the process of introducing informatics into education. It will have to be recognized, promoted and developed, so that local needs may be better determined in order to pinpoint training objectives. Educational research work can be linked to an incitement structure for software production. It will also have to include an assessment of the educational software used.

Evaluation. The final problem to be raised is not the least. Regardless of the objectives set and the modalities adopted for educational software production and teacher training, it is necessary to assess the efficiency and continuity of such systems through the use of various evaluation measures (Dress et al., 1987.).

Introducing informatics as a subject

Optimum education entry level. Almost all the Arab states have introduced informatics as a subject only in the second level of their education systems. The main reasons for this are the high costs incurred in spreading the use of informatics to lower educational levels, the level of maturity of the secondary-school students and the serious lack of manpower needed to teach informatics in the primary level and intermediate level schools.

Informatics curricula for general education. Informatics curricula in second-ary-level education have to include the following components (Chamma'a et al., 1986): knowledge and skills of hardware use; knowledge and skills for the use of applications packages (for example, word processing, spread-sheet, graphics and databases); computer-based instructional applications (to help use informatics for learning about all disciplines); knowledge and skills of programming; and emphasis on the socio-economic effects of informatics in the society. The last component has often been missing from the informatics curricula of many Arab states.

Programming languages. Two basic questions ask what is the most suitable programming language for each educational level in the Arab states and should the programming languages be Arabized or not? In order to address these questions, the following suggestions are made (Mandurah and Rehab, 1989; Al-Jaberi et al., 1987.). At the primary level (Grades 1–6), only the Arabized LOGO programming language should be used. At the second level (Grades 7–12), programming in BASIC is highly recommended. Using Arabized BASIC is still a debatable issue, although some Arabized versions of BASIC are being used in several Arab states (for example, ALKHAWA-RIZMI and SAKHAR BASIC). Other Arabized programming languages have also been introduced for specific hardware (for example, Al-FARABI and Al-QAWL.). Although some experts have recommended the use of PASCAL (since it is a structured programming language) for students in Grades 10–12, BASIC still prevails as the most economical language to be used in teacher training and student education at the second level.

Teacher training in the field of informatics in education. The experiments in progress concerning the introduction of informatics into the education systems of the Arab states have confirmed that the availability of adequate hardware, good curricula and techniques is not enough to ensure the successful introduction of informatics into education. In addition, informatics teachers, as well as those using informatics as an educational tool, should already have received a sound training (Mandurah and Rehab, 1989; Dress et al., 1987.).

Training of teachers in informatics involves two categories of teachers: those who have already been trained in a particular subject and who will be offered complementary training in informatics, and those already (initially) trained in informatics. As far as the first category is concerned, senior officials in several Ministries of Education in Arab states are tempted to restrict complementary training in informatics to teachers of scientific subjects, particularly to those specializing in mathematics or physics. Experience has shown that such a trend is neither justified nor advisable. As for the second category, the personal interest of the recruited teachers in the teaching profession has to be supported by a training workshop in teaching methods and practices.

It should be noted here that almost all Ministries of Education in Arab states have difficulty either in keeping in service qualified teachers who are specialized in informatics or in bringing trainee teachers up to the desired standard. In an attempt to solve such a problem, a few Arab Universities have already launched specialized programmes in their colleges of education for graduate teachers in informatics. Also, the Ministers of Education in the Arab Gulf states decided at their 1989 Bahrain conference to establish such programmes in their states.

Training of teachers in the use of informatics as an educational tool concerns teachers of all school subjects who will have to use computers and introduce informatics into their educational practices. Basic training and complementary training for in-service teachers should be considered separately. As far as basic training is concerned, the use of informatics and its educational applications should be made available to the maximum number of teachers in all subjects. This is needed to extend computer literacy to all school teachers. As for complementary training, it may be provided to some teachers only so that they may participate later in the teams entrusted with the development of educational software.

Many Arab states have already held many basic teacher training workshops. However, the majority are still far from witnessing the participation of their trained teachers in educational software development teams. Regional co-operation appears to be the best possible solution to this problem, as will be explained in detail below.

Regional co-operation among Arab states

Current situation

Several organizations have contributed to the development of strategies and plans for the introduction of informatics into the second level of the education systems of Arab states. These organizations include UNESCO, the Arab League Educational, Cultural, and Scientific Organization (ALECSO), ISESCO and the Arab Bureau of Education for the Gulf States (ABEGS), as well as such funding agencies as the United Nations Development Programme (UNDP) and the Arab Fund for Social and Economic Development (AFSED).

The following activities conducted by the above organizations are cited as examples (*Experiences of...*, 1989; Mandurah and Rehab, 1989). In Qatar (1985), ALECSO and ABEGS held a technical work-shop to discuss the use of informatics, both as a subject and as a tool in the educational systems of the Arab states. In Algeria (1985), UNESCO held a technical workshop for experts, in order to discuss basic issues on the use of informatics in the education systems of Arab states. These issues included: 'Informatics and Arabization', 'The Production and Distribution of Quality Educational Software for Arab Countries' and 'Manpower Development and Training'. In Morocco (1987), ISESCO held a symposium on the 'Educational Applications of the Computer'. The participants were able to reach an agreement on a unified strategy for the introduction of informatics into general education in Islamic Countries. In Tunis (1987), ALECSO – in co-operation with ABEGS and AFSED – published a model plan for the use of informatics in education systems of the Arab states. In Bahrain (1988), ABEGS held a technical workshop on the use of informatics in education. The participants agreed that every Arab state must adopt a national plan for the introduction of informatics into its educational system. Participants also recommended that ABEGS should establish a centre for the development of the use of informatics in the education systems of the Arab Gulf states.

In May 1986, UNDP approved the funding of a preparatory assistance project, to be undertaken by UNESCO, to make investigation missions to the Arab states, in order to establish the feasibility of a regional project for the introduction of informatics into the region's education systems. The project design document, as well as the reports on the field survey (published in 1986) carried positive findings and confirmed the feasibility of such a project (Chamma'a et al., 1986).

The need for regional co-operation

Regional projects for the introduction of informatics into the education systems of Arab states are needed for the following reasons (UNESCO, 1986; Fakhro, 1987). The sclution to the special problems associated with the Arabic linguistic-cultural environment, education and informatics is likely to be similar for the majority of the requirements of the countries of the region. The relatively low level of development of informatics technologies in the region makes it paramount to establish regional projects in order to optimize the return on the financial and human effort investments. The return will be in the form of impact on the education system of the Arab states. The increasingly expensive requirements to develop courseware, software and training materials for this educational process, in any language, make it essential that resources, know-how and products be shared in a complementary fashion to ensure the long range growth and survival of informatics in the region's education systems. The proper and speedy utilization of relatively limited international know-how and expertise that can be brought to assist in the implementation of such regional projects is needed.

Possibilities for regional co-operation

UNESCO's proposed regional project. Based on a survey by UNESCO consultants in 1986, it was concluded that many Arab states were wining to collaborate in any regional effort that would bring about the transfer of know-how and technology, and in the resolution of some of the more chronic technical problems arising from the introduction of informatics into education. These states emphasized the need for urgent action on any level to initiate work in this area. The majority visited indicated that policy on a high level has already been enacted to pursue actively programmes and projects in informatics, particularly in education (UNESCO, 1986; Chamma'a et al., 1986). However, the changing regional programme priorities of the UNDP and its financial constraints prevented this project from being funded by the UNDP.

ALECSO's regional plan. In 1987, ALECSO proposed to the Arab states a model national plan for the introduction of informatics into their education systems. This plan has already been approved by AFSED (*Experiences of...*, 1989).

ABEGS proposed regional centre. In 1988, ABEGS proposed to the Arab Gulf states the establishment of a centre for the development of the use of informatics in the education systems of these countries (Mandurah and Rehab, 1989).

AFSED regional centres. In 1988, AFSED approved the funding of a project for the establishment of two regional centres for the development of Arabic educational software and Arabic administrative software, respectively. The two centres, in two chosen countries of the region, have yet to be launched.

Obstacles and prospects for regional co-operation

In the absence of any common international or regional forum for collaboration at this stage, many Arab states have embarked on a limited attempt to push ahead with the introduction of informatics into education. These countries have also indicated their willingness and desire to join in collaborative regional or sub-regional projects, once that becomes a reality. It must be noted, however, that any regional or sub-regional project has to be geared to benefit each state individually, before one can expect them to share their vital resources on a regional level (UNESCO, 1986).

As a concluding remark, it must be emphasized that such a regional project will have little chance of success without the active participation and full involvement of such funding agencies as UNDP and AFSED.

Latin America

Marco Murray-Lasso

Latin America is a region composed of developing countries in various stages of development. One of its characteristics is the mixture of a small minority of wealthy people living together with a large majority of poor people, with a relatively thin middle class. The difference between the 'haves' and the 'have-nots' is very marked and one of its manifestations is the application of information technology in education. One can find private bilingual schools using the most recently developed technology, both hardware and software, in the same city block as a state school which has no budget to acquire chalk and paper, and for which such items have to be provided by the Parents' Association.

Most of the region is heavily in debt to international financial institutions, foreign governments and private foreign banks, and because of the service of this debt, there is a large negative flow of capital from the region to the developed world. Mexico, one of the large countries in the region, has been in the news recently because of a deal with many foreign financial institutions, by means of which the country's foreign debt was consolidated, because it was widely held that Mexico could not afford to repay it. This deal is a candidate for use as a model for several other Latin American countries which are similarly indebted to the advanced nations, a condition which has created a financial nightmare for all countries in a similar situation. Teachers have fared worse than the average worker and education budgets per student have suffered correspondingly. The Mexican situation, is not significantly different from that of such other large debt-ridden countries as Brazil, Venezuela, Argentina and Peru. Other countries, such as Paraguay, Haiti, Ecuador and Nicaragua, are going through even worse times.

Widening the gap between the 'haves' and the 'have-nots'

One of the consequences of the situation described above is that state schools are seen to be of such low quality, because of the lack of human, financial and material resources, that the economically powerful have created a private school system that differs greatly from the state system. It is not uncommon in the private schools to find a computer laboratory with thirty to fifty computers, in which a computer co-ordinator provides interactive contact of one to two hours weekly for every student. Although the use of the computer is often not very creative and a lot of time may be spent with games of little educational value, some of the better schools provide an educational use of the computer as creative as that of the advanced nations.

In contrast, state schools either have no computers or one computer for the whole school, giving the students essentially no interaction with the machines. This, coupled with the fact that the students of the private schools often have a computer at home which gives them the opportunity of additional interaction, is spreading the 'information culture' much more rapidly among the economically powerful than among the poor. The result is an increasing widening of the cultural and economic gap between the 'haves' and the 'have-nots'. Thus, what we are seeing in Latin America is that a technology, which was believed to have the potential for closing the gap between the social classes, is in fact widening it.

What we have described within a country is, of course, also happening between countries. The more advanced nations are using information technologies to further their cultural and economic advantages over the less developed countries. This was widely recognized at UNESCO's Education and Informatics congress (International Congress..., 1989*a*).

Trends in the use of computers in Latin America

One of the principal complaints about the use of computers in education in Latin America is the lack of detailed information (Oteiza M. 1987). Since there are wide differences between countries in the region as well as within individual countries, this section can only indicate some general trends which are due to the social and economic situation that typically prevails in the region. The first that can be pointed out is the much higher student/keyboard ratio than that of developed countries. Part of the story has to do with the much broader base of the population pyramid, due to the higher birthrate in the region. Thus, a higher proportion of the population is of school age in Latin America than in the developed countries. Furthermore, because of the difficult financial conditions that the Latin American countries are experiencing, the budget per student allocated to the introduction of computers into state schools in Latin America is considerably less than that in developed countries and of such a proportion that the ratio of students per keyboard makes it impossible to achieve a reasonable interaction of the students with the machines. Hence, in countries such as Mexico, the style of use of computers in state schools has definitely been chosen as 'group interaction' ' as opposed to 'personal interaction'.

In the Mexican approach, the teacher is the one who touches the keyboard and the computer serves as a prop to sustain the discussion about the topic which is being taught. Because the whole group has to be able to see the screen and since there is only one computer in the front of the classroom, the text has to be displayed in very large letters, thus making it very difficult to exhibit detailed explanations or illustrations. In other countries, where it is desired to maintain personal interaction with the computers, budget restrictions force the introduction of computers into schools to be limited to pilot studies or select groups. As mentioned above, the situation in the private schools is quite different and the style of use of the computer in school is generally of the personal interactive type. Besides these differences, relating to personal and group interaction, there are various ways of thinking about the use of computers in education.

The most popular approach to the use of the computer in education in Latin America is its application in administration (Aguilar Villalobos and Diaz Barriga, 1987, 1988). This includes the central government education authority and the universities. The next most popular application is the teaching of programming, especially at secondary and university levels. Depending on whether we are considering general or vocational/professional education, topics may include generalities about the computer, computer history and some general programming languages, such as BASIC or Pascal, or more specialized languages, such as FORTRAN for engineering or COBOL for business. Generally, some additional topics, such as flow-charting, algorithms or database also included. In addition to teaching programming, some teachers use the computer in the secondary school as a tool and introduce such packages as word processors, spreadsheet and database managers, as well as graphics packages of various kinds.

So far we have been referring to the use of the computer in regular school work. The teaching of computing through extracurricular programmes is also popular in Latin America. In Mexico, for example, there is a programme for children up to 16 run by the Mexican Academy of Sciences in conjunction with the Ministry of Education's National Library System, in which children learn Logo, word processing, spreadsheets and databases, out of school hours, on computers located in public libraries (Mexican Academy..., 1984–1989).

In Latin America, many believe that Logo is a good vehicle for the introduction of computers into education, particularly at the primary level, and some translations into Spanish the Logo language (developed in Chile and Argentina) have become relatively popular. In Costa Rica, the National Project on Computers in Education is centred around Logo. Logo has been found very useful for teaching hearing-impaired children who are integrated with regular children in public schools in Mexico City (Mexican Academy..., 1984–1989). Nonetheless, BASIC is still by far the most popular language used in education in Latin America, probably due to the fact that it is almost always the resident language in the microcomputer and does not have to be bought separately. In fact, using the BASIC resident in ROM and centring the teaching around simple programming projects, one can avoid having to buy disk drives, which are often more expensive than the computer itself and more prone since they have moving parts, to maintenance problems.

Some primary schools, besides Logo and BASIC, use CAI packages. These are, however, often in foreign languages or are in very poor translations; they are used mainly by private schools. The development of educational software in either Spanish or Portuguese has been very limited (Aguilar Villalobos and Diaz Barriga, 1987). Many factors explain this, such as the fact that the development of educational software, especially at the primary- and secondary-school level, is not seen as good business when compared to the traditional markets of the industrial and service sectors. This is because of the scarcity of computers for schools and of funds to acquire software, which is considered very expensive by the education community. Some of these factors also apply outside Latin America, as was shown by the preliminary survey on The Use of Information Technologies in Educational Systems (USEIT) conducted by UNESCO (International Congress..., 1989*b*, pp. 19–28). Some countries, notably Costa Rica, have very ambitious goals and are receiving help from manufacturers and foreign educational institutions. Others, such as Brazil and Cuba, are going it alone and doing well. It is widely acknowledged that Brazil is the most advanced country in the region in informatics and this is largely due to its aggressive and independent policy, supervised by a Ministry of Informatics. There are thus some places in the region where the way in which computers are being used in schools is very similar to that in advanced countries. This, however, is the exception rather than the rule; in general, Latin America lags considerably behind the advanced countries in the application of computers to education.

Some countries, such as Mexico, Argentina, Cuba, the Dominican Republic, Costa Rica, Venezuela and Brazil, have national policies for the introduction of computers into education, but in spite of the fact that they state that this introduction has a high priority for the country, the budgets allotted as a rule do not reflect the stated importance (Oteiza M. 1987; International Congress..., 1989*b*, pp. 19–28). Brazil, Costa Rica and Cuba are, however, exceptions; their national programmes have the enthusiastic support of the highest government officials, both in word and deed. Brazil has been able to create an indigenous microcomputer industry that manufactures a high percentage of the computers used in education. Mexico has also had similar programmes but has not persevered with them.

In general terms, there are very few teachers in Latin America who have received training for the appropriate use of computers in education. One study (Aguilar Villalobos and Diaz Barriga, 1987) estimates that no more than 2 per cent of the teachers have received training in the use of computers in education. Most teachers have received no training whatsoever and those who have received training have in many cases only received a few hours of superficial instruction. As in other regions, both developed and less developed, the lack of trained teachers is seen as one of the most difficult obstacles to the success of the use of computers in education. It is not difficult to diagnose the principal reasons why training programmes for teachers in

Latin America have been so scarce. The salaries the teachers earn usually force them to hold more than one job, leaving very little time for other activities. Educational authorities are pressed by the financial situation to get as many teaching hours from the teachers as they possibly can; hence, almost no time is allotted to in-service training of any sort. Much of the training is therefore done in the teachers' own time, which, because of the multiple-job condition, is practically non-existent. Those of us who have been involved in organizing symposia, seminars and similar meetings, have felt the difficulty in getting the teachers to attend the meetings, because lack of permission from their superiors. Although this complaint is also voiced sometimes by teachers in developed countries, the difference in the degree of the problem is quite substantial. The training question in Latin America is more a social and economic problem than one of having the initiative needed to organize courses.

One area in which the Latin American region competes in a relatively favorable light with the advanced countries is in the area of research. Because universities, whether state or private, are part of the) lite of Latin American society, they suffer from lack of resources much less than the primary and secondary schools. We thus see a good amount, comparatively speaking, of research activity in Latin American universities, with work of a quality similar to that of advanced countries (Academia Nacional..., 1987; Mexican Academy..., 1984–1989). In spite of this, the field of evaluation of this research leaves much to be desired (Oteiza M. 1987).

Some things that can be done

There has been relatively little international co-operation in the Latin American region notwithstanding the fact that many of the countries share the same language and cultural background. Some of the forms of co-operation, such as the use of computer networks for communication, have been much discussed, but little real action has followed. The same situation seems to be true for the development of educational software: the Instituto Latinoamericano de Comunicacion Educativa (ILCE) has done a fair amount of software development in the BASIC language for a special computer named Micro-SEP (based on a Radio Shack Color Computer). However, due perhaps to the special characteristics of the Mexican national project, which, as previously mentioned, is centred on group interaction, the programmes have been implemented only in Mexico (Sesión Anual Ordinaria.., 1987).

As has been mentioned at numerous meetings, there are obvious advantages to international co-operation in the area of computers in education, a fact that almost everybody acknowledges, but winds up not doing much about, notwithstanding several existing projects by the Organization of American States (OAS), UNESCO and the ILCE. There seems to be a need to research in detail why this should be so. Considerably more work is needed in the area of standardization, not only of equipment and the educational software that will run on it, but even more important, of educational aspects that are independent of the computer. Not even in the area of teaching mathematics, which appears to be a perfect candidate for international interchange of computerized educational materials, is there much real activity; discussions between countries in Latin America or with countries from other regions seems to be full extent of activity.

Perhaps it is necessary to create the conditions for the establishment of an educational computing market that would somehow resemble the textbook market. In the textbook market, at least at the university level, part of the success of some texts is due to the existence of international editorial boards which start by agreeing what a series of books should cover and at what levels, and move on to agree on such matters as style, adequate vocabulary for all the countries that use the same language, notation, level of rigour, etc. If similar editorial boards were established for educational materials, perhaps the road towards more collaboration would have fewer bumps. Other ideas that have been advanced in many meetings are the establishment of clearing houses of educational materials and information. In Colombia, the Grupo de Investigaci;n sobre Informática Educativa of the Universidad de los Andes publishes the *Boletín de Informática Educativa: Sistema de Información sobre informática Educativa (SIIE)*. ILCE has had a Documentation Centre since 1970.

An idea that has been tossed around is the joint development, between several countries, of a special educational computer with related peripheral equipment, aiming at large productions and low costs. Another activity ripe for international collaboration in Latin America, given the common language, is the joint preparation of training materials for teachers on the use of computers in education. As mentioned before, the need in Latin America for training teachers in computers in education is great, and its surface has not even been scratched. If we were to practise what we preach, we should be able to see the great potential of the computer as a help in this training. The possibility of sharing costs and of teachers receiving this training at their own pace – given the very limited free time they have on their hands – makes such a project doubly appealing.

References

Academia Nacional de Ingenieria [of Mexico]/National Research Council [of the United States] (1987) *Microcomputer Applications in Education and Training for Developing Countries. Proceedings of a Meeting on the Use of Microcomputers for Developing Countries.* Boulder, Colo. Westview Press.

Aguilar Villalobos, J. and Diaz Barriga, F. (1987) Experiencia en Computación Aplicada con Fines Educativos. *Revista Tecnología y Comunicación Educativas,* Vol. 2, Nos. 9–10, pp. 43–60. (1988) *Revista Tecnología y Comunicación Educativas,* Vol. 3, No. 11, pp. 43–57.

Al-Jabiri, M. R., Dress, F. As-Safar, I., Charter, I.M.C., El Asri, A.H., Ysewijn, P., al Khalifa, S.S., Houfaneh, M.M., Diallo, A. and Weaver, B. (1987) Elaboration of the Computer Science Curricula for General Education. In: *The Educational Applications of the Computer,* pp. 158–63. (Proceedings of the symposium organized by ISESCO in co-operation with the faculty of education of Mohammad V University, Rabat, 5–9 January, 1987).

Al-Kasimi, A. and Rida, A. (1987) Report on Computer Use in ISESCO Member Countries. In: *The Educational Applications of the Computer* pp.25–30. (Proceedings of the symposium organized by ISESCO in co-operation with the faculty of education of Mohammad V University, Rabat, 5–9 January, 1987).

Anderson, J., Boonme, N., Mahabala, H.N., Nishinosono, N. and Teodoro, E. (1986) *Developing Computer Use in Education: Guidelines, Trends and Issues.* Bangkok, APEID/UNESCO. (doc. BKAM/86/M/83–1200).

Barrington, J. (1989) Survey of events: Pacific Basin. *Comparative Education Review,* Vol. 33, No. 2, pp. 288–9.

Chamma'a, S., Fakhro, S., Nussair, Ziyoute, M. and Zouain, G. (1986) *Introduction of Informatics into the Education Systems of the Arab Countries.* Paris, UNESCO. (Reports of field visits to countries of the Arab Region)

Computers in Education: An Outline of Country Experiences (1985) Bangkok, ROEAP. (doc. BKA/85/M/254–1200.)

Computers in Education: Inventory of Training Institutions, Publications, Societies in Asia and the Pacific. (1986) Bangkok, ROEAP. (doc. BKA/86/M/498–500.)

Dress, F., Al-Jaberi, M.R., White, A.L., Rahman, A.H.A., Alvi, F., Al Musbahi, A.Z. and Wynands, A. (1987) Training of Instructors in the Field of the Educational Applications of the Computer. In: *The Educational Applications of the Computer,* pp. 152–7. (Proceedings of the symposium organized by ISESCO in co-operation with the faculty of education of Mohammad V University, Rabat, 5–9 January, 1987).

Experiences of Arab States in the Introduction of Computers into Schools. (1989) Cairo, Egyptian Computer Society.

Fakhro, S. (1989) A Proposed Model Plan for the Enhancement of the National Projects for the Introduction of Informatics into the Intermediate and Secondary Schools of the Arab Countries. *Risalat ul-Khaleej al-Arabi* (Riyadh), No. 29, pp. 83–95.

Fasano, C., Hall, N. and Cook, J. (1988) *Information Technology and Educational Services.* Canberra, Department of Employment, Education and Training.

Fitzgerald, D., Hattie, J. and Hughes, P. (1986) *Computer Applications in Australian Schools.* Canberra, Commonwealth Department of Education.

Frampton, A. (1989) Educational Computing in New Zealand. *Information Transfer*, Vol.9, No. 1, p. 37.

Gheith, M., Al Abd Allah, I.Y., Tagg, W. Loethe, H., Rida, A.R., Loum, S., Hassan, Y.S. and Al Haj Amar, B.O. (1987) Strategy for the Introduction of Computer Sscience in General Education. In: *The Educational Applications of the Computer*, pp. 147–51. (Proceedings of the symposium organized by ISESCO in co-operation with the faculty of education of Mohammad V University, Rabat, 5–9 January, 1987).

Gorny, P. (1989) Curriculum-Proposal for the Integration of Informatics into Engineering Programmes Offered at Colleges and Universities in Developing Countries. *Higher Education in Europe* (Bucharest), Vol. XIV, No. 2, pp. 51–9.

Gorny, P. (1991) Anforderungen an die Lehrerbildung Informatik. In: Burkert, J. and Perschke, R. Weiterentwicklung des Informatikunterrichts – Folgerungen aus der Sicht von Lehrerbildung und Wissenschaft, MatDiealien zur Schulentwicklung Heft 16. Hessisches Institut für Bildungsplanug und Schulentwicklung. Wiesbaden 1991. pp. 139–147*a*.

Guthrie, G. (1983) Policy Issues in Planning Secondary Teacher Training in Papua New Guinea. *South Pacific Journal of Teacher Education*, Vol. 11, No. 1, pp. 33–42.

Guthrie, G. (1985) The Role of the Teacher in National Development. *Papua New Guinea Journal of Education*, Vol. 22, No. 2, pp. 265–81.

Hall, N. (1982) Computers in Education Course. In: *Proceedings of the Fourth Annual Conference of the Computer Education Group of Victoria*. Melbourne, CEGV.

Hindson, C. (1985) Primary Teacher Training in Kiribati: the Biggest Little System in the World, *South Pacific Journal of Teacher Education*, Vol. 13, No. 2, pp. 44–53.

International Congress: Education and Informatics – Strengthening International Co-operation/Congrès international: (Éducation et informatique – vers une coopération internationale renforcée, Paris, 1989. (1989*a*) *Final Report*. Paris: UNESCO.

International Congress: Education and Informatics – Strengthening International Co-operation/Congrès international: Éducation et informatique – vers une coopération internationale renforcée, Paris, 1989*b* *Proceedings/Les Actes*, Vol. 1, pp. 1–383, Paris: UNESCO.

Laws, K. and Horsley, M. (1988) Practicum Experiences in the Cook Islands. *South Pacific Journal of Teacher Education*, Vol. 16, No. 2, pp. 43–55.

Lewis, R. (1990) The Ownership of Change: an Experiment in Experience Exchange. In: A. McDougall and C. Dowling (eds.), *Computers in Education. Proceedings of the IFIP TC 3 Fifth World Conference on Computers in Education – WCC90*, pp. 791–6, Amsterdam: Elsevier Science Publishers B.V.

Lovis, F. B. and Tagg, E. D. (eds.) (1988) *Computers in Education. Proceedings of the 1st European Conference on Computers in Education, Lausanne, 1988.* Amsterdam: North-Holland Pub. Co.

Lyudmila Zhivkova Institute. n.d. *Children in the Information Age: Opportunities for Creativity, Innovation and New Activities.* Sofia.

Mandurah, M. and Rehab, O. (1989) A Comprehensive Study about Computer Applications in Education with Emphasis on Past Experiences and Future Projects of the Arab Gulf States. *Risalat ul-Khaleej al-Arabi* (Riyadh), No. 29, pp. 99–183.

Mexican Academy of Sciences/Mexican Society for Computers in Education (SOMECE). 1984–1989. *Proceedings of the First through Fifth International Symposia on Computers in the Education of Children and Youngsters.* Mexico City. (in Spanish.)

Oteiza, M., F. (1987) Informatics and Education: the Situation in Latin America, *Prospects*, Vol. XVII, No. 4, pp. 547–52.

Owens, L. and Phillips, B. (1987) An Australian Teacher Education Workshop with Staff in an Indonesian College: Some Cultural Thoughts on Cross Cultural Communication. *South Pacific Journal of Teacher Education*, Vol. 15, No. l, pp. 29–49.

Papagiannis, G. J. and Milton, S. (1987) Computer Literacy for Development: an Evolving Metaphor. *Prospects*, Vol. XVII, No. 3, pp. 355–66.

Regional Seminar on Computer Educational Software Development, Evaluation and Dissemination, Tokyo, 1988. (1988) *Final Report.* Bangkok, PROAP/Japanese Council of Educational Technology Centres.

Sesión Anual Ordinaria del Consejo Directivo del ILCE (1987) *Tecnología y Comunicación Educativas*, Vol. 2, No. 8, pp. 18–35.

UNESCO (1986) *Introduction of Informatics into the Education Systems of the Arab Countries.* Paris, UNESCO. (Project design document)

UNESCO Principal Regional Office for Asia and the Pacific (1990) *Guidebook for the Development, Distribution and Evaluation of Educational Software.* Bangkok, UNESCO.

Wacquant, L. J. D. (1989) The dark side of the classroom in New Caledonia: Ethnic and Class Segregation in Noumea's Primary School System. *Comparative Education Review*, Vol. 33, No. 2, pp. 194–212.

CHAPTER FIVE

Prospects for international co-operation

Rhys Gwyn

The prospect of developing better means of international co-operation in respect of education and informatics is an attractive one. Given the very evident importance of informatics both in socio-economic development and as an educational tool, it makes a great deal of sense. To share developmental ideas and development costs, so as to ensure that young learners of all nations have the opportunity to benefit equally from the advances which informatics applied to education can bring to the classroom, is a vision entirely worthy of the UNESCO mandate.

Indeed, it is a vision which UNESCO has begun already to bring about, through important activities at regional and international levels, and we shall look at some of these in a moment. With luck and with collaborative goodwill all round, we may find in a few years time that the internationalist approach really has succeeded. Certainly it has some powerful forces behind it, not least of which is the power of the technology itself.

It is important to remember just how wide the range of technologies dealt with is. When discussing informatics in the classroom, we are no longer faced with the microcomputer alone, powerful tool though that is. Rather, we are looking at the whole gamut of information and communications technology – advanced processors, graphics adapters, networks, satellite communications – which is already installed in a great many classrooms and in use by pupils. Together these technologies make it possible for children in classes thousands of kilometres apart to work together almost as easily as though they were in adjoining classrooms. Such co-operation exists today and is an extremely attractive *modus operandi* in the classroom.

Moreover, it does not particularly need the permission of governments for it to happen.

As a consequence, there is already a *de facto* internationalization at the grass roots levels of many secondary and even primary classes which is far in advance of much thinking at official levels. Where the children are concerned, there is no problem (though in saying this, we have to note that the number of classrooms which currently enjoy international communication, while quite large in actual number is no more than a tiny fraction of classrooms worldwide).

We should not underestimate the power of the technology to drive policy in this way, from grass-roots up. Indeed, the underlying argument of this chapter is that the technology push is one of the most important characteristics of the whole informatics-in-education phenomenon, and that this push *is likely, for the foreseeable future, to be a more powerful force than the formulation of official policies*. The latter, it seems, are doomed to follow behind as realization of what the new information technologies have to offer to the classroom slowly permeates upwards.

However, our focus in this chapter is necessarily upon policy, specifically, the extent to which policies for internationalization may draw upon what has been learned from policies at national levels.

Two perspectives: the ideal and the real

There are two possible perspectives on this question: simplistic or ideal, identifying a goal towards which it is worth striving, and a realistic view, identifying the many hurdles which have to be overcome before we can ever hope to achieve the goal of internationalization.

Since we do not live in an ideal world, I deal relatively briefly with the first view.

The ideal approach

In an ideal world, all the rich countries would have far-sighted policies for the development of the classroom uses of informatics. These policies would be based on a number of factors.

There would be, for example, a constant monitoring at national level of the directions in which hardware and software development were going. As a consequence, ministries would know, a year or so in advance, what were likely to be the technological platforms upon which the next round of developments would be based. Research and development (R&D) programmes would be well in hand to ensure that appropriate software applications, tailored to educational needs, would be available as the new technologies themselves became available; these R&D programmes would lean heavily upon pedagogical research. Financial plans would be in place to ensure a phased release of new levels of technologies into classrooms, so that any one classroom could expect a complete replacement of its new information and communications technologies (NICT) within a five-year cycle. Moreover, there would be an on-going programme of teacher training, and of teacher-trainer training, to support the optimum take-up of the new developments in the classroom.

While this comprehensive and planned development was being undertaken by the rich nations, they would also take pains to pass on the benefits of their investments to the developing world. Working through an agency such as UNESCO, the rich nations would make available their pedagogic research, their software development, their support materials and their teacher-training programmes. They would do so because this was educationally a worthwhile thing to do and because they genuinely wished to provide equal educational opportunities for children all over the world. They might, perhaps, not provide the hardware as well, but evidence suggests that the hardware investment is not the most difficult part of the burden to bear. In such a climate of internationalism, there would be a slow but steady movement towards the eventual equalization of educational opportunity across the globe.

This is, of course, an ideal scenario. It is, therefore, an unrealistic one. There are at least two important factors which have to be recognized for the barriers to international co-operation which they in fact are.

THE COMPETITIVE ADVANTAGE

We must first recognize that an effective, functioning policy for the use of informatics in education is a potentially important strategic weapon in economic development. This fact is not recognized as explicitly as it might be, even by the developed nations – or if it is, their levels of investment do not suggest as much. But it is recognized that maintaining a competitive edge in the uses of NICT, and preferably in their development also, is a prerequisite of maintaining economic advantage. A clear indicator of this recognition is the very high level of investment made by the European Community across a wide spectrum. This includes investment in both leading-edge technology development and in training for technology; such investment is targeted entirely at creating competitive advantage for Community economies (and Community economy, which is something else) as against the economies of North America and the Far East.

THE LACK OF CO-ORDINATED POLICIES

But there is, in fact, another barrier to a sharing of resources and development strategies between the rich nations and the emerging world. Despite what we have just said about the importance of NICT education and training in relation to national development, it seems that the rich nations currently do not have, in fact, much to offer in the way of co-ordinated policies.

This last remark is in no sense intended to be cynical; it is offered as a statement of fact. The steam has gone out of the movement for what used to be called 'IT in Education'.

This movement was at its strongest in the mid-1980s, and it was strong at both national and international levels. It was a period of enormous interest in the massive national programmes developed, par excellence, in France and the United Kingdom. These, and similar initiatives in certain states of the United States and some of the Canadian provinces, were given wide exposure by, for example, OECD in respect of the international scene while the Commission of the European Communities sponsored a whole series of conferences at the European level at which national Ministries vied with one another to demonstrate their commitment to the insertion of the new technologies into their education systems. It was a time of real excitement, of a real sharing of ideas, albeit among the haves rather than between the haves and the have-nots.

Similar developments were launched in Central and Eastern Europe. Countries such as Bulgaria made a major commitment to developing educational uses of NICT and large pan-European conferences were launched, with the aid of UNESCO. In the then USSR, a massive programme to introduce information technology across the schools of the entire country was set in motion.

The sweeping socio-political changes affecting Central and Eastern Europe in the last few years, and more recently in the Russian Federation, make it difficult to comment with precision on the current situation in these countries. In Western countries, however, it is clear that the impetus has gone. The showcase national programmes of France and the United Kingdom are no more; insofar as there is any continuity, they have been replaced by lesser programmes, mere holding operations which pay lip-service to the importance accorded the NICT in education, but not much more.

A number of things appear to have gone wrong. It is a time of recession and education budgets are hard-hit generally. In such times, it is not really surprising that the urgency of an area such as NICT, which is notoriously demanding of resources, may seem rather less than it did in a time of relative affluence – when school roofs need repairing and books are in short supply, it is not easy to commit large proportions of educational budgets to glossy new machines.

Moreover, one suspects that the enthusiasm of ministries began to decline once it became apparent just how expensive the new technologies really were. From a very early stage, there was a tendency to believe that an educational policy for NICT in education could be created more or less by making large numbers of machines available, and that it was not really necessary to address the major pedagogical issues raised by the use of the new technologies in the classroom, or even question much what kind of software was really required (the French programme was an honourable exception, or at least it was until budgets began to be slashed). It is incredible, for example, that throughout its existence, the much-vaunted Microelectronics Education Programme (MEP) in the United Kingdom did not see fit to make available a basic requirement such as a database program suitable for secondary school students and that the most important work in this area was done by the far-sighted co-ordinator of the MEP's Primary programme (itself an afterthought).

What became apparent was that the investment had to go on after the first round of machines had been bought. Microcomputers do wear out physically; what is more to the point, they become obsolete and need to be replaced on a planned cycle. Such replacement is expensive, to say the least. Moreover, there was a much greater investment needed, not only in software development as we have already seen but also in the very expensive field of teacher training and above all retraining (where some effort was in fact made). At the same time, areas such as research into the pedagogical implications of the uses of NICT were scarcely touched upon (as always there are exceptions, in this case for example work in Sweden on expert systems for use by pupils). The development that did occur, for the most part, lacked any solid basis of research.

It was clear that the budgetary demands were very great indeed and the impetus for development, somewhere, was lost. Somehow, the big national programmes were 'no longer necessary'; they had served their initial – consciousness- raising – purposes; responsibility, in the United Kingdom certainly, could now safely be passed over to the local (funding) authorities who could be entrusted to get on with the job. At least, that was the theory; the realities of recession tell a different story.

As a consequence, it is currently difficult to identify any clear national policies in the rich nations which could serve as a basis for the ideal solution of shared international dialogue. This is not to say that the dialogue is not possible. It is a dialogue that can be constructed, but not on the basis of a neat transfer of solutions that have been worked out by the developed nations at an official level and which are tailor-made for the needs of the developing world.

Reality is something different, and something more complex.

The real approach

Planning for the real world has to take account of a number of factors which do not fit easily into the ideal scenario.

First, what drives development in the world of information technology is software advance. Hardware advance is, of course, extremely important, and improvements in processor design and speed, in video displays, in dynamic memory and in external storage capacities contribute greatly to what actually becomes available to the user. But this is *only* the technology platform, and what is technologically possible in the field of microcomputing already outstrips our apparent capacity to exploit it to the full. What really moves us forward is the software development, because it is this that gives us access to the power of the technology. It is the ever more powerful databases, spreadsheets, wordprocessors, desktop publishing and graphics, and communications packages which serve as our point of entry to the phenomenal capacities of the current microprocessor.

Second, the thrust for software development does not come, nor will it come, from educational needs. Software development is mega-business, as important a commercial market as any, and the driving force for this market comes from the needs of commerce and industry. While many software companies – and hardware producers too – are very sympathetic towards and supportive of the needs of education and training, the real commercial interests lie elsewhere. (The fact that educators worldwide very often appear to think that the NICT industry owes them free hardware and software does not perhaps help to convince the commercial sector of the importance of the educational market.)

The implication of these two points is that any policy for development of the educational take-up of the NICT, be that policy national or international, must recognize that educational needs must be met as best as can be within a development climate which is driven by quite other considerations.

This is, as they say, the bad news. The good news is that the bad news is not necessarily bad news at all. A realistic policy for international development can be built, and built quite well, upon the recognition of the nature of the commercial marketplace for software. But it will not be a policy for co-operation simply between national ministries. Rather, it will have to be co-operation between groupings of ministries – perhaps even a global grouping – on the one hand and the software industry on the other. And to make such a co-operation work, the co-ordinating role of a body such as UNESCO is essential.

To substantiate such a claim, we need to look a little more closely at what has been learned from the experiences of the past decade.

Lessons from experience

Observers of the scene are in fact able to draw a number of important conclusions from the experiences of development at national and local levels since the early 1980s. These concern the substance of NICT development, its organization and, inevitably, its financing.

As we examine some of these learnings here, it is with the aim of identifying the most fruitful areas in which to explore the potential for international co-operation. Such co-operation will not be built easily, and it is essential to begin with areas which are likely to produce identifiable results.

Substance

Issues concerning the substance of NICT uses in education are addressed elsewhere in this book. It is necessary, however, to go over them briefly because they are central to the argument about co-operation with the software industry and central also to the view of international co-operation put forward here. Four points in particular stand out, concerning the role of CAL, informatics as a discipline, informatics as a tool and the on-screen environment. It may be that the third and fourth of these, especially, prove to be the most fruitful areas for international co-operation.

THE ROLE OF CAL

It is clear that CAL has a great deal to offer in the classroom. However, we need to be clear also about the sense in which the term is being used here.

There is the very general sense in which all learning activity using NICT may be regarded as computer-aided learning. But the more usual sense, and the one used here, is that which is more accurately caught by the American expression 'computer-aided instruction', i.e. those kinds of programmes in which the technology is utilized to provide a teaching (or training) function of one kind or another. Currently, such materials have reached a high standard of sophistication and they encompass, for example, reinforcement programs which have developed from early drill-and-practice approaches to interactive video programs which provide very clear training in both principles and practice in many areas. CAL/CAI has come a long way since its inception.

Experience from the substance of developments at national levels suggests, however, that this may not be the most fruitful area for the development of international co-operation. Two factors need to be considered very carefully.

One is that, despite the successful production of many CAL/CAI resources the research base is still relatively small. Very little is known about the interaction between, for example, individual learning styles and strategies of CAL program construction, or about the transferability of principles between instructional design based on static materials and that based on dynamic materials such as interactive video.

A second factor, which is perhaps more effectively a barrier to international transferability of CAL/CAI materials, is that they tend to be highly culture-specific.

This is not a matter of language alone: one thinks, for example, of programs used very successfully in the United States to promote reading skills in young learners, programs which could not possibly be used in the United Kingdom for a whole range of reasons which are almost indefinable but which have to do more with tone and with style than with the pedagogic principles employed. Other examples abound. It is well-known, for example, that interactive video materials designed in one European country for training in business practices cannot be adopted for use in another European country by the simple expedient of dubbing. Everything is 'wrong': furnishings, clothes and body language which are appropriate to one country appear immediately foreign in another. As a consequence, program-makers cannot dub but find in practice that they must re-shoot virtually all sequences.

The more important the human element in the training being given, the more difficult becomes the transfer from one national setting to another. Experience from interactive video-based training suggests that only in those cases where what is being imparted is the understanding of a purely scientific or technological *process* can such training shake off its cultural constraints; even then care has to be taken over the actual style of instruction being delivered.

There are doubtless many cases where CAL/CAI materials exist which are capable of being adapted from one country to another. In particular, it seems to be an area in which it would be well to encourage the maximum sharing of research into instructional design and into learner preferences. But if we are looking to initiate a more global approach to international co-operation and to identify strategies of collaboration capable of relatively rapid dissemination to the widest possible audience, then it may well be the case that we should not be looking to begin with CAL/CAI.

INFORMATICS AS A DISCIPLINE

When we examine the possibilities for co-operation in informatics as a discipline, the potential at once appears higher.

While the *use* of NICT applications is not culture-free, there is a great deal in the discipline of informatics which relates to formal reasoning and which is therefore less closely tied to cultural demands. However, we do have to take account of a number of different interpretations which may be put on the word 'informatics' itself.

A relatively straightforward case is that of the teaching of programming. Any chosen programming language is a closed world and the operations which are possible within that world are determined by its built-in logic. Very often, the 'words' of the language are a sub-set of English and it would be interesting to know to what extent this in itself may constitute a cultural barrier, but the set is always a very small one when compared with a natural language. The concepts upon which computer languages depend (representation of variables, repetition, testing for conditions, recursion and so on) transcend the natural language element.

It would seem likely, therefore, that this is an area in which, for example, training methodologies developed in respect of a particular language in one country might be relatively easily transferred into another. Nor is informatics confined to the teaching of computer languages. It involves the teaching of algorithmics and the point just made about particular languages is as valid for algorithmics also. Similarly, informatics involves an understanding of computer systems and their component parts (such as processor, dynamic memory, storage memory and display) and processes (such as input, processing and output). Here also there is a very high potential for sharing tested strategies for presenting information to learners and for developing understanding.

This is an important area – it would be a mistake to think that informatics is a domain to be studied only by those intending to follow careers in computer science. Taught properly, informatics gives all students an understanding of technology-based processes which are by now indispensable elements of modern life, and we may argue strongly for its inclusion in all secondary school curricula.

It is difficult to draw a neat line between this area, informatics as a discipline, and the next, informatics as a tool. The distinction between them is blurred and the fact that they are treated separately here does not imply quite so strong a separation in practice.

INFORMATICS AS A TOOL

When we do focus upon informatics as a tool, the prospects for international co-operation begin to look very interesting indeed.

We start with a definition: by 'informatics as a tool' is meant the use of NICT applications to facilitate learning in areas of the curriculum other than informatics itself. It is at this point that the relationship between software development and the needs of industry, commerce and research suddenly becomes highly relevant to the needs of the classroom.

The driving force behind commercial software development is the constant need for better and faster tools for the processing of information. If we set aside the specialist needs of advanced scientific research, the models of information processing which the NICT make available to the world of industry and commerce are well known: they are the database and the spreadsheet, the wordprocessor and the design package. Add to these communications software and we have the basic products of the commercial software industry. Hundreds of millions of dollars are invested, each year, in the constant refinement of the market leader packages in these fields and as a consequence, those packages are very sophisticated indeed.

However, it is not only the *kinds* of application that are by now well established. The ever-improving sophistication of computer applications resides very much in the increasing smoothness of the user interface and the cleverness of the graphics output; underneath, we find a range of information processing *functions* which in fact do not change so very much. As a consequence, there is fundamentally something of a plateau in our current understanding of the ways in which computer applications in general use can process information.

This provides us with a most convenient perspective on educational development. In primary and secondary schools, there is more to what goes on than merely the processing of information although information processing remains a very important activity indeed at classroom level and an activity which is undertaken across a high proportion of curriculum areas. In the natural sciences, in history, in geography and in the social sciences, the ability to process and to interpret information is one of the key skills to be developed.

In areas such as these, the tools required by pupils and students are no different from those required by the managers of business and industry. If we set aside for a moment any consideration of the actual complexities of functions required within, say, a spreadsheet or database program, the fact remains that the basic processes of data analysis undertaken by school pupils are the same as those undertaken by adults whose livelihood depends upon their ability to transmute data into usable information. Databases are searched and sorted; the information which they contain is represented graphically or fed into text-based reports. Whether the user is 15 or 35 makes relatively little difference.

The same is true of wordprocessing and of desktop publishing: again, the basic functions used by pupils are the same as those used by adults.

This continuity in the ways in which informatics as a tool is used in the school and in the workplace is of enormous consequence to educational development.

In the first place, it means that a great deal of software – as suitable for use in the classroom as for use in the office – has been developed and is readily available at low cost. In many packages, the basic applications of database, spreadsheet and wordprocessor are combined into the one 'integrated' shell, again inexpensively available.

Second, skills acquired in these areas in the classroom are directly relevant to skills required later in the workplace.

Third, because the basic applications and functions within the applications are well established, it becomes possible to identify exactly what these skills are and to design appropriate training curricula and support materials.

Finally, in this area we are dealing with *software functions* and with training in the use of software functions; in other words, we are looking at an extension from teaching informatics as a discipline. Very importantly for the internationalization of collaborative effort, then, these functions are largely culture-independent and serve therefore as an excellent basis for co-operation across cultures.

This last point is critical and requires some elaboration. It is not the point that database use (for example) in the classroom is in itself culture-free. We may illustrate by reference to the use of databases, focusing upon three possible pedagogic approaches open to the teacher using databases in the classroom.

In the first approach, the teacher makes available to the children a very large database of, let us say, census material. The children are taught the skills of interrogating a database; they learn the differences between sorting and searching, and they learn to search on single and multiple fields. They learn how to maximize the efficiency of a multiple criteria search by selecting the narrowest criterion first. They learn also how to extract reports from searches and how to print summary reports. All of this is excellent skill training – it should be clear how closely it relates to training in informatics as a discipline – and will it enable pupils to become adept at database interrogation.

The second teacher uses the first approach to ensure that the pupils have understood how to operate with a database, but then goes on to provide the pupils with an empty database structure with which to study a chosen topic – an analysis of the different kinds of trees growing within one kilometre of the school for instance. The pupils then undertake field work to ascertain what trees exist and to record their species, characteristics, location and so forth. They next enter their findings into the database which has been prepared by the teacher. This too is excellent training: the pupils learn the value of careful field work, of accurate data capture, and of data entry and verification. All of this will strengthen their understanding of the functioning of databases and will perhaps give them greater insight than the pupils in the first example.

The third teacher also goes through the first stage to make sure that the pupils have the necessary skills and may also use the second approach. But this third teacher introduces a new dimension: the pupils are told that now they must construct a database of their own – not just by capturing the data for a given structure, but first by working out for themselves the structure of fields that they want to adopt. Decisions on the field structures are left to the pupils; they are expected to learn from their mistakes and to develop their databases through successive refinements. They thus have to undergo the entire process of database definition and construction as well as of data capture and verification, and later interrogation.

It is clear that in each of these three cases the pupils will learn much about databases. But it is vital to note that the third teacher goes far beyond the first two, not so much in respect of the skills inculcated but in respect of the role of the teacher and the status of knowledge itself. The third teacher is introducing into the classroom a complete transformation of the roles traditionally ascribed to teachers and pupils.

In the first two cases, knowledge is under the control of the teacher, who is either totally the provider of what is to be known (teacher 1) or the arbiter of the categories into which knowledge is to be fitted (teacher 2). Teacher 3, by contrast, makes a very different statement. In this case, *the teacher is the provider of skills, but knowledge becomes something which children can themselves create.* This is a change of the profoundest significance which puts even the youngest learner on a continuous line of development towards becoming a creative and autonomous researcher. Knowledge is no longer the preserve of the postgraduate scholar or something to be handed down from on high by the teacher. It becomes a construct, be it shared or personal. Moreover, when this approach is used, it demands of pupils a reflection on the processes whereby knowledge is brought into being which they rarely experience in more traditional settings. It is, quite simply, a higher order, a metacognitive, experience – but also, of course, it is far more challenging of the teacher's authority. The teacher using this approach has to be very confident about the technology (so as to act as consultant and adviser to project work) but must also have a very clear grasp of cognitive develop-ment if a proper sequence of learning activities is to be created.

It should be clear from these illustrations that choices about the ways in which databases are used in the classroom are not merely pedagogic choices: they are essentially cultural choices as well.

However, we are now looking *at the ways in which these tools are used and not at the functioning of the tools themselves.* The functions themselves are culture-independent. If therefore we separate classroom uses from func-tions, we get a clearer perspective on development.

It is here, we suggest, that we find one of the most productive areas for international co-operation. Given that the kinds of software we have been discussing are in use worldwide, there is a great deal of scope for co-oper-ation over training in their function, that is, co-operation which leaves decisions about pedagogical application to be taken within national con-texts. Moreover, such co-operation should be one in which it is possible to enlist support from the major software publishers; we return to this point below.

THE WORKING ENVIRONMENT

A fourth lesson learned, relative to substance, concerns the computer envi-ronment itself.

Much progress has been made since the days when all computer users were faced simply with the operating system prompt on the screen. There are still many occasions when experienced users of the NICT will find it more convenient to work from the prompt, but current environments offer a far more easily understood view of the workspace.

Both of the major families of hardware currently in use in the Western Hemisphere offer a graphic-based environment. These are known generically as Graphic User Interfaces (or GUIs for short); another term is WIMP (windows-icon-mouse-programs). The reality of the market-place is that the products of one company, the Microsoft Corporation, are used exclusively in Apple products and dominate in the general the personal computer and compatibles family. While this situation represents a virtual monopoly for Microsoft, it is a positive advantage for the user (especially the learner) in that it represents a *de facto* standard, not merely within one of the hardware families but across both. As a consequence it is very easy for the educational user to move between hardware platforms, and it is also easy for training materials to be developed which require very little modification from one platform to the other.

In the early 1980s, one of the major problems faced by trainers and materials developers was that different programs tended to present different operating faces to the user. As a consequence, it was necessary to switch between quite different general skills as one moved from program to program. One might require all application commands to be preceded by a ' / ', while another required the use of various combinations of keys used in conjunction with the Control key. Some would have menus available across the top of the screen, some down one side, some at the bottom. When one had mastered the commands relative to one application, there was no necessary transfer of learning to another.

When GUIs began to appear however, they brought with them a far greater transferability of learning in respect of basic processes such as filing and editing commands. Now, with the wide dissemination of the Microsoft *Windows* environment for personal computers and the complete dominance of its counterpart in the Apple market, that transferability is complete. What has been learned for one application becomes a useful starting point for learning another.

This is not to say that there is no room for improvement in the present level of GUIs – there is. But it does mean a very great economy of training. Once the principle of drop-down menus is understood, it applies across all software applications which run under *Windows*. The file functions menu is always the leftmost, with the edit function on its right. The scrolling functions, mouse pointing, selection of text or cells, formatting: all of these processes are immediately recognizable within a new application and they provide an entry point to the learning process which takes the user already many steps towards application competence.

This chapter is not the place in which to extol the products of any one software manufacturer. However, the remarks made here about GUIs do bear out the more general point that co-operation with the industry is in fact supportive of educational development. It is no exaggeration to say that the appearance of industry-standard GUIs is as important a development as any from the educational point of view. We shall suggest later in this chapter that a very considerable basis for international co-operation has been laid by this development.

Organization

With hindsight, much has been learned also about organization from the educational developments of the 1980s. Perhaps the most important point of all is that an organized response at both the national and international levels is in fact required. Spectacular advances were made in France and the United Kingdom simply because national programmes were launched. This gave a lead to development; it signalled that the take-up of NICT by schools was seen as important, and it generated a certain amount of software development and of teacher training.

What was done was not necessarily enough. The Microelectronics Education Programme (MEP) in England and Wales, for example, used up a great deal of its resources in setting up a regional organization outside of existing structures. Funds which might have been more usefully spent upon more software development and upon teacher training were spent upon the staffing of fourteen regional centres, of which eventually no more that three or four (by common consent) made any significant contribution to development. Very little funding was put into the institutions responsible for teacher training, so that when the MEP was wound up, these institutions had to find the means to take over training responsibilities which they might have discharged from the outset. The software development programme also – with the very honourable exception of the programme for primary schools – achieved relatively little of significance, and what it did achieve, it achieved late in the life of the programme. The French experience was perhaps more positive, largely because of the emphasis placed from the outset upon teacher training at a significant level.

However, much valuable development took place alongside these national programmes. In many of the states of the United States, for example, state authorities initiated numerous programmes of in-service training for their own teachers, often taught by specially-appointed support staff; similar development took place in the British local education authorities (LEAs). Unfortunately, as economic recession bites, many of the British programmes have been curtailed.

Hindsight suggests that the organizational response to what was seen as an urgent need in the early 1980s was not well thought through. The responses mounted in France and the United Kingdom were essentially emergency ones, accompanied by a great deal of noisy concern about the need to 'get ahead' of other national programmes. From this experience, the lesson learned overall was that a national organization, however urgently it may be needed to support innovation, should not neglect existing structures. What tended to happen was that 'special' structures were put in place which were expensive to establish and which left an insufficient mark when their time was expired. Nonetheless the signals sent out by the setting up of the national programmes did initiate a great deal of development.

FINANCE

A major part of the problems experienced stemmed from a failure to appreciate the true nature of the investment required.

The worst error – assuming that provision of financial support for purchase of hardware was the most significant part of an effective strategy – resulted in quite large sums of money being made available for equipment. This thinking ignored several factors.

In the first place, no national programme appears to have accepted the need for a cyclic approach to hardware purchase itself. The assumption seems always to have been that once machines were installed in a school, a responsibility had been discharged and there was no need to do anything further; this was very much the flavour of development in many of the British LEAs. From the very outset of the 'IT in Schools' movement, however, it was evident that hardware capacities were in a state of constant evolution and that there was no apparent end to that evolution. What is purchased this year is already challenged by next year's technology advance. Since this is still the case in respect of the hardware platform, it would seem that there is an important lesson still to be learned. It is a difficult lesson, which in a country with a large schools population calls for a very strong-willed determination to meet the equipment challenges of the NICT in schools on a semi-permanent basis and to allocate 'rolling' budgets accordingly.

Second, hardware purchase was emphasized at the expense of software development. Here, there was initially something of a dilemma. The schools were provided with machines before educational software had been developed, so that there was little opportunity for appropriate use. On the other hand, until teachers had the opportunity to become acquainted with the technology, they had no basis on which to specify the software needed. It was a classic 'chicken-and-egg' situation. This dilemma was not resolved easily and its eventual solution came, in fact, only with the availability of software intended for commercial use which was found to be appropriate for the classroom also. Once this availability was understood, the need for specialist software development was considerably reduced.

Thus, this particular problem is no longer one of the non-availability of software. Rather, it is one of the need for policy-makers to accept that investment in software purchase is the strategic investment; it need not be larger than the hardware investment but it is the more important of the two, not least because it is the investment which determines the nature of the work actually undertaken in the classroom.

Third, it is essential to realize the importance of the investment in teacher training. This may appear obvious, but the size of this particular investment represents a challenge to authorities at national and local levels. No hardware purchase or software purchase is of any value unless teachers are trained in its use. Moreover, the challenge is not one-off; just as the hardware needs to be replaced and new versions of software need to be acquired to keep up with processor improvements, so do teachers need to cycle through training programmes throughout a professional lifetime.

This is a new factor in the situation facing educational funding. Prior to the information technology explosion of the early 1980s, teachers had operated in a relatively stable technological environment. Other twentieth century developments such as wireless and television, the record player, tape-recorder and the videocamera have all created their own educational opportunities but have not radically challenged the role of the teacher or altered the *modus operandi* of the classroom. NICT are different: not only are they an ever-more-powerful technology but they create a quite new kind of pedagogic challenge to the teacher, involving a major adjustment to concepts of the teacher's role. Just to keep up with this challenge, teachers may reasonably expect to be provided with up-date training at regular intervals during a career, training geared to both the learning of new applications and new refinements in the environment, and the development of new pedagogic skills.

In respect of initial teacher training, there is the added challenge of keeping the trainers themselves fully up-to-date with development. This is by no means a minor task. Although the teacher-trainer corps is by definition smaller than the corps of classroom teachers at secondary and primary levels, it is more senior in age and, as a consequence, the challenge of adjusting to new pedagogical roles is all the greater.

Training is expensive. One of the major lessons to be learned about the financing of national programmes for the use of informatics in schools is that the training issue needs to be addressed fully. If it is not, investment in the areas of hardware and software will be wasted in part if not entirely. Of the developed countries of Western Europe, only France could reasonably claim to have addressed this issue in anything like adequate terms in the innovative period of the 1980s.

Areas and mechanisms of co-operation

Establishing appropriate and effective mechanisms for international co-operation is by no means an easy task. Co-operation does not just happen as a consequence of bringing people together. We need to recognize this fact as an essential preliminary to the search for solutions.

For over a decade, a number of approaches to international co-operation have been tested out. We have seen already how the Commission of the European Community created a relatively effective dialogue between Member States of the Community in the mid-1980s. The OECD's Centre for Educational Research and Innovation (CERI) supported conferences which contributed significantly to exchanges of perspectives between the developed countries of the world, the club of the rich nations. UNESCO has provided support for the sharing of know-how in more than one region of the world; this has included extensive coverage of the European scene as well as of the developing regions. Also, the UNESCO-sponsored Intergovernmental Informatics Programme (IIP), which was created in 1985, has strengthened international co-operation and supported national efforts in training specialists, developing infrastructures and facilitating the design of nation polices.

Nor is this kind of activity the sole preserve of the inter-governmental bodies. Among the multi-nationals, International Business Machines (IBM) for example, has mounted a regular series of seminars which have brought together industry representatives, Ministry officials and practitioners at the European level. Similar support to the education sector is given by Apple Computers.

There is no question that all of these activities have led to valuable exchanges of learning between participants, and no question either that these exchanges have influenced development in a positive manner. What may be useful, however, is to examine some of the problems associated with the use of the international seminar or workshop as a means of influencing change and to see what this tells us about strategies for the future.

A question of ownership

The dilemma confronting the development and adoption of educational innovation on a national scale is well known. It is a question, essentially, of ownership. In brief, if innovation is introduced top-down, at the behest of ministries, there is the danger that it is not accepted, or that it is accepted only partially, by the teachers who must make it effective in the classroom. Conversely, if innovation is introduced at the classroom level, it runs the risk of remaining localized, of not being legitimatized within the national system and of creating (possibly unacceptable) diversity within that system. Furthermore, behind this dichotomy lies the classic tension between national authority on the one hand, with its macro view of what it wishes the education system to deliver and of how it wants it delivered, and the teacher in the classroom on the other hand, with his or her view at the micro level, as an individual professional, of what best serves the learning needs of the children in that class. The micro and the macro views are not necessarily in harmony at any one time in any one system.

Either approach to innovation carries with it its own particular risks. These risks extend to attempts to disseminate understanding of innovation between cultures through mechanisms such as conferences.

International conferences are expensive to mount and expensive to attend. Participation is necessarily limited. When they are mounted within the framework of a major inter-governmental organization such as UNES-CO, it is right and proper that national delegations be made up of ministry representatives, empowered to put forward official points of view. However, it is only realistic to acknowledge that ministers and their officials, by definition, are not likely to be persons familiar with the day-to-day uses of NICT in the classroom. To put the point quite starkly: ministers and their officials are not necessarily the persons best equipped to learn, or to learn most effectively, from exposure to innovations in other countries. The problem is that of bridging the gap between what the minister hears at a conference and what actually happens six months later in the minister's home country.

To say this is not to argue international conferences should be attended only by classroom practitioners. That would be ridiculous: there is a real need to represent the national point of view, and even if the practitioner is better placed to learn from the experience of innovation in other countries than are ministers and their entourages, he or she has no power at all to promote the innovation in the home country at anything other than purely local level. Another, more effective, approach needs to be identified.

The international conference can be made to work, perhaps especially at the regional level. One of the most effective models was one adopted by the Commission of the European Community (CEC) in the mid-1980s. In this period, CEC mounted a series of conferences which succeeded in bringing together both officials (decision-makers at national level) and practitioners with an active involvement in innovation. National officials clarified policy; practitioners demonstrated classroom innovations. The chemistry of the exchanges which took place was considerably enhanced by the mood of the times: it was the period in which the aura of excitement and of creativity which surrounded the 'NICT in education' movement still prevailed and, as a consequence, there was considerable commitment to a shared learning in which all were involved. Thus, ministry officials and national inspectors discussed the issues and examined software alongside curriculum developers, innovation team leaders and classroom teachers, and this on a transnational basis. It was a heady experience, by no means confined to the CEC conferences mentioned: something very similar was to be observed, for example, at conferences organized by far-seeing authorities in Bulgaria (the Plovdiv and 'Children in the Age of Information' conferences).

That mood of excitement, sadly, is no longer with us, and the harsh winds of economic recession blow cold on all innovation, especially innovation which costs money. Nonetheless the value of the model remains: the international conference can be a real force for international co-operation if it can bring together both those who influence and make decisions and those who are closely involved with the introduction of the NICT at the levels of the classroom and of the local system. It is not an easy thing to do, and the protocols of such a mix are inevitably different from one culture to another. But it can be done – perhaps not on the grand scale involving a large number of countries, but on a regional basis, with relatively large teams from a relatively small number of countries, there is much transfer of learning that can be achieved.

However, we should not lose sight of one other important element in the chemistry of the CEC conferences in the 1980s: this was the period when a number of the participating countries had their own national development agencies for information technology in education and, as a consequence, these agencies were able to offer some support to both Ministries and the teaching profession in a way that maintained the momentum of innovation. This support was not as effective as it might have been, but it served as a focus for the on-going debate.

The different actors

Different actors, clearly, have different contributions to make to the international dialogue, and it is always necessary to respect the specific characteristics of any given kind of actor.

This is particularly true of the inter-governmental organizations. In the case of CEC, for example, it is essential always to recognize the sensitivity of the debate about the Community's legal competence in the field of education (as distinct from training) and to recognize therefore that any actions promoted by the CEC within the Community must be seen always to complement actions at the national level and to support dialogue between the independent education systems of the Community. Despite the implications of membership of the European Community for member states, there is no question of the CEC's attempting to promote a unified 'Community policy' for education.

OECD/CERI is, as the name makes clear, focused upon research and evaluation. Moreover, it exists within the larger framework of an association of member states which is quite different in kind from that which constitutes the European Community, with its far more binding treaty implications. As a consequence, it is not realistic to expect an organization such as OECD/CERI to bring together practitioners who do not have the research focus or, for that matter, individuals who do not have an accredited status as representatives of national viewpoints.

Similarly UNESCO, which has made a major commitment to developing better understanding of the impact of NICT upon education worldwide, is bound by its Charter. It is not the role of UNESCO, any more than it is that of CEC or OECD/CERI, to tell sovereign governments what to do, but rather to foster the dialogue between nations and to do the utmost possible to disseminate learning and to facilitate exchange. This mission, of course, UNESCO has discharged, and is discharging, with considerable effectiveness.

Within these kinds of constraints each of the major inter-governmental organizations does have the power to engage with a range of different activities. Later in this chapter, we shall look at ways in which a more efficient mode of international co-operation might be built upon better co-ordination between such activities, and also between them and the more formal work of these organizations at governmental levels.

But inter-governmental organizations are not the only international actors on the scene. Actors of a different kind have rather more flexible roles to play. The international foundations, for example, can operate in a variety of ways, as has been demonstrated by the European Cultural Foundation (ECF), and particularly by its Institute for Education and Social Policy. Acting within budget frameworks which are by no means limitless, ECF has done a great deal since the early 1980s to disseminate a wider understanding of NICT: it has organized conferences, contributed to others, undertaken research and published findings. In these and other ways it has acted within Europe as a valuable channel of communication between policy-makers at national and international level on the one hand, and researchers and practitioners on the other, and in the process has contributed a valuable catalytic effect upon development.

Similarly, the leading manufacturers have all made, and continue to make, significant contributions to the international debate. Indeed all of the major manufacturers have made commitments such as seminars, and act strenuously to maintain their dialogues with both policy makers and practitioners. Conferences are supported, and groups and schools may be donated equipment and software to enable needed development to take place.

It must be recognized, however, that manufacturers are not charitable foundations. While many do place considerable resources at the service of educational development, the *raison d'être* of the manufacturing organization must be, in the last analysis, that of maintaining a profitable business. This is something which educational practitioners find difficult to understand; there is a tendency for teachers to believe that the major manufacturers have unlimited resources from which to pour free machines into schools. In practice, a school is a potential customer just like any other.

But while all of these actors invest heavily in various forms of international dialogue, one still remains sceptical of the real – and above all, *continuing* – impact upon development at national levels. Relative to the expenditure involved, returns often appear to be disappointingly low. There are exceptions, such as the CEC conferences mentioned above, but overall one is left with the feeling that there must be a more effective way of going about the business of international co-operation.

A significant part of the problem is that, as we have seen, the great inter-governmental organizations can do little more than advise, guide and educate their member states. Moreover they act, in the main, independently of one another. A formal dialogue may exist, and the one organization may (or may not) be represented at a meeting organized by another, but observers attending in ones and twos are scarcely the equivalent of a full dialogue between organizations. As a consequence, there is little – if any – overall coherence to international activity.

The separateness is easy to understand. Each organization is a political creation with its own specific mandate. Memberships do not overlap and interests do not necessarily coincide – indeed, we saw at the outset that, as between countries, interests may well conflict. These remarks are based on a personal experience of over twenty years of participation in a great many European conferences, workshops and projects. The total expenditure upon these activities will have exceeded the GNP of more than one developing nation. Yet the experience leaves one with the very strong feeling of less than value for money – with the feeling that, between us, we do not succeed in doing as much as we might – as much as we must – in the service of international co-operation.

And 'international co-operation' in this context, we need to remind ourselves, means making schools better as places of learning. The protocols of dialogue between Ministries of Education at the official level are of no importance whatsoever when measured against the right of the children of the world to the best education we can make available to them. When that world is one where NICT are an important force for socio-economic change at national levels (and therefore for socio-economic disparity between nations) as well as for the economic advancement of the individual, the need to safeguard that right becomes ever stronger.

We are not doing well enough; we must do better.

But what do these fine sentiments mean in practice?

Improving present practice

It is beyond the capacity of a single writer, however presumptuous, to solve all of the problems of international co-operation which arise in respect of the educational uses of NICT. In attempting to say even anything meaningful about the issues, one is necessarily driven back upon a simplified view of the world.

Simplicity, however, is no bad thing if it helps us to identify both those issues which are at the heart of the matter and the broad outlines of a strategy which could lead towards effective co-operation.

It may be helpful to identify five issues. First, we need to be clear about the goals of international co-operation. Second, we need a focus on the content areas most usefully addressed, and here we do well to look at a range of basic skills. Third, we need to see how existing modalities can be put to best use. Fourth, we need to be clear about the contribution of industry. Fifth, we need also to examine the need for a new mechanism at international level, one that will act as a catalyst for co-operation and ensure that duplication of effort is kept to a minimum.

The goals of co-operation

The goals of co-operation may appear to be obvious, but they are worth restating. The whole point of international co-operation in respect of the educational uses of the new information and communication technologies is to ensure that the NICT are used, along with education generally, as a weapon in the fight to eradicate inequality. Global inequality exists at every level. There is inequality between nations, between regions of the world, between social groups, between individuals.

Inequality will never be eradicated; to think that it can be, is to dream the impossible. But in an age of global communication, when the effects of a cyclone, a tidal wave, an earth quake or of civil war are on the television screens of the world within the hour, an age, in other words, in which we cannot pretend not to know the extent of inequality and of the suffering caused by inequality, we have no excuse for failing to combat that inequality. And in a world where the use of NICT is one of the most powerful of economic weapons (as well as of weapons in the strict sense of the word) countries of the developed world must share the educational advantages of NICT; sharing these advantages would be as important a weapon as any in the fight against global inequality in the field of education, since the advantages in question have to do with basic literacy, basic numeracy and basic information handling skills.

We should not underestimate the extent to which knowledge is power. We are here confronting two levels at which this is the case.

The first level is that of the individual. NICT offer such a powerful extension of the knowledge-handling capacities of our limited intellects that to withhold that extension from any child is to deny him or her an important element of control over his or her destiny.

The second level is that of the nation. The war in the Gulf demonstrated clearly the importance of information and of information processing as a strategic and as a tactical weapon, but the demonstration applies equally to economic competition. The ability – to take just one example – of the weather satellite to provide predictive information of the likely coffee harvest yield in Brazil in any given year is of economically strategic importance to more than one country in the developed world; the availability of a sophisticated workforce able to take advantage of this and of a vast range of similar information, and to turn that information to strategic advantage, is a major factor in the maintenance of economic dominance.

In global terms, the issues about sharing understanding of the educational potential of NICT are as simple, as stark as described here. Either we contribute to the solution or we contribute to the problem. There is no middle way.

A focus on basic skills

But what does this mean in terms of the education and training that needs to be shared between developed and developing worlds? We have already acknowledged that inequality exists and will continue to exist. The task for our generations is not to eradicate inequality, because that is impossible, but to reduce inequality. If we accept this simple fact, and adhere to the virtue of simplicity in defining our goals, we may even find that our task, quite suddenly, becomes manageable at least in conceptual terms.

What we mean is the following. We have argued that the pattern of development of commercial software in the first world has shaken down, by now, into certain patterns. While there exists and will continue to exist a very wide range of computer software applications, the battles, essentially, are fought over the three key areas of wordprocessing, databases and spreadsheets. We have seen that the structure of the software industry is built around the three most important elements of the processing of text, the processing of factual data and the processing of numeric data. Design packages are also important in many industries, while an additional element, the generation of the screen environment within which the other elements exist, constitutes a very important part of the development effort and of the market. Together these elements are the foundations of the information industry.

We have also argued that while any one successful computer application goes through a constant process of revision and upgrading, the underlying functionalities of the different families of applications are well known. As a consequence, it is not difficult to construct training programmes and training materials in respect of these functionalities, resources which can be translated and used in many different cultures. (Note: we are here referring to the *functionalities* of computer applications, not to the *manner* in which they are used.) Collaborative international effort would be best directed to a sharing of know-how, of materials and of resources in these areas, leaving training in their use, an issue which invokes many culture-specific consider-ations, to be determined nationally or locally.

We have seen also that hardware cost is only a part of the total investment needed in respect of NICT in education. An advantage of the very simple strategy put forward here is that it produces economy in what may easily become another, very expensive area of investment, namely the training and re-training of teachers. There is just no need for each country to re-invent the training wheel in respect of NICT functions and recognition of this basic fact would open the door to a great deal of useful collaboration.

A serious and co-ordinated effort towards making the necessary soft-ware available at no cost would handsomely repay the effort in terms of making the educational benefits of NICT available worldwide.

A question of language

In saying this, of course, we ignore one very important question, which is that of the many natural languages of the world and, perhaps even more important in practical terms, the different scripts in which language is recorded.

We have to recognize that this is the most important question of all. The language of NICT, whether we like it or not, is a sub-set of English, and sooner or later this nettle must be grasped.

In very broad terms, the choice is simple. International collaborative effort can do one of two things. First, it can wait until computer applications are written which can present to the user an interface in any one of the major natural languages of the world, in the appropriate script. Second, it can be launched now on the basis of an acceptance of English, perhaps more specifically of the Roman alphabet, as a necessary element in the use of NICT.

The first is the culturally pure approach, preventing, as far as possible, the economic dominance of the English language in the world at large from reaching into the classroom.

The second is the pragmatic approach. It recognizes that, purist consider-ations apart, the English language and Roman script are facts of global life, that mastery of English is a vital weapon for advancement both of the individual and of the nation state, and that the effective use of NICT virtually requires the ability to use that sub-set of English which governs file saving, copying, printing and the like.

The heart favours the first approach. But the head says otherwise. The difficult experience of Japan in matters of script is a salutary warning which has to be heeded. It is hopelessly unrealistic to think of waiting for a wide distribution of hardware and software while will incorporate all of the scripts of the world; even in Western Europe, the diversity of accents possible is a headache, especially in respect of electronic communication. If progress is to be made in respect of international co-operation over the educational uses of NICT, then the cost of that progress has to be the further advance of English generally and of Roman script specifically as the tools of advance. The argument, however, is not an easy one to accept.

Using the modalities

The picture presented here is a simplistic one, hedged around with a number of 'ifs': if the analysis of the key applications is accepted, if it is agreed that application functionalities can be taught in ways which are not culture-specific, if it can be accepted that realism dictates the acceptance and use of the 'English' interface – if these and other conditions can be met, then perhaps we can begin to make progress.

But if they are met, then the task, in conceptual terms, is not a daunting one. It is not difficult to construct training programmes, curricula and materials. It is not difficult to translate training manuals into national languages. It is not difficult to create CD-ROMs, inexpensively, which would serve as a vehicle for the dissemination of resources such as sample databases and spreadsheet files of varying levels of complexity. It is not difficult, in short, to engage with the transfer of training know-how on a relatively large scale, if only the will is there.

Collaboration of this kind can achieve very considerable economies. It is not the end of the battle, of course. There is still the provision of hardware to be considered, and this is not a small problem. But computer hardware is not the wildly expensive item it once was, and powerful machines can be made available at relatively low cost; an agreement to accept Roman script as the working medium would further help the cause of standardization and of economy.

We recognize, of course, that immediate agreement to co-operate extensively across the international community would not change situations overnight. Everything that is said in this chapter has to be set against the more urgent imperatives of combating hunger, disease and poverty, and we would do well to acknowledge that we are looking at development perspectives which extend over fifty years rather than five. We must acknowledge also that the best electronic technology in world is no more than expensive junk in a setting where there is no electricity supply.

At the same time, these arguments have their mirror image. The appropriate use of NICT is itself a long-term weapon with which to combat hunger and disease and poverty. It is itself a weapon in the economic emergence of the poorer nations of the world. The question may well be not: 'Can the poorer nations of the world afford to introduce NICT into their educational systems?' but rather: 'Can the poorer nations of the world afford *not* to introduce NICT into their education systems?'

Indeed, the question may well go further. In contemporary Europe, recent momentous political changes have lead to expressed fears of great movements of peoples, away from the relatively disadvantaged East into the affluent West. Such movements would be entirely understandable, just as they would be entirely disastrous for the very affluence which trigger them off. Given the central economic importance which we have here ascribed to NICT, the real question may be: 'Can the *rich* nations of the world afford not to introduce NICT into the education systems of the poorer?' The educational modalities exist, but they are separate and unco-ordinated. Is it too much to ask for a greater degree of international co-operation among the international organizations themselves? How real is the dialogue between OECD/CERI, the Commission of the European Community and UNESCO? How much effort is put into the avoidance of overlap and the maximum sharing of know-how and of findings from educational research? If real co-operation is to take place between the education systems of the world, it is probably to the inter-governmental organizations that we must look first.

Drawing upon industry

The world and regional organizations, however, are not the whole of the equation. It is equally important to involve the information industry as fully as possible in the debate.

To its credit, as we have seen already, that industry has invested and does invest heavily in its support for education. What however is needed most of all is the involvement of the industry in a dialogue at a more strategic level. That dialogue would involve the inter-governmental agencies, representatives of ministries, research teams and of training agencies, and the major manufacturers themselves. The latter would contribute to the debate their inside view of the direction which technology development is taking at any given moment. There is no need for any such contribution to divulge commercially strategic information, but rather to impart the kind of guidelines which would enable educational planning to take place in a constructive and co-ordinated manner. Without that contribution, the debate would be conducted in a vacuum, and it is an essential ingredient in the planning process.

A facilitating mechanism

But where does such a dialogue take place? We are not talking here of occasional conferences, sometimes within one framework, sometimes within another. What is needed is nothing short of a semi-permanent commission, funded by all of the inter-governmental agencies and by industry but existing in the space between them, a commission charged with the bringing together of all of the support mechanisms for development which have been outlined here, with maximizing economy of development and with the making available, to all countries which request it, the guidance and the materials necessary as a basis for development. Such a commission would develop and publish training guidelines and training curricula; it would make available resource materials to support training; it would work with the industry to ensure that new technology development was matched by support for education systems in its use; at the same time, it would advise the industry on the specific needs of education and ensure that the hardware platform required for development was available to education systems at minimum cost.

This is no more than the outlines of a vision; the complexities of setting up such a commission (or organization, or foundation, or agency) would be great. Essentially, however, this is the kind of development that is needed if international co-operation is to mean anything. The technology itself would be an important element in the functioning of such a body.

One aspect of development upon which we have touched only lightly is the potential of electronic communications. The global electronic network is embryonically in place: where the telephone goes, there the computer can go too. Clearly, this leaves out many areas of the world, but in principle there is be no major centre of population which cannot be reached by electronic network.

Already this facility is being exploited by schoolchildren in many countries of the world. Using relatively simple electronic mail facilities, individuals and classes are able to communicate with each other and, very excitingly, to work together on joint projects which involve, for example, the construction of comparative databases on a number of social or historical topics. Work of this kind introduces an immediacy and a sense of reality into learning about other countries which is not always obtainable from book-based lessons; moreover, it requires that the children participating pay special attention to the process of communication, whether in their own or another language, and that they engage in real negotiations with their partners before commencing work on any one common topic.

The fact that this kind of international collaboration can be achieved by children merely highlights the potential for the use of electronic communication in the more general developmental sense. The kind of international agency we have postulated here would need to use precisely this kind of facility for its communication with national agencies. Using electronic mail, materials, databases and programs can all be communicated instantly and easily to a wide number of correspondents; printed copy, in fact, can often be dispensed with.

The technologies exist; what we have to do is learn to exploit them, and to do so in a way that helps all schools and all pupils to benefit from the technology advances of recent decades. If we do not, then those who are already disadvantaged will fall even further behind.

The context in which support for international development is to be found is a fragmented one, and this is counter-productive to development as well as being wasteful of time and energy. The author of this chapter has considerable experience with collaboration at the European level of development, and that experience leads, once again, overwhelmingly to the question: surely we can do better in our modalities of co-operation?

We owe it to our children, and to the children of our children, to make the effort. Not just at the European level, but globally.

If we do not, posterity will think the worse of us.